First in the Field
A Story of New South Wales

by

George Manville Fenn

First in the Field
A Story of New South Wales
by George Manville Fenn

Copyright © 2023

All Rights reserved.

ISBN: 978-93-60466-09-1

Published by

DOUBLE 9 BOOKS

2/13-B, Ansari Road
Daryaganj, New Delhi – 110002
info@double9books.com
www.double9books.com
Tel. 011-40042856

ABOUT THE AUTHOR

George Manville Fenn was a very productive author of novels, a writer, an editor, and an educator from England. He was born on January 3, 1831, in Pimlico, London. He mostly learned on his own; he taught himself Italian, French, and German. During the years 1851–1854, he went to Battersea Training College for Teachers and then became the head of a state school in Alford, Lincolnshire. In the early 1850s, Fenn started to write short stories and pieces for newspapers and magazines. The Old Forest Ranger, his first book, came out in 1856. Afterward, he wrote more than 100 books, many of them for teenagers and young adults. He was one of the most famous writers of his time, and his books were well-liked and read by many people. He-- also worked as a reporter and writer for Fenn. Among the newspapers and magazines, he worked for was The Boy's Own Paper, which he ran from 1866 to 1874. He worked hard to make children's books better and was a strong supporter of education and reading. The Englishman Fenn passed away on August 26, 1909, in Isleworth.

CONTENTS

Chapter One
One Afternoon 9

Chapter Two
After the Fight 16

Chapter Three
A Startler 21

Chapter Four
Preparations 31

Chapter Five
Outward Bound 34

Chapter Six
On the other Side 47

Chapter Seven
Preparing to Start 51

Chapter Eight
To the Bush 56

Chapter Nine
Nic's Experiences 70

Chapter Ten
A Morning Dip 75

Chapter Eleven
How to Ride 80

Chapter Twelve
A Black Peril 88

Chapter Thirteen
Nic's Mission 93

Chapter Fourteen
"Sweet, Sweet Home" 104

Chapter Fifteen
After Nature's Remedy.. 111

Chapter Sixteen
Life at the Station.. 115

Chapter Seventeen
A Strange Encounter 126

Chapter Eighteen
A Fright.. 135

Chapter Nineteen
Nic Shows His Teeth.. 140

Chapter Twenty
Leather's Other Side.. 146

Chapter Twenty One
A Day's Fishing 159

Chapter Twenty Two
A Woolly Patient and a Scare 165

Chapter Twenty Three
A Squatter's Life 173

Chapter Twenty Four
Leather Speaks Out.. 178

Chapter Twenty Five
Nic Takes the Helm.. 184

Chapter Twenty Six
"When the Cat's Away" 187

Chapter Twenty Seven
Brookes Strikes Back 194

Chapter Twenty Eight
And all in Vain.. 201

Chapter Twenty Nine
A Night's Work 208

Chapter Thirty
The Quest 217

Chapter Thirty One
Black Sympathy 223

Chapter Thirty Two
A False Scent 226

Chapter Thirty Three
In a Trap 235

Chapter Thirty Four
Trust for Trust 243

Chapter Thirty Five
Nic has Suspicions 252

Chapter Thirty Six
In Sanctuary 256

Chapter Thirty Seven
Castles in the Air 264

Chapter Thirty Eight
Nature at Home 266

Chapter Thirty Nine
A Double Surprise 270

Chapter Forty
The Doctor Plays Magistrate 277

Chapter Forty One
Right Wins 285

Chapter One
One Afternoon

"I say, don't, Green: let the poor things alone!"

"You mind your own business. Oh! bother the old thorns!"

Brian Green snatched his hand out of the quickset hedge into which he had thrust it, to reach the rough outside of a nest built by a bird, evidently in the belief that the hawthorn leaves would hide it from sight, and while they were growing the thorns would protect it from mischievous hands.

But the leaves opened out slowly that cold spring, and a party of boys from Dr Dunham's school, the Friary, Broadhurst, Kent, was not long in spying out the unlucky parents' attempt at house-building and nursery. Still, the thorns did their duty to some extent when Brian Green of the red head leaped across the big dry ditch, rudely crushing a great clump of primroses and forcing them down the slope, for when the freckled-faced lad thrust his hand in to grasp the nest a sharp prick made him withdraw it, while this action brought it in contact with a natural *chevaux de frise*, scarified the back, and made a long scratch on his thumb.

"I wish you'd keep your tongue inside your teeth, Nic Braydon!" cried the boy fiercely. "You won't be happy till I've given you another licking. Look here what you've made me do!"

"I didn't make you do it," said the first speaker. "Why don't you let the birds alone?"

"Because, if you please, Miss Braydon," said the bigger lad mincingly, "I'm not so good as you are. Oh dear, no! I'm going to take that nest of young blackbirds because I want them to bring up and keep in a cage. I'm going to transport them to the shed in the playground."

The first boy winced sharply at his companion's words, and the four lads present burst into a derisive laugh at his annoyance; but he smothered it down, and said quietly:— "Then you may as well leave them alone, for they're not blackbirds."

"Yes, they are, stoopid."

"No, they're not."

"How do you know?"

"Because I found the nest when it was first built, and saw the eggs and the old bird sitting."

"Oh, that's it, is it? Oh, I say, isn't he a nice, good little boy? He doesn't want me to take the young birds because he wants to steal them himself."

The others laughed in their thoughtlessness as their schoolfellow winced again, and Brian Green still hung on to the bank, sucking the scratches on his bleeding hand and grinning with satisfaction at the annoyance his innuendoes caused.

"I say, boys," he cried, "they don't transport people for life for stealing young blackbirds, do they?"

There was a fresh roar of laughter, and the boys watched Dominic Braydon, who stood frowning, to see if he would make some sharp retort, verbal or physical, and perhaps get thrashed again. But he concealed his annoyance, and said quietly:

"That's a thrush's nest."

"You don't know anything about it, Convict," said Green.

The boy winced again; but he went on:

"Well, I know that. Blackbirds make rougher nests, and they're not plastered inside so neatly with clay as that is. Then the eggs are different: blackbirds' are all smudgy, dingy green; those were beautiful blue eggs, with a few clear spots on one end. Yes, look," he cried; "there's half one of them."

As he spoke he leaped down into the ditch, and picked up a fragile, dried-up portion of an egg and showed it to his companions.

"Yah! Old Botany Bay don't know what he's talking about," said Green, dragging a hedge-stake from the top of the bank, and wrenching the upper part of the dense hawthorn growth into a gap, through which he pulled the nest with its contents, four half-fledged birds, looking, with the loose down at the back of their heads, their great goggle eyes and wide gapes, combined with the spiky, undeveloped feathers and general nakedness, about as ugly, goblin-like creatures as a painter could have desired.

"There!" cried Green, dropping the hedge-stake and leaping back over the ditch; "aren't those blackbirds? Oh, murder!"

There was a great roar of laughter, for the clumsy leap resulted in two of the callow birds being jerked out heavily into the bottom of the ditch, and upon their recovery one was found to be dead.

"Never mind," said Green; "three are better to bring up. Now then, in you go, ugly."

He placed the bird in the nest with its companions, down by which it snuggled itself at once, so that the three completely filled the bottom.

"Fits splendidly, boys. I shall make old Botany Bay get worms for me and chop them up to feed them."

"You ought to be ashamed of yourself;" said the first boy, frowning. "You know you let those young starlings die."

"You ought to be ashamed of yourself;" retorted Green, "getting yourself put in a school among young gentlemen. I don't know what the doctor was thinking about to take a convict's son."

"My father is not a convict," cried Dominic angrily.

"Oh, isn't he, just. Transported for life. We know, don't we, boys?"

"Yes—yes," was chorused.

"Of course he was," cried Green. "You can't keep these things quiet. Pretends his father is a settler. Yes; the judge settled him for life."

The boy looked round for applause, and received it sufficiently to make him go on with his banter.

"Just as if we weren't sure to find out the truth. Calls him a squatter. Yes; the government made him squat pretty quickly."

There was another laugh as the boys wandered on along the edge of the great common, where the quickset hedge divided it from the cultivated land, high above which a lark was circling and singing with all its might.

"I want to know why the doctor lets him stop amongst gentlemen's sons."

"I know, Bry Green," said a mischievous-looking, dark-eyed boy; "it's because his father pays."

"He wouldn't be here long if his father didn't," said Green laughingly.

"Unless he supplied the doctor with sugar and soap and candles and soda and blue."

There was a roar of laughter once more, in which Dominic Braydon joined, and Green turned so suddenly on the last speaker that the young thrushes were nearly jerked out of the nest.

"Do you want me to give you a wipe on the mouth, Tomlins?" cried the boy angrily.

"Oh no, sir; please don't, sir," was the reply, with a display of mock horror and dread; "only you said gentlemen's sons, sir,—and I thought what a pity it was Nic Braydon's father wasn't a grocer."

"My father's a wholesale dealer in the City," said Green loftily; "and it's only as a favour that he lets old Dunham have things from his warehouse at trade price."

"Ho, ho, ho! here's a game!" cried the dark boy, throwing himself down on the velvety turf and kicking out his legs in his delight.

"My father isn't a poor parson," continued Green contemptuously; "and if any of you fellows like to call on me during the holidays, any one will show you Alderman Green's big house on Clapham Common. We keep a butler, footman, coachman, and three gardeners."

"And the gardeners make all the beds," said Tomlins, at which there was another laugh.

"You're a little idiot, Tomlins," said Green loftily.

"Yes, sir; but I can't help it," said the boy meekly. "You see my father never brought home turtle soup from the Lord Mayor's dinner so as to make me big and fat."

"You won't be happy till I've rubbed your ugly snub nose against the next tree," cried Green. "Get up, you gipsy-looking cub!"

He stepped quickly as he spoke to where the boy still lay upon the green and kicked him viciously.

"Oh!" yelled the boy, who began to writhe now in earnest as he fought hard to control himself, but in vain, for he rose to his knees at last with the tears coming fast, and then limped slowly along, sobbing bitterly.

"Serve you right," cried Green. "Teach you not to be so jolly saucy. Now then, none of your sham. I didn't hurt you much. Go on."

"I—I can't yet," sobbed the boy.

"Oh yes, you can. None of that. Here, carry these."

He thrust the nest of young thrushes into the boy's hand, and forced him to proceed, limping heavily.

"Look at the little humbug," cried Green, as they all went on, with Dominic Braydon hanging down his head and gazing hard at the ground to keep from darting indignant glances at the tyrant who had bullied and insulted him till it had been almost beyond bearing. He felt a choking sensation in the throat, and an intense longing to do something; but his ways were peaceful, and Green, was heavy, big, and strong. In addition, he was cock of the school, to whom every one had yielded for a long time past; and Dominic Braydon had still fresh in his memory that day when he had resisted a piece of tyranny and fought at the far end of the school garden, where an unlucky blow on the bridge of the nose had half blinded him and made him an easy victim to the enemy, who administered a severe drubbing and procured for his adversary a birching for fighting—it was before caning days—and a long series of impositions for obstinacy, a trait the doctor said that he absolutely abhorred—Dominic's obstinacy consisting in a stubborn refusal to confess who had beaten him. This his schoolfellows called honourable; but Green had other opinions, and set it down to the fear of getting another thrashing for telling tales.

But Green was not quite correct.

And so on this bright spring half-holiday the boys went on along the side of the common toward the dense furze clump, Green hectoring, throwing stones at everything he saw, from the donkeys and geese to the yellow-hammers which flitted along the hedge, stopping now and then to twitter out their quaint little song about "a little bit o' bread and no cheese," and looking as much like canaries as they could as they perched upon some twig.

"I'll give you a bit o' cheese and no bread," cried Green, as he hurled stone after stone, but fortunately with the worst of aim. "Now then, you Tomlins, stop that miserable snivelling, and walk upright; you're not hurt."

The boy hastily wiped his eyes, as he mentally wished that he was big and strong.

"And don't you drop those birds, or I'll give you another," shouted Green, as he sent another pebble flying.

The boy stifled a sob, and followed limping.

"Lean on me, Bob," said Dominic.

"Thank you," sobbed the boy; and then in a whisper, "My hip hurts as if it was put out."

"Not so bad as that," said Dominic in a low tone; and he helped the boy along till Green looked back, saw what was taking place, and shouted:

"Now then, none of that, Convict. He's only shamming. Let him alone."

"Don't let him touch me, Nic," whispered the boy piteously; "I can hardly walk."

Dominic said nothing, but his brow was full of lines; and he looked down at the ground and supported his companion by tightly holding his arm.

"Do you hear?" roared Green, stopping now. "I told you to leave that little sham alone."

"I'm not shamming, Nic," sobbed the boy in a whisper; "it hurts dreadfully every time I move my leg."

"Oh, you won't, won't you?" cried Green menacingly. "I shall have to give you a lesson too, Master Braydon, and transport you into a better state of mind. Stand aside, will you?"

As he came up he struck Nic a back-handed blow across the chest, forcing him backward and making Tomlins utter a cry of pain.

"Now then, none of that," continued Green. "Go on, and take care of those birds,—go on!"

The boy in his dread and pain, wincing in the expectation of a fresh kick, staggered on for a few paces, and then with a cry of misery fell forward flat upon his chest.

"Mind those birds!" yelled Green, starting forward, and bending down he flung the wretched boy over on to his back so as to extricate the bird's nest.

But he was too late; the unfortunate callow songsters had been saved from a lingering death by starvation and imprisonment, the sides of the clay-lined nest being crushed in, and the breath out of the tender little bodies.

They were quite dead, and in a fit of vindictive rage Green flew at the innocent author of the mischief.

"You miserable little beast!" he roared; and his foot was raised to deliver a savage kick. "Get up!"

But instead of Tomlins getting up, Green went down. For, quick as thought, Dominic rushed at him.

"Let him alone!" he cried hoarsely; and the fierce thrust he gave sent the young tyrant into a sitting position upon a cushion-like tuft rising from the closely cropped grass.

But that tuft was only cushion-like in appearance. There were geese feathers about, but they did not form its contents, for it was stuffed with keen, stiff thorns such as can grow to perfection upon a Kentish common; and if Brian Green had been an indiarubber ball he could not have rebounded more suddenly than he did.

Raising the now empty nest he threw it with all his might at Dominic, and both his fists after it.

The nest missed; the fists took effect, alighting as they did upon Dominic's breast and shoulder, and completely driving all thought of consequences out of the boy, who retaliated with such good effect that, as the lookers-on cheered and shouted encouragement, the fight raged fiercely. Even Tomlins forgot his sufferings, and watched every fluctuation of the struggle with an intense longing to see the school tyrant effectually mastered and dragged down from the pedestal whence he had so long dominated and ill-used all around.

The others shared his feelings, and a couple immediately constituted themselves seconds during the few minutes the fight went on fast and furious, Dominic always being ready to dash into the affray after being dragged up at the close of the wrestling bout which ended each round, while Green grew more and more deliberate, as buzzing sounds came into his head, ringings into his ears, and it began to dawn upon him that Nic Braydon had the hardest face he ever touched, and that it was of no use to keep on hitting it, for it always returned to be hit again.

At last, to the intense delight of the boys, it became evident that the result of the encounter must be a sound thrashing for Brian Green, and Nic's second kept on whispering to him to do this and do that to bring it to an end.

Then came a most exciting finish, in which Nic was following up blow with blow, and Green, backing slowly away, guarding himself ineffectually, and growing confused and helpless, was wondering whether Nic had had enough, when the fight came to a sudden termination, and fists dropped down to sides, for the sonorous voice of the doctor arose from close at hand with:

"Young gentlemen, what is the meaning of this disgraceful scene?"

Chapter Two
After the Fight

Three boys began to explain at once; but the doctor, who was walking with his wife and two daughters, and had been attracted by the struggle going on, held up his hand.

"That will do! that will do!" he said in his most dignified manner and with his deepest-toned voice. "I have seen enough. Disgraceful! disgraceful! It would have been bad enough in the village lads and the farm labourers' boys; but in the young gentlemen of the Friary it is outrageous. Silence!" he nearly shouted, as Nic began to speak. "I tell you I saw enough. You, sir, were attacking Green with a violence that was nothing less than brutal and savage. I am shocked, quite shocked. Such conduct cannot be borne. Ladies present too, exposed to seeing your ruffianly violence."

"But, sir—" began Nic.

"How dare you speak, sir, after I have ordered you to be silent! Your half-holiday is cancelled. Back all of you to the Friary; I will see you on my return. Now, my dears, we will resume our walk."

The doctor turned upon his heels, and went off with his ladies talking in a loud voice about botany, the words *Ranunculaceae* and *Caryophyllaceae* being plainly heard as he stopped and picked a yellow blossom and a tuft of weed, the young ladies glancing back twice at the boys who had been guilty of so disgraceful a breach of scholastic etiquette as to have their fight take place upon an open common and let it be seen.

Nic stood arranging his jacket and torn-off collar, looking down rather dismally at Green, and wishing that he had not hit him quite so hard; for his adversary was seated upon the grass where there was no furze, embracing his knees and resting his brow upon them, softly swaying his head from side to side.

Tomlins was the first to speak, for the others were looking after the doctor, and were—especially the two seconds—wondering what the doctor would say when he came back, and how severe their punishment would be.

The fight had done the little dark-eyed fellow good. It was like so much liniment rubbed into his bruise to see the brutal tyrant of the school well thrashed; and feeling that with such a protector as Nic he had no more to fear from Green, he was not above giving expression to his thoughts.

"Never you mind, Nic Braydon," he said. "I shall speak out when the doctor has us up. It wasn't your fault, but bully Gooseberry Green's. He began it, knocking me about, kicking me—a brute. I shall tell the doctor everything just as it happened."

At this Green raised his face to dart a vindictive, threatening look at the little fellow, but he had not paused to think about the state of his face, which was comic in the extreme, and instead of alarming Tomlins made him forget his lameness more and more, and sent him into a fit of laughter.

"Here, boys, look at Gooseberry's phiz. He seems as if he'd been washing it and left it too long to soak! My! what a swelled head!"

The others joined in the roar of laughter, and Green's face was hidden again directly.

But Nic had not laughed. He was hurt bodily and mentally. There was a feeling of regret, too, uppermost, which made him resent this unseemly mirth as cowardly to a fellow enemy.

"You be quiet, Tomlins!" he cried.

"What for?" retorted the boy. "You haven't been kicked as I have. I shall laugh at Gooseberry if I like. He began it all, and he has got his dose, and serve him right. Here, let's get back. Old Dictionary turned his head just now. I say, Greeny, like to have another kick. I'm such a little one, I shan't hit you again."

"Wait a bit," muttered Green.

"Oh, certainly; I'm in no hurry. Only you may as well do it when Nic Braydon's here, because he can give you my compliments afterwards, and leave my card in each of your eyes. Poor old chap! I'm so glad you've been licked."

"Will you be quiet, young un!" cried Nic angrily. "It's mean and cowardly."

"Well, that's the stuff he deals in," said Tomlins. "He likes that better than anything else."

"That's no reason why you should," cried Nic. "Let him be, I tell you."

"Oh, all right, I've done; but I suppose I may say I'm very sorry for him."

"No, you *mayn't*," cried Nic. "Here, come on back, Greeny; we've had it out, but we needn't be bad friends. I'm sorry we fought; you'll shake hands, won't you?"

Green made no movement, and Nic drew closer and held out his hand again.

"Come on," he said; "I'm sorry now; shake hands."

But Green did not move. He sat there crouched together, till Tomlins went behind him.

"He's asleep," cried the little fellow. "I'll give him a job like he gave me, and wake him up."

Green spun round upon the bottom of his spine and faced his little tormentor, who started back with a cry of mock alarm.

"Here, hi, Nic!" he shouted. "Hold him back. He's going to bite."

Nic made a rush, not to protect Tomlins, but to seize him and drag him away.

"If you tease him again, I'll kick you too," he whispered. "Let him be; he's beaten. You don't want to hit him now he's down."

"Yes, I do," said the boy, struggling to free himself. "I owe him a lot, and it isn't safe to hit him when he's not down. Oh, I say, don't; you're hurting me."

"Serve you right. Come away."

"Here, boys, help!" cried Tomlins, making a grimace. "Convict's setting up for—Ah!"

He did not have time to finish his sentence, for Nic caught him sharply by the shoulders and gave him an angry shake.

"If you say that again, I'll serve you worse than Green did. No, I won't;" he said in repentance. "There, go on back."

The boy was silenced, and in a startled way joined his schoolfellows, while Nic once more went close up to Green.

"Let me help you up," he said. "Here, shake hands, Green. It was only a fight, and you might have won."

There was no answer, and Nic took his adversary by the arm, half forcing him to rise; but Green did not turn his head, nor raise his face to gaze in that before him, though he unresistingly allowed himself to be helped along the side of the hedge, so as to reach the lane that led to the high road and the village, at one end of which the park-like grounds of the doctor's establishment stood.

"He'll come round soon," thought Nic. "He's sure to feel sore after such a licking."

"I say, isn't old Convict a rum one," whispered one of the boys who had been seconds.

"Well, he always was," said the other. "What do you mean?"

"Why giving Green a licking, and then going to help him like that."

The other boy looked at the battered pair, and let them pass on in front, following afterwards with the others.

"It's the proper thing to do, isn't it?"

"Yes, with some fellows," said Tomlins, who was listening. "I should do it to either of you chaps if I'd licked you."

The pair looked at each other and laughed.

"Hark at Mouse Tomlins," said one of them.

"Ah, you wait. I shall get bigger some day, and then I shall do just as Convict Braydon does; but I shouldn't to old Green. You see if he don't hit foul before long, and serve poor old Convict out."

"Don't you be so fond of calling him Convict; he doesn't like it," said Braydon's second.

"Well, he shouldn't be a convict then," retorted the boy.

"And you shouldn't be a cocky, conceited little donkey," said the elder boy.

"But I'm not," said the little fellow, laughing; and then wincing and crying, "Oh, my leg!"

"And he's not a convict."

"But Gooseberry Green says his father is, and that he was sent over to Botany Bay, and that's what makes poor old Braydon so mad."

"His father and mother are both out there somewhere, because Nic told me so, and he says he's going out there some day; but his father can't be a convict, or else he wouldn't be at a good school like this. It's all Green's disagreeableness."

"I'm jolly glad he has got a licking," said the other, "though I seconded him; but I wish he hadn't spoiled our afternoon. If Nic Braydon would come too, I'd go and get into the Hurst. The doctor won't be back for two hours safe, and he's sure not to send for us till eight o'clock. Let's get him to come."

"Well, you ask him."

The boy hurried on and overtook the adversaries.

"Here, Nic Braydon, let him go on by himself. We're going to finish the afternoon together. We don't see any fun in going back yet."

Nic turned his face to his companion, who burst out laughing—a laugh in which he was joined by the others as they came up, Tomlins being the most facetious.

"I say, look at his open eye," cried the little fellow, "and the crack on his lip. I say, don't laugh, Nic; it'll hurt. Don't he look like enjoying himself!"

"Be quiet, Tomlins!" cried Nic's second.

"All right; I've done."

"I say, will you come, Nic?"

"No; I'm going to see Green back to the Friary."

"And then," cried Tomlins, "they're going to have a can of hot water and sponge one another, and make friends and live happy ever after. I say, wouldn't they both look nice in a glass case!"

Nic smiled in spite of himself; and went on back to the Friary, where the man-servant also indulged in a grin as he saw the battered, pair, who partook of their tea with pain, and looked thoroughly unpresentable when at eight o'clock they were summoned to the doctor's study to be lectured severely, Nic getting the greater part of the scolding, which ended with the ominous words:

"I will say no more, Dominic Braydon, for I don't like to come hastily to decisions; but I am afraid that I shall be forced to expel so evil-tempered, virulent, and quarrelsome a boy. Now retire, sir, to your dormitory. I will see you after breakfast in the morning."

Nic went slowly up to the room he shared with Tomlins and the boy who had been his second, feeling that the doctor was cruelly unjust in refusing to listen to explanations which he had on his side been extremely unwilling to make.

"Nobody seems to understand me," he said to himself; "convict, always convict. And, suppose I am expelled, what shall I do? what will my father say? It seems sometimes more than I can bear;" and for hours that night he lay awake, feeling no bodily pains in the fiercer ones of the mind, and always dwelling upon his position—quite alone in England, with father, mother, and sisters at the other side of the world, at a time, too, when it might take a year for a letter sent to bring back its answer; so that it was getting far on toward the early dawn when he ceased thinking about the far-away land of the convict and kangaroo, and went off fast asleep.

Chapter Three
A Startler

Constant dropping will wear a stone, says the old proverb; and if you doubt it, go and look at some step where the rain has dripped from gutter or eave, and see what a nice little hollow is worn. The constant dropping of unsavoury words wears the mind too; and these remarks and banterings about Australia and its convict life in the early days of the century began to have their effect upon Nic Braydon.

He was a good deal younger when his father, an eminent physician in London, awoke to the fact that he had been curing other people at his own expense, that he had worked and studied and been anxious over patients in his dingy house in Finsbury till he was completely broken in health; and he knew enough of his own nature to be aware that, if he kept on as he was, he would in a year or two be a confirmed invalid, if he were still living. In other words, he had worn the steel spring of life till it had grown thin in some places, and rusted and eaten away in others for want of use.

Then he said to himself like a wise man, "I advise others and neglect myself. I must be my own physician now."

He knew perfectly what he ought to do—take to some open-air life in a healthy country, where his avocations would give him plenty of outdoor exercise; and just at that time he met the newly appointed, governor of the penal colony of Australia at dinner. He heard a good deal about the place, went home and read, and inquired more; then, striking while the lion was hot, he sold his practice, house, and furniture, provided all that he could think of as necessaries, communicated with the government, and, after placing his son Dominic, then aged ten, at the Friary with Dr Dunham, he sailed with his wife and two daughters for the far-off land.

Now, Nic's notions about all this had grown a little hazy, while the teasings of his companions grew keener and sharper day by day, and mastered the facts; so that at last he had often found himself wondering whether there was any truth in his schoolfellows' words, and his father had, after all, done something which necessitated his leaving the country.

That seed did not take root; but it swelled, and shot, and gave him a great deal of pain, making him grow morbid, old, and thoughtful beyond his years. He became more sensitive; and when at last the doctor seemed to side against him, and treated him as he thought harshly, Nic began to find out thoroughly that it is not good for a boy to lose the loving help and companionship of father, mother, and sisters, and he grew day by day more gloomy, and ill-used as he believed, till at last, after the sharp reproof from the doctor about his quarrelsome disposition and ill-treatment of his schoolfellow Green, he began to feel it was time he set off to seek his fortune, never once pausing to think that the doctor had only judged by appearances. He had seen Nic attacking Green quite savagely, and not having been present earlier, and, truth to tell, not having sufficiently studied the inner life of his boys, he had looked upon Nic as an ill-conditioned, tyrannical fellow, who deserved the severest reproof.

So Nic thought it was time to seek his fortune.

Who was the miserable ass who first put that wretched idea into boys' heads, and gave them a mental complaint which has embittered many a lad's life, when, after making some foolish plunge, he has gone on slowly finding out that castles in the air, built up by his young imagination, are glorious at a distance, but when approached the colours fade? They are erected with no foundation, no roof; no walls, windows, doors, or furniture—in fact, they are, as Shakespeare says, "the baseless fabric of a vision."

So much by way of briefly moralising on the fact that for, a boy to make up his mind to go and seek his fortune means, in say nine hundred and ninety-nine thousand nine hundred and ninety-nine cases out of a million, trying to climb upward in search of a castle in the air, or tying a muffler round the eyes before making a leap in the dark.

So Nic wanted good advice, change, and something to drag him out of the belief that he was one of the most ill-treated young personages in the world.

But something came just a fortnight after the fight.

Nic's brow was all in puckers, his cheeks were pushed up in folds by his fists, his elbows rested upon his desk, and he was grinding away at a problem in Euclid—with thoughts of Green, Tomlins, the doctor, and a sore place upon one of his knuckles, which had partially healed up and been knocked again and again, all netted and veined in among right, acute and obtuse angles, sides, bases, perpendiculars, slanting-diculars, producings, joinings of AB and CD, and the rest of it—when one of the doors opened, the servant went up to the desk of the usher in charge, and the hum in the big schoolroom ceased as the usher tapped the desk before him.

"Braydon."

"Yes, sir."

"The doctor wishes to see you in the study."

Nic had started up, and now the wrinkles in his brow grew deeper, and then disappeared as if by magic, for he had caught sight of Green grinning at him with satisfaction in every curve of fat, self-satisfied-looking countenance; and putting on an air of calm indifference he moved toward the door.

As it happened he had to pass just in front of Green's desk, and the lad raised himself a little, put out a leg to cause a stumble, and whispered:

"Birch. Keep the door shut, and don't—"

Green was going to say "howl," but he illustrated his meaning by uttering a cry wonderfully like that sent forth by a cat under similar circumstances.

"What's that?" cried the usher.

"I trod on Green's foot by accident, sir," said Nic.

"Green should not leave his feet lying about all over the floor," said the usher, trying to be facetious, and then looking satisfied, for his joke was received with a roar, which was increased at the sight of Green's ghastly smile as Nic went out of the schoolroom.

"That's birch for him," he muttered, as he passed through the baize door, which shut out the noise of the school from the rest of the house; and the boy drew a deep breath as he crossed the hall toward the study, connected in his mind with scoldings and reproofs of the severest kind. "What have I been doing now?" thought Nic, as he laid hold of the handle after knocking and hearing a deep-toned "Come in."

Then he started and stared, for there was a fine-looking middle-aged lady seated near the doctor's table, who turned to look at him searchingly as he stopped short.

"I beg pardon, sir. You sent for me?"

"Yes, yes, Braydon: come in. This is Lady O'Hara."

"Yes, I'm Lady O'Hara. Look at that, now. A great strapping fellow! And he told Sir John that it was his little boy."

Nic stared, for this was spoken loudly, in a pleasant rich voice, with an intonation that decidedly fitted with the name.

"Yes, yes," said the doctor, who was smiling and very courtly; "but Dr Braydon forgot that his son has been with me over five years, madam, and he has grown bodily, and mentally, I hope."

"To be sure. Shake hands, Dominic. Why, you ought to be Irish, with a name like that."

"Lady O'Hara!" cried Nic excitedly, as he grasped the hand extended to him. "Do you know my father?"

"Oh, don't make jam of my fingers, boy, and I'll tell you," cried the lady, with a pleasant grimace. "Ah, that's better. Yes, of course I know him. He lives next door to us, about a hundred miles away."

The doctor chuckled, and Nic stared.

"Sit down, Braydon, sit down," said the doctor. "Ah! that's better," said the lady, in a fresh, cheery way. "Well, now, look at that, doctor. Here am I, come at his father's wish to take care of him, and he's big enough to take care of me."

"But—I beg your pardon," cried Nic—"you know my mother, madam?"

"To be sure I do, and the two girls; and here's a batch of letters I've brought."

"Oh, tell me, please," cried Nic excitedly, taking the letters with trembling hand,—"my mother and Janet and Hilda, what are they like?"

"Gently, gently," cried the lady; "where will I find breath to answer your questions? Why, the poor boy's like an orphan, Dr Dunham, living all these years away from home."

"Mrs Dunham and I try to make this my pupils' home," said the doctor, with dignity.

"Yes, I know," said the lady, smiling a broad, pleasant smile, and showing her fine white teeth; "but sure, doctor, there's no place like home. It's very pleasant out yonder with Sir John, but I long for wild old Galway, where I was born. Well, Dominic, and do you know what I've come for?"

"You said something about taking care of me, madam," stammered Nic.

"Ah, and don't stammer and blush like a great gyurl, and don't call me madam. I am a very old friend now of your dear mother, and I've come to take you back with me over the salt say—I mean sea, doctor, but I always called it say when I was a gyurl. I was in England a great deal after I was married, but the fine old pronunciation clings to me still, and I'm not ashamed."

"Why should you be, Lady O'Hara?" said the doctor in his most courtly manner, as he rose. "There, you would like to have a quiet chat with Dominic Braydon. I will leave you till lunch is ready."

"Oh, I don't know about lunch," said the lady, hesitating. "Yes, I do. Dominic here will lunch with us, of course?"

"Of course," said the doctor, smiling; and there was a curious look in his eye as Nic glanced at him sharply.

"Sure, then, I'll stay," said the lady. "But wait a minute: I shall be obliged to answer the question when we get back over the say. Did I say say or sea then, Dominic?"

Nic coloured a little.

"Oh, there's no doubt about it," cried the lady. "It was say, doctor. Now then, tell me: has he been a good boy?"

The doctor wrinkled his brow and pursed up his lips.

"Ah! ye needn't tell me. I can see—about half-and-half."

"Well, yes—about that," said the doctor.

"To be sure," said the lady; "and I'm glad of it. What's wrong with him?"

"Oh, I don't like to tell tales out of school," said the doctor jovially. "Not quite so much of a student as I could have wished. His classics are decidedly shaky, and his mathematics—"

"Look here, doctor: can he write a good plain English letter, properly spelt, and so as you can read it without puzzling because he hasn't dotted his i's and crossed his t's?"

"Oh! yes, yes, yes," said the doctor; "we can do that, eh, Braydon? But there's rather a long list of black marks against his name," he continued severely. "For instance, there has been a tendency toward fighting."

"There, that'll do, doctor.—Come and give me a kiss, my dear.—Sure, doctor," she continued, after Nic had obeyed, "he's coming out to a new country, where that part of his education will be of the greatest value to him."

"My dear madam!" cried the doctor, staring.

"Oh, I mean it, sir. It's a new country, full of savages, black and white, and the white are the worst of them, and more shame for us we sent them there, though I don't know what else we could have done. Dominic, my lad, do you know we're going to make a convict of you?"

Nic gave a violent start, and darted a reproachful glance at the visitor.

"There, leave us together a bit, doctor," she said quickly, "and I'll be bound to say when lunch is ready we shall both of us be as hungry as sailors with talking, for I've got to question him and answer all his."

"To be sure, to be sure," said the doctor. "Then, if you will excuse me, Lady O'Hara, I will adjourn to the schoolroom."

"There, Dominic," cried the lady as soon as they were alone, "now we can talk like old friends. But tell me what made you start and colour like a great gyurl when I talked of making a convict of you?"

Nic was silent.

"Won't you tell me?" cried the lady, smiling at him in a winning, frank way, which unlocked the boy's lips at once and made him feel eager to confide in one who took so much interest in him.

"Yes, I'll tell you," he cried: "it's one of the boys—the biggest. He has set it about that my father is—is—is—"

"A convict?"

Nic nodded, and his brow contracted.

"The impudence!"

"And he nicknamed me Convict. And it isn't true, Lady O'Hara? Pray, pray tell me."

"About your father, Dr Braydon? Be ashamed of ye'self, boy, for ever thinking it. Your father's the finest gentleman in New South Wales, and the best friend that Sir John and I ever had in our hard life yonder."

Nic drew a long, deep breath. Something seemed to be swelling up in his throat, and he reached forward to catch hold of and retain the plump white hand, which returned his pressure.

"And so the big fellow called you Convict, did he, because your father's over the water!"

"Yes."

"And I see now: that accounts for the fighting?"

Nic nodded.

"I bore it as long as I could," he said eagerly; "and it began about something else."

"Sure, and why did you wait for that? You should have done it at once. I would."

Nic stared in wonder and admiration at his new friend.

"But tell me: did you give him a great big beating?"

"Yes, I'm afraid so."

"Then don't be afraid any more. It would do him good. There, I was thinking I was going to have the care of a tiresome young, monkey of a boy; but I promised your dear mother, and should have taken you back. But, do you know, Dominic, you and I are going to be great friends."

"I hope so," said Nic.

"I'm sure of it. There, I don't want to know any more about you. I only say that you're just the lad for over yonder, and your father will be delighted. Now, then: ask me anything you like."

"May I?"

"To be sure."

"Then what is my mother like now?"

"Look yonder," said the lady, pointing to a great mirror. "Now think of your face made thinner and more delicate, and with soft curls of silky grey hair, beside a very white forehead; and a gentle expression, not a hard look, like yours. That's your mother."

"And my father?" cried Nic eagerly.

"Look again," said the lady, "and fancy your face in thirty years' time, with dark grey hair, all in little rough half-curls, and a great many lines in the brown skin all over the forehead, and about the eyes."

"Yes," said Nic eagerly, as he stared at himself.

"And a look of a man who is strong as a horse; and that's all. No, stop: I forgot his birrd."

"His bird! Does he keep a bird?"

"The young ruffian! he's making sport of me," said the lady. "I said birrd: b-e-a-r-d, birrd. And it's all tinged grey and black. That's your father."

"And the girls?"

"Oh, just two bright sun-browned colleens, like you, only better looking. What next?"

"What sort of a place is it?"

"Place? Oh, there's a wooden house on a slope looking down a bluff at the edge of a great plain, from which you look over the Blue Mountains."

"Yes, they call them blue because they're green, I suppose?" said Nic, with a smile.

"And people say it's only we Irish who make bulls," cried the lady merrily. "No; they call them blue because in the distance they look as clear and blue as the loveliest amethyst. Ah! it's a beautiful place, Dominic, as you'll say."

"And big?"

"Big?"

The lady laughed softly.

"Yes, boy; it's big. There's plenty of land out yonder, and so the government's pretty generous with it. Here at home they count a man's estate by acres: we do it in square miles out there."

"Look here, Dominic," said the lady, after answering scores of questions, during what seemed to Nic the happiest hours he had ever spent in his life, "I've been thinking."

"Yes, madam."

"Say Lady O'Hara, boy," cried the visitor petulantly; and then, with a sad smile full of pathos on her quivering lip, she added softly, "I can't tell ye to call me mother: my son died, Dominic, just when he began to know me; but look here," she cried, brightening, though the lad could see tears in her fine dark eyes, out of which she seemed to peer as from passing clouds. "Sure, I tell ye I've been thinking. Your father said it was time you left school to finish your education out there."

"Education?" faltered Nic.

"Oh yes; but not book learning, boy: hunting, and shooting, and riding, and stock-keeping, and farming, and helping to make Australia a big young England for John Bull's sons and daughters, who want room to move."

"Yes, I see," cried Nic.

"To be sure you do. Well, then, the ship sails in a month from to-day: so what's the good of your stopping here for a month?"

"But I've nowhere else to go," said Nic.

"Oh! yes, you have. You and I have got to be great friends—there, something more than that. I shall just borrow you of your father and mother till I have to give you up at Port Jackson. So, what do you say to my taking you away with me at once?"

"Lady O'Hara!"

"Don't shout, boy: this isn't the bush. Will you come?"

Nic sprang from his chair.

"Look at that, now!" cried Lady O'Hara, showing her teeth. "Hadn't we better have a bit of lunch first?"

"Oh! yes, yes, yes, of course. But, Lady O'Hara, will you take me?"

"Take ye? Why, what an ungrateful young rapparee it is, wanting to leave the home of five years like that!"

"Home!" cried Nic piteously. "Oh, Lady O'Hara, it hasn't been like home. I haven't been happy here."

"Sure, I know, boy, and it was only my fun," said Lady O'Hara, laying her hand upon the lad's head: "as if a boy could be quite happy away from all who love him, and whom, in spite of his thoughtless way; he loves! Then you shall come and live with me at the hotel, and help me do all my shopping and commissions, beside getting your outfit and the things you're to take out for your father. Come, Dominic, is it a bargain?"

"Do—do you really wish it?"

"Why, of course, boy, or I wouldn't ask you. Ah, here's the doctor and his lady. Sure, madam, I'm glad to make your acquaintance," said Lady O'Hara, with grave dignity. "Dominic Braydon and I have been arranging matters, and I should be obliged by your having his boxes seen to and sent off to-morrow."

"To-morrow?" said the doctor.

"Yes," said the visitor, in a quiet, decisive tone; "and as for your pupil— your late pupil—I shall take him away with me directly after lunch."

Both the doctor and his lady began to make excuses about the impossibility of Braydon being ready at so short a notice; and Lady O'Hara turned to the boy.

"Do you hear that, Dominic? You can't be ready in the time. What do you say?"

"I can," replied Nic.

"Of course you can, boy. There, doctor, I've come to take him, so now let's have lunch."

The lunch was eaten, and the doctor and Mrs Dunham having nothing more to say, Nic hastily packed up his things, and then ran to the schoolroom to say good-bye. Ten minutes later he was in Lady O'Hara's carriage, with the cheer given by the boys humming in his brain and a peculiar sensation of sadness making itself felt, though all the time his heart was throbbing with exultation, and the intense desire to go on faster and faster, far away from school, and to make his first plunge into the unknown.

Lady O'Hara did not speak for some time, but took out her little ivory tablets, and sat back in the carriage conning over the memoranda they contained, while her companion read and re-read his letters. Then, shutting them up, she returned the little book to its case and faced round.

"Well," she said, with a merry look, "have you done breaking your heart, Dominic?"

"Yes," he said gravely.—"I can't help feeling sorry to come away, and I'm afraid the boys liked me better than I thought for. It isn't so nice as I fancied it would be."

"No, I suppose not," said his companion; "nothing ever is so nice as we thought it would be. Like to go back for a month till the ship sails?"

"What!" cried Nic.

"I'll tell the man to drive back, if you like."

"You're saying that to tease me, Lady O'Hara."

"True, my boy, I was."

"And you know I wouldn't go back. All I want now is to get on board and start on our long journey."

"Ah, and that's, as I told you, a month hence. There, Dominic, you must mind I don't spoil you before I get you home. Now talk to me and tell me about yourself."

Chapter Four
Preparations

It was like a new beginning of life to Nic Braydon, and he lived for the next three weeks in a round of excitement. The principal way in which he spent his time was shopping with Lady O'Hara, who saw that he had a regular outfit of suitable articles of clothing, all of the most durable and useful make.

"You're not going to a land of filled shirts and dancing pumps, Dominic," said the lady; "you're going out to work as your father has done, and is doing now."

"I shall not mind work," said Nic sturdily.

"I know that, boy. But business. Now I think I've got through all the clothing—Sir John's, yours, and some that the doctor asked me to order. Now, what next?" she continued, turning to her tablets. "Oh, I see: a light gun that will carry shot or ball, a rifle for your father, and another for my husband. Then there are knives, axes, and fishing tackle. Really any one would think I was a man to execute such commissions. But I'm an old traveller, Nic, and have helped my husband over his wants for many, many years."

So that day was devoted to selecting guns, Lady O'Hara handling and testing the various pieces in a way that made the gunmaker open his eyes and Nic stare.

"You have a gallery, I suppose, where I can try any piece I select?"

"Oh! yes, ma'am—I beg pardon—my lady," said the gunmaker.

"Then I'll try those two rifles, and those three shot guns—no, those two. That other is only just long enough in the stock for me. It would not suit a man. Stop; you shall try it, Dominic. Well," she continued, smiling; "so you think it very unladylike for a woman to handle a gun, eh?"

"I—I did think something of the sort," said Nic hesitatingly.

"Of course you would; but I have often had to handle a gun, Dominic. A woman who goes out with her husband into all kinds of savage places needs to be able to use a piece."

"Then you have been in savage places?" said Nic.

"Often, my boy; and it is a dangerous place we are in now. And you'd like to ask whether I ever shot any one, eh?" she said, smiling. "No, I never did, and I hope I never shall. It was the power of being able to use a piece that has saved me from having to use it, Dominic. Wild people and ruffians don't care about attacking people who can defend themselves."

The gunmaker was ready with the charged guns, and he had led them into a long gallery with targets, where the lady astounded the man by her ability and knowledge of what a gun ought to be.

Then Nic had his first trials, and made so poor a business of it that Lady O'Hara said to him laughingly:

"Sure it must be a bad gun, with a crooked barrel. Let me try."

The reloaded gun was handed to her, and she raised it, lowered it, and raised it again and again to try the balance and weight.

"It comes up very nicely," she said, balancing it in her hands.

"It is really one of our best make, my lady," said the gunmaker.

"But my young friend does not seem to find that it shoots straight. Now then."

She raised it quickly to her shoulder, glanced for a brief instant along the barrel, and the white mark at the end of the gallery was speckled like a currant dumpling, while the gunmaker smiled with satisfaction.

"It was my fault," said Nic dolefully. "I suppose I can't see straight."

"Perhaps not," said Lady O'Hara drily. "How many times have you fired before?"

"Never till to-day, only little brass cannons," said Nic.

"And they're poor things for educating the hand and eye," said the lady. "Shooting looks easy, Dominic. You think you have only to pull the trigger; but it's like other things, my boy, it wants learning."

They walked back into the shop, where the guns and rifles selected were ordered to be packed with an ample supply of the best flints and ammunition in proper cases for the journey; and the gunmaker smiled his thanks, and wished for more masculine lady customers.

There were more peaceful purchases to be made, though. Cases of seeds were ordered, and the seedsman undertook to pack and send in the autumn a couple of bundles of fruit trees for experimental purposes.

"For I want your father to try and make a good English garden out there, Dominic," said Lady O'Hara enthusiastically. "Australia must become the home of many of our people; and though it is right on the other side of the world, we don't want it to remain foreign, but English."

Those four weeks went like magic, and when only two days remained the list of purchases was pretty well complete, and included horses, cows, and sheep of select kinds, and a couple of retrievers, setters, and Scotch collie dogs.

They had been twice to the East India Docks, from which the ship was to sail, and now another visit was to be paid to make sure that the various packages had been delivered on board, to see to the live stock, and to have another look at the cabin.

"There, Dominic," said her ladyship at last, "I think I may say that I have—that we have—done all our work. Now two days to pay a few visits, and then we go on board for our long, long journey. How do you feel—ready for the start?"

"Quite," said Dominic eagerly.

"That's right. We start with the knowledge that our home is ready made out yonder. What must it have been for the brave folk who acted as pioneers, not knowing what they were going to find?"

That was mental food for the night; but Nic's busy days precluded his being troubled with sleeplessness, and he lay down to dream of the far-off home, and woke to say, in his intense eagerness:

"Only one more day, and then—off!"

Chapter Five
Outward Bound

"But why not go on board to-night?" asked Nic.

"Because," said Lady O'Hara drily, "it will be better to leave it till to-morrow."

Nic wondered, and said nothing, but he knew afterwards. The fact was, he did not think about anything for long. There was too much to see and do. One thought crowded out another. This minute he would be wondering how the dogs were, the next whether cows were ever sea-sick, and this made him wonder whether Dominic Braydon, off on his first voyage, would suffer from that most unpleasant ailment. There were the new clothes to think about, and the guns. It happened, too, that while he was thinking about them Lady O'Hara, looking worried and tired, entered the hotel room.

"I hope that man sent the guns all right," said Nic.

"He did, for I received a note from him and a receipt for their delivery."

"I'm glad of that," said Nic. "I was anxious about them." Lady O'Hara looked amused. Then, watching the boy closely, she said:

"By the way, Dominic, I don't think I told you I meant that gun with the short stock for you."

"For me?" cried Nic, flushing with excitement. Then hastily, "Oh no, I don't want to shoot people."

"You may if they want to kill you or those whom you love, my boy. But in any case you may want to shoot snakes and the wonderfully beautiful birds which you will see in the bush. A gun is a necessity for a settler, and so are those."

She pointed to a parcel on a side table.

"Fetch those here, and open the paper."

Nic fetched the strongly done-up packet, opened it with trembling fingers, and laid bare a beautifully finished axe and a sheath knife of the finest steel, with stout buckhorn handle and leathern belt.

"Not drawing-room presents, my boy," said the lady, smiling, "but suitable for a young settler. There, you can squeeze those in your portmanteau; the gun you can have when we get over the sea."

"But, Lady O'Hara!" faltered Nic; "the gun—such an expensive one."

"Of course it is. Who'd buy cheap rubbish to take abroad? You want the plainest and the best that money can buy."

"Yes, but I meant—"

"That they were too costly to accept? Not a bit, my boy. We owe your father a deep debt. Didn't he doctor and save both our lives? And he's a dreadfully obstinate man to deal with; but I can do as I like with you, so now hold your tongue."

"But I must thank you, Lady O'Hara."

"No, you needn't. Now then, Dominic—dear, dear! three syllables to say every time I speak to you. What a tiresome, long name, though it does sound Irish."

"Latin," said Nic.

"Irish; and don't contradict me, sir. Sure I had an uncle in Galway, who was Dominick O'Hara, with a k to it. I shall call you Nic."

"Yes, do, please."

"I will. So now then, Nic, you haven't a husband to meet when you get over yonder—a fierce-looking governor, who barks at people; and when I get back he'll be asking me what I forgot to bring. Now, my dear boy, do tell me what I've failed to get."

"I can't," said Nic laughingly; "you seem to have bought nearly everything."

"Ah, ye're no use to me at all, at all, boy. I'm sure there's something I ought to have bought, and I shall remember it when we're hundreds of miles from land. I know: it was another pair of razors for Sir John!"

"But you bought those seven in a case, with the days of the week on them, Lady O'Hara."

"Sure, and I did, Nic. Good boy. You are of some use, after all. My poor head's nearly worn out with thinking, and I'm bothered entirely. Nic, I mean to go to sleep for a week as soon as we get on board by way of a good rest. Now then, do try and think for me, Nic; what was the other thing I forgot?"

Nic shook his head.

"I could think of hundreds of things that might be useful out there."

"No, you couldn't," said the lady shortly. "You've never been there, and you'd be taking out all kinds of things that would be just of no use at all, the same as I did when I first went. I've got something on my brain, only it's buried under a heap of other things. Well, never mind; it will shake up to the top at last when it's too late."

Lady O'Hara's head was bothered till the last moment, when the hotel bill was paid, the hackney coach and driver in his coat of many capes at the door, and landlord, landlady, and servants all waiting to bid the amiable, bluff-spoken Irish lady God-speed in her long journey to the other side of the world. Then the door banged; and, followed by a cheer, the coach was driven off, Nic feeling in a peculiar state of mind, a mixture of high spirits, low spirits, and pain; for Lady O'Hara plumped herself back in her corner, took out a handkerchief, covered her face, and burst into a fit of sobbing, rocking herself to and fro as she cried aloud till Nic could bear it no longer. He had been fidgeting and wondering what to say or do, growing more and more wretched, till, at the end of ten minutes, he laid his hand upon his companion's, and said simply:

"Oh, Lady O'Hara, pray, pray don't cry."

"Sure, and I won't," she exclaimed impetuously, as she hastily wiped her eyes; "but I couldn't help it, Nic. It hurts me when people are so kind and sorry to part from you, and ye feel that ye may never see them again. I'm afraid I'm a very silly old woman. Give me a kiss, my dear, and I won't cry another drop. There, it's all over now, and that's cleared my head. It doesn't feel bothered a bit. What's forgotten's forgotten, and I don't think my darlin' will be very cross with me. If he is, I shall call you to witness that I've worked very hard."

"That you have," cried Nic.

"There, the work's done, and we'll have a rest, and enjoy our voyage. And do you know what sort of a ship we're going in, Nic?"

"Yes; the *Northumbrian*."

"Of course; but do you know what she is?"

"East Indiaman."

"That's true enough; but has nobody told you what we shall have on board?"

"No."

"Then I'll tell you now. We might have waited for the next, but that would have been for a month, and I want to get back home again, Nic; so, as Sir John's name was enough to get me what I wanted, I settled we'd go in the *Northumbrian*, which is taking out a lot of convicts."

Nic's brow grew rugged.

"But there's a big draft of the 300th Regiment and their officers too, and they'll take care of us, boy, so you won't mind."

"Oh! no," cried Nic, "I shall not mind."

In fact, he failed to see what there would be to mind, for it did not occur to him that it might be unpleasant and awkward for the governor's wife.

The bustle of departure had commenced when they reached the dock, and the quay swarmed with the friends and relatives of the company of infantry off on foreign service, while dock officials were busy issuing the orders which began to take effect a few minutes after Nic had seen Lady O'Hara into her cabin and hurried back on deck to gaze on the novel scene.

For hawsers were being secured round posts, men were leaving, a couple of boats were out ahead ready to tow, and soon the great three-masted vessel began to move slowly along by the quay to the great gates, with the soldiers cheering and waving their caps, and shouts and cries rising from those being left behind, till the gates were passed, and the long narrow channel between stone walls gave place to the river, with its tide at the height; the faces began to grow smaller and smaller, and soon the *Northumbrian*, with her littered decks and bustle and confusion, began to drop slowly down with the tide.

There was plenty to see as well as plenty to learn. The first thing was to be able to see in peace, and to do this Nic found he had to learn to get out of the way of the men busy lowering down packages, getting rid of the litter of the deck, and blunderingly making matters shipshape—blunderingly, for the crew, almost without exception, were suffering from the effects of their holiday ashore, and were working the mate and boatswain into a state of red-hot indignation at the slow progress made. The latter, too, a big, burly, red-faced man with stiff whiskers, was every now and then asking people how he could be expected to have clear decks when his ship was being turned into a farmyard.

This recalled the live stock on board, and Nic went forward to have a look at the cattle in their pens, where they were contentedly enough munching away at the hay placed ready for them, while the dogs, which recognised Nic, began to tug furiously at their chains, and made their eyes seem ready to start from their heads as they tried to strangle themselves by straining at their collars.

Nic was leaning over the pen in which they were chained up, patting and caressing them, when a gruff voice cried fiercely:

"Those dogs yours?"

"Not exactly. They're for Sir John O'Hara."

"Then I wish he'd got 'em. Who's to move with all these things on board?"

"What's, the matter, Buller?" said a bronzed man, coming up.

"Matter, sir? everything. There isn't a man aboard fit to pull a rope, and I can't move without breaking my shins over cats and dogs, and all this here Tower mynadgery. Is the skipper going to start a farm?"

"Get on, man, and don't make so much noise."

"Noise, sir!" growled the boatswain, for it was he; and he looked hard at a couple of officers in undress uniform, whose attention had been taken by the dogs.

"It's enough to make any one grumble. I'm 'customed to tea and rice and a few passengers. I don't understand all this—ship turned into a live-stock show, a barracks, and a farm all in one."

He went off growling, and the mate turned to the officers.

"A bit rusty, gentlemen," he said, smiling. "It will soon wear off, as we get shipshape."

"Sooner the better," said one of the officers, who turned to the dogs, and had a look at them before speaking to Nic.

"Yours?" he said.

"I have charge of them."

"Then you are a passenger?"

"Yes; I'm going out with Lady O'Hara."

"The governor's wife! Well, how do you think you will like the sea?"

"Oh, very well," said Nic. "Of course I shan't like it when it's rough."

"Nor anybody," said the officer, "eh, Harvey?"

"I shall not," said the gentleman addressed, as he pulled the setter's long ears.

"So long as it isn't rough. Well, as we are to be fellow-passengers all through the voyage, we may as well be friends and go through our introductions. Who are you?"

Nic told him.

"Going to join your people, eh? Well, that's pleasant. We are going to leave ours."

"Who are you?" said Nic, taking his new acquaintance's tone.

"I?" said the officer, laughing at the manner in which the question was put. "Lieutenant Lance, His Majesty's 300th Light Infantry. This is Ensign Harvey of my company. Both at your service, sir, and our company too."

"Thank you," said Nic, laughing; "but I'm not likely to need it."

"Unless the birds want to take *flight*," said the ensign.

Nic looked at him inquiringly.

"He means the gaol birds, youngster," said the elder officer, laughing, "if they rise against us. Not a very nice arrangement for your lady coming out in a ship like this."

"Is there any danger?" said Nic anxiously.

"No," said the ensign, rather importantly; "we shall see that there's not."

"Then you are here to guard them?" asked Nic.

"Bah, no! We are going to join our regiment. There is a warder guard. Of course, if there was any necessity—"

Nic looked rather startled, and the lieutenant said, smiling:

"There'll be nothing to mind, my lad. The winds and waves will trouble you more than the convicts; but they're not pleasant fellow-passengers to have, on board."

Nic did not think so the next morning, when, after guard had been mounted under the lieutenant's charge, just as they were getting well out of the mouth of the river, with the soldiers stationed at intervals with loaded muskets and fixed bayonets, orders were given, and the stern-looking warders ushered up the convict gang of fifty men from below to take their allotted amount of air and exercise in the forward part of the deck; for almost without exception they were a villainous-looking lot, their closely cropped hair and ugly prison garb adding to the bad effect.

Talking was strictly forbidden, every movement being carefully watched, and not least by Nic, at whom the prisoners looked curiously as they passed, one man putting on a pleading, piteous aspect, as if asking for the boy's compassion, and twice over his lips moved as if he were saying something.

But somehow, though the man was not bad-looking, and formed one of the exceptions to the brutally fierce faces around, his pleading look did not excite Nic's pity, but caused a feeling of irritation that he could not explain.

This happened again and again, when, attracted by the daily coming up of the men on deck, Nic found himself watching them, unconscious of the fact that he was watched the while.

Every now and then the chief warder, a stern, fierce-looking man with a cutlass in his belt, shouted out some order; and as it was obeyed by this or that man the boy soon began to know them as Number Forty-nine or Hundred and eighty, or some other number. One particularly scoundrelly-looking fellow, who made a point of catching his eye whenever he could, for the purpose of winking, thrusting his tongue in his cheek, or making some hideous grimace, and following it up with a grin of satisfaction if he saw it caused annoyance, was known as Twenty-five; a singularly brutal-visaged man with a savage scowl, who never once looked any one full in the face, was Forty-four; and the mild, pleading-looking man, who annoyed Dominic by his pitiful, fawning air, was Thirty-three.

"Well, sir, what do you think of them?" said a familiar voice one day; and turning sharply, Nic found himself face to face with the chief warder.

"Think? I hardly know," said Nic. "I feel sorry for them."

"Just what a young gent like you would do, sir. Pity's a good thing, but you must not waste it."

"But it seems a terrible thing for these men to be sent out like this."

"Seems, sir. But is it? You see, they needn't have been sent out. They only had to behave themselves."

"But some of them may be innocent."

"Yes, sir," said the warder drily; "but which of 'em? Look at that fellow coming round here now, slouching along, and never looking at anything but the deck. He'll never look you in the face."

"Yes, I've noticed that."

"Wouldn't pick him out for an innocent one, would you?"

"Well, no," said Nic; "one seems to shrink from him."

"And right enough too, sir. He got off with transportation for life; but I'm afraid he deserved something worse."

"Did he kill anybody?" said Nic in an awe-stricken whisper.

"Yes; more than one, I believe, sir: sort of human wild beast. I never feel safe with him, and we all take care never to have Forty-four behind us. Try again, sir."

"Well, this one coming now," said Nic. "He's rather common-looking, but he doesn't seem so very bad. One would think he could be made a better man."

"Twenty-five, sir. Well, he'll have every chance out yonder. He has only got to get a good character over his work, and the governor and them will soon let him go up country as a signed servant, and when he has served his time he can start farmer on his own account. Makes faces at you, doesn't he?"

"Yes," cried Nic eagerly.

"Ah, he won't now I'm here."

Nic smiled, for the man screwed one side of his face as he passed, thinking that the chief warder would not see, but he did.

"You, Twenty-five! How dare you? Extra punishment for that. Pass by, sir."

"No, no, don't punish him," whispered Nic. "He did not mean any harm."

"Not going to, sir," said the warder drily; "but one must keep them in their places. He's a comic sort of blackguard. Not much harm in him."

"I thought not," said Nic eagerly.

"And precious little good, sir," added the warder. "But he may turn out right. Housebreaking, I think, was his offence. When he gets out to the convict lines they'll teach him to know better; and some day he'll have a house of his own, if it's only a bark hut—gunyah they call 'em out there—and then he'll know the value of it, and be ready to upset any one who tries to break in."

"Then you have been out before?"

"Oh yes, sir. I know the country pretty well, specially the part where your father is. I've been there."

"And you know my father?"

"Oh no, sir. I never saw him. But it's a fine place, and you'll like it. I wish I was you, and going to begin life out there in the new land."

"Then you think I shall like it?" said Nic.

"You can't help it, sir. But if I was you I should be careful. You'll have a deal to do with the convicts."

"Oh no," cried Nic. "I am going straight up the country to my father's place."

"Yes, sir, I know; and that's why I was presuming to give you a bit of advice—that is, as a man who has had twenty years' experience."

"I don't understand you."

The warder laughed.

"I suppose not, sir. Well, it's like this. Your father has taken up land, and keeps sheep and cattle, I suppose?"

"Yes, thousands."

"And employs men?"

"Of course. He has said so in his letters. He is obliged to have several."

"And if he was in England he could engage farm labourers easily enough."

"Yes."

"How's he going to engage them out there, sir?"

"The same as he would in England."

"When there are none, or only a few, and they all want to be masters themselves? No, sir; you'll find there—with perhaps a black or two who can't be trusted to work, only to do a bit of cattle driving or hunting up strayed stock—that your father's men are mostly convicts, 'signed servants, we call them—that is, assigned servants."

"What?"

"That's it, sir: men who are assigned by the prison authorities to gentlemen."

"Oh!" ejaculated Nic; and the warder smiled at his surprise.

"That's it, sir, and I say a good thing too. Here's a new country with plenty of room in it, and the judges and people at home sentence men to be transported for fourteen or twenty-one years, or perhaps for life."

"Yes, I know all that," said Nic, nodding his head.

"Then, sir, the law says lots of these men are not all bad, and they're sorry for what they've done; so if they are, and show that they want to lead a new life, we'll give 'em a chance. Then all those who have earned a good character in the convict lines and mean work are assigned to settlers who want labourers and shepherds and stockmen; and if they behave themselves, and show that the punishment has cured them of their bad ways, all they've got to do is to report themselves from time to time; and so long as they don't try to escape out of the country they can do pretty well as they like, and plenty of them out there are doing far better than they would have done at home."

"That's very good," said Nic.

"To be sure it is, sir; and that's why I say to you, be a little careful, and not be ready to trust the convicts. Plenty of them you'll find good fellows; but there are plenty more who are very smooth and artful, and only waiting their time. But you'll soon learn which are sheep and which are goats. Now, here's a chap coming round here—Thirty-three, sir. What do you say to him? He's got fourteen years for robbing his employers. Embezzlement they call it. Now, he's been a well-brought-up sort of man—good education, always well dressed, and lived on the fat of the land. He looks at you, I suppose, when I'm not here, as much as to say, 'Isn't it cruel to shut me up with these ruffians and murderous wretches? I'm a poor, innocent, ill-used man!'"

"Yes, that is how he always does look at me," cried Nic. "Yes, sir, and at everybody else; but if he was an innocent, ill-used man, he'd wrinkle up his forehead and look bitter and savage-like, ready to treat everybody as his enemy. That chap's a sneak, sir, and I've no hesitation in saying he deserves all he has got. Don't you listen to him if ever he speaks, and don't you break no rules by petting him with anything good from the cabin."

"I certainly shan't," said Nic. "I don't like him."

The warder turned sharply, and looked hard at Nic, as he said, smiling:

"You'll do sir. Dame Nature's made you a bit of a judge of men, and what you've got to do is to sharpen up that faculty, as people call it. I'm not bragging, but I've got it a little, and I've polished and polished it for twenty years, till I'm not such a very bad judge of convicts. You give me a gang, and in a week's time, if there's an innocent man, or a man who wants to do the right thing, or one who's been always wrong and could be worked up into the right, I'll pick him out. Here you, Twenty-five, I've got my eye on you, and you'd better make an end of those monkey faces, unless you want the cat."

"The cat?" said Nic.

"Yes, sir, with nine tails. That's the punishment for convicts who won't behave themselves, assigned servants and all. You'll soon know all about the lash when you get out to your father's station."

"I'm sure I shall not," said Nic indignantly. "My father is too humane a man."

"That's right, sir. You always believe in and stick up for your father; only recollect you're going to a new country, where there are thousands of convicts, the scum of our own land, and the lash is part of the law, and the law is very strict. It's obliged to be, for the protection of the settlers. See how stern we are here where we have them all under our eye. You're obliged to be harder where they're free like and scattered all over the country."

"Yes, you're stern enough," said Nic indignantly, "threatening to give a man the cat-o'-nine-tails for making faces."

The warder smiled, his hard, stern face lighting up as he gazed admiringly at Nic.

"Bah! that was only talk, sir, just as one would threaten a boy. Twenty-five's a man of five-and-thirty, but he's only got brains like a boy. I could make anything of him."

The warder nodded good-humouredly, and then his face grew hard-looking as an iron mask, as he shouted out orders to first one and then another of the men under his charge; while the soldiers, standing here and there, rested on their muskets, and looked grimly on at the evil-looking prisoners pacing the deck.

Nic walked aft with his forehead puckered up and his mind hard at work thinking of the home that he was going to, and feeling somewhat damped by the warder's words; and as he reached the quarter-deck he went to the side, after noticing that Lady O'Hara was talking to the officers, and resting his arms upon the bulwark he leaned there gazing away at the sunlit sea, flecked by the flying-fish which flashed out, skimmed along for some distance, and then dropped back into the water.

"Convicts—convicts," he thought. "What a place for Lady O'Hara it is here with these men aboard! Suppose they should rise some night—suppose they should rise at home where mother is, and the girls—suppose—"

"Why, how now, my thoughtful young philosopher? What are you thinking about?"

Lady O'Hara had laid her hand upon his shoulder, and the boy was silent for a few moments.

"Well, what is it? Not going to turn sea-sick, after behaving so well all across the bay."

"No," said Nic; "I'm quite well."

"Then what makes you look so glum?"

"I was thinking about the convicts."

"And a very unpleasant subject too, Nic. Don't think about them, boy. They used to make me ill when I first went out yonder. It seemed so horrible to have them mixed up so with one's daily life."

"Yes, that's it," cried Nic; "that's what I've been thinking. I suppose father will have some at his station?"

"Not a doubt about it."

"Well, it seems so shocking, and—and unsafe."

"Not a bit of it, my boy. That's just what I used to think, but I don't now."

"But I shall never get hardened to it, Lady O'Hara."

"Sure, I hope not, Nic. I don't like hardened people. You think by my words that I'm hardened to it. There, don't turn red, boy. I can read what you thought. I'm as soft as you. Sure, I wept all night when that poor boy died over there, and kept crying out for his mother when he was delirious; and it was no use to say to myself, he should have thought more of his mother and her teachings when he grew wasteful and dissipated and stole his master's money, for I couldn't help thinking that he was back in the old days and felt in trouble, and called for his mother; and who should a boy call to but his mother at a time like that?"

Nic sadly thought of how little he had seen of his, and the governor's wife went on.

"No, Nic, I'm not a bit hardened; I only look now at things from a sensible point of view, and say to myself, 'Here are these men who have done wrong, and the law has sent them out for a punishment; those who are very bad will be unable to do any more mischief, while those who have any good in them have chances given them to lead a new life.' Why some of them are getting to be well-to-do bodies, Nic, and married and have children, who will grow up better people in a new land. Don't you fret about the convicts, boy; but take them as you find them. When you have to do with the bad ones, keep them at a distance; and when you have to do with the good and repentant, just shut your eyes to the past and open them as wide as you can to the future. Sure, Nic, I'm the governor's lady with a title, and everybody's glad to be my friend, yourself included, my boy; but how do I know what I might have been if I hadn't been tenderly cared for when I was young? You'll like some of the transported people, Nic, my boy. I've got some out there whom I look upon as friends, and just because I see that they've put the past behind, and are doing what these sailor lads do here, keeping a bright look-out ahead. Yes, Nic, they're looking to the future, and so am I and you. What a place this world would be if we hadn't a future before us every one! There, you will not fret nor worry yourself about any dangers we are likely to meet with from the convicts now."

"Oh no," said Nic eagerly; "you have done me no end of good, Lady O'Hara. But—"

"Well, but what, boy? Out with it, and don't hesitate."

"Are they ever likely to rise against us over there, or here aboard ship?"

"Sure, I don't know, Nic," said Lady O'Hara coolly. "Very likely, my boy. They are always thinking about it, I know."

"But if they do?"

"Well, we shall just have to rise too, and teach them manners. We've got right on our side, and they haven't; so we are sure to win."

"But you don't seem at all alarmed, in spite of all that I have said."

"Sure, and why should I be, Nic, or you either? They may rise, and a hole may burst out in the bottom of the ship, and we may run upon a rock, and there may be a storm, and there are plenty of other maybe's, Nic. But let them be, my dear boy. You and I have got our duty to do, and let's do it, and while we're doing that, leave all the rest. Nic, boy, faith's a grand thing. I'm full of it, and ye're just a little wanting; so get it as fast as ye can; it's a fine thing in the making of a true man."

Chapter Six
On the other Side

The voyage was long but uneventful. They sailed on, in fine weather, down and down into hot inter-tropical sunshine, and reached the Cape, took in fresh stores, and then sailed on south, so as to get into the region where the winds are chill, but blow strongly in the right direction, carrying the big ship onward in its course.

Week succeeded week in slow monotony, broken by a little rough weather, but that was all. The soldiers were drilled on deck till Nic pretty well knew the ordinary routine, and Lieutenant Lance laughingly asked him if he would like to take command. The convicts came up morning by morning and had their exercise in the old monotonous way; and Nic went round with the doctor to see the men in their quarters and visit patients. But there was no rising or mutiny, nothing to break the even course of the voyage but a little tossing among the huge waves that came rolling from the south-west, threatening to engulf the ship, but only dived beneath it, raising it upon a rolling bill, and then gliding onward to give room to the next. Nic saw the albatross till he was tired of watching its gliding flight. He fished and had very bad fortune, but better when he joined in with the sailors, who good-humouredly made room for him to help haul after they had hooked a shark, drawn the fierce fellow alongside, sent a loop down over its head right to the narrow part in front of the tail, and so got a double hold.

Then came the evening when all was excitement, for the skipper announced at supper that in all probability they would see land next morning, and a thrill ran through every breast.

He was correct: land was in sight at daybreak, and Nic was standing on deck to see it, hardly willing to be dragged away to breakfast, and back again with Lady O'Hara and the officers, all eager after their long, long voyage—for ships did not reach Australia in less than six weeks in the days of King George the Third—to see the land that was to be their home for many months, in some cases years, to come.

That afternoon they sailed out of the rough water between the great headlands into the lake-like expanse of the glorious harbour; and before long, after signalling, boats were seen approaching, their white sails glistening in the clear air.

"Smell, Nic," said Lady O'Hara, "home at last, boy! What do you think of the sunny land?"

"Think?" cried Nic huskily — "it is glorious! I never saw the sky so blue, the land so green, and everything so beautiful. But pray, pray don't talk to me. I want to try and make out whether my father is in any of those boats."

"I should say yes: in that," said Lady O'Hara, who spoke in a deep, subdued voice.

"Which — which?" cried Nic.

"That one, with the union jack at the stern."

"What, with the men in white?"

"Yes; it is the boat from the man-o'-war yonder. The governor is in it, please God; and your father, as his friend, will most likely be with him."

Just then one of the officers handed her a telescope, and went forward to order up a guard of men to receive the governor.

Lady O'Hara did not seem herself. She was no longer the bluff, outspoken woman, but appeared trembling and nervous, as she stood resting with one hand upon the rail.

"I can't use it to-day, Nic, boy," she said. "You try the glass."

Nic took it, rested it on the rail, had a long look, and focussed and re-focussed it, without avail.

"I — I can't see with it," he said huskily. "It is so dim. The glass is not clear."

"Try again," said Lady O'Hara; and Nic looked at her sharply, her voice was so changed.

But he raised the glass once more, and this time brought it steadily to bear upon the boat rowed by the man-of-war's men.

"Now, Nic, tell me what you see," said Lady O'Hara. "Some soldiers with muskets and bayonets. I can see the scarlet quite plain."

"Yes, yes: the marines. What else?"

"There's an officer just in front of the flag."

"One officer?"

"Stop a minute. Yes, there's another: he seems to me a bigger man."

"Look — look again."

"It's so far off that I can't quite make out, and the glass won't keep steady; but I think he has a big white beard. Yes, and he has taken off his hat. His head is white."

Lady O'Hara half closed her eyes, and the captain, who was near, saw that a smile came upon her lip.

"But you see some one else, Nic?" she said faintly.

"Yes," said the boy in a very husky voice; "but it must be a seaman: there is some one in a straw hat."

"And who will that be, Nic?"

"A sailor, I suppose."

"I do not say. Your father generally wore a straw hat. Can't you make out his face?"

"No," said Nic, taking his eye from the glass quickly, and gazing at the boat, which seemed to have suddenly gone back some distance.

"I want to look without the glass," he added, after a minute or so; and then, forgetful of the glorious panorama spread around beyond the blue lake-like harbour, he held on by the rail, gazing hard at the approaching boat, seeing neither of the others, only that one with the white jacketed men who made the water flash at each dip of the oars.

Then by degrees Nic began to make out the faces, which grew clearer and clearer, till the figure wearing the straw hat rose up and waved it, and the officer in uniform rose up then and took off his hat.

At that moment Nic was conscious of the fact that Lady O'Hara was close by him, waving a white handkerchief.

Then he seemed to see nothing but a blurred picture of boats drawing nearer, as the great *Northumbrian*, with her sails hanging almost motionless, glided slowly onward through the calm water.

He was conscious, though, of the gangway being manned, and of a guard of soldiers being drawn up to receive the governor, the officers and the captain and mates being ready too.

At last the boat came close in alongside; a sharp order was shouted, the guard presented arms, and a big burly grey officer stepped easily on board, raised his hat to the officers, and then took Lady O'Hara's hands in his, gazed at her for a moment, and then quietly drew her arm through his, while she drew a deep, long breath, and stood there proud and happy.

Nic just saw her, but only as it were out of the corner of his eye, for he was tremblingly watching the gangway for the next comer—a tall, spare, grey, aquiline-looking man with face of a warm sun tan, and eyes that seemed to pierce the boy through and through, as he held out his hand and cried "Father!"

"Yes, my boy. Then you knew me again? Why, Nic, lad, what a great fellow you have grown! Lady O'Hara, welcome back."

"And glad to be back," cried the lady, shaking hands, and after a glance at Nic, asking the question hovering on his lips, "And how are they at the Bluff?"

"All well, and send loving greetings."

"Which I'll answer for myself, and very soon," cried the lady.

"And all well?" said the governor, with a look round as if addressing every one.

Lady O'Hara answered.

"Yes, all well. An excellent voyage, and you'll thank the officers for their kindness to me and Dominic Braydon here. Gentlemen, I am going ashore in the boat, but I shall not say good-bye. My husband bids me say that he will be glad to see every one who can leave the ship this evening at dinner. What time, my dear?"

"Six, gentlemen," said the governor; and after a little official business the party descended into the boat, and, feeling as if it were all a dream and impossible, Nic sat there being rowed ashore toward Government House, holding his father's hand for the first few minutes till he fancied that he was noticed, and then listening to him as he pointed out the various buildings ashore, and the vessels afloat, two of them being men-of-war, whose rigging was gay with bunting in honour of the governor's lady's return.

"Well, Nic," said his father at last, as they gazed searchingly in each other's eyes, and with the most satisfactory result, "do you think you will like Australia?"

"Like it?" cried Nic. "Why, of course, father: isn't it home?"

"Yes, but rather a rough, unpolished place."

"What does that matter!" said Nic proudly. "Shan't I be with you all again?"

Chapter Seven
Preparing to Start

In those days it did not take long to see the town. There were some shabby-looking stores and shops, a few settlers' houses, the hotel, taverns, and plenty of tents. The substantial parts were the buildings erected for the soldiery and convicts. But these latter were busy enough, gangs of them being marched out every morning under a strong guard to work at road making, quarrying, and other tasks; and as Nic, boy like, went round everywhere during the few days of his stay at the governor's house, he ran up eagerly, as soon as a convict gang appeared, to see if he could encounter his old shipboard friend the head warder, and whether he could recognise any of the convicts who came out in the *Northumbrian*.

But they and the soldiers seemed to have been absorbed in the large body of men in the convict lines and barracks, and he looked in vain for the fierce, swarthy ruffian, his comic, grimace-making friend Twenty-five, and the pitiful, pleading countenance of Thirty-three.

Still, there was a great deal to see, and the time went rapidly as he watched the convicts at work with their armed guard always on the *qui vive* to shoot down any man who attempted to resist their warders or make for the bush.

There were the blacks too, fairly plentiful in those days, hanging about the place ready to help drive sheep or cattle, or do any light work which did not entail much labour.

The hospitality at Government House was everything that could be desired, and here the lieutenant and ensign were welcomed again and again during their stay.

The last day came, when, after making all his preparations, the doctor announced that they would start at dawn the next morning.

"Why not stay another week?" said Lady O'Hara.

"You know," said the doctor: "those at home are eager to see us back; and Nic here is longing to find out what home is like. When shall we see the governor and you?"

"Before many months are over. That road is begun, you see, and we shall work up in your direction. Perhaps we may run over for a flying visit before."

That evening Nic accompanied his father to where the various goods purchased for him by Lady O'Hara had been stored at a kind of warehouse; and here Nic found a large, light waggon in the course of being loaded by a couple of fierce-looking, bearded men, whose bare arms were burned of a reddish tan.

The elder of the two, a man of about fifty, was standing up in the waggon pulling at a great packing-case, while his companion, a well-built fellow, who looked strong and active as could be, was hoisting up the case, helped by a shaggy-haired native, whose face shone as if it had been blackened and polished like a boot. The white, or rather the reddish-brown, man attracted Nic's attention at once, as he stood there with his muscles standing out, making him resemble an antique statue; but it was the embittered, proud, and resentful look in his face which struck the boy.

It was quite evident that he was attempting a task for which he was not equal, and that, instead of the case being deposited in the waggon, it would the next minute go down with a crash to the ground; and, as soon as this was seen, Nic involuntarily ran to help, and his father shouted as he, too, ran and seized one side of the case, with the result that the black grinned and made way, to stand looking on.

"Jump down, Brookes!" cried the doctor. "You ought to know better. Get the case up first, and then put it in its place."

"Know better?" growled the man. "I know how to load a waggon; but who's to do it with a fellow like that and a nigger? One's got no muscle, and t'other's like a black-pudd'n."

"Get down—quick!" cried the doctor.

"I'm a-comin'," growled the man; and he descended slowly, placed a shoulder under the end of the chest, and it was turned over on to its side.

"Jump in, Leather, and work it into its place."

"Oh, I can do that," grumbled the elder man; but his companion sprang up lightly, hoisted one end of the case, and walked it bit by bit to where it was to stand, before leaping down again.

"Is this our waggon, then?" asked Nic.

"Yes, boy. We take the load back with us. I think we shall just get all up in one load."

"Are the roads good?" asked Nic, as he gazed at the heavy packing-cases; and the elder man grinned, while the labourer addressed as Leather, (a name which accorded well with his tanned skin), glared at the speaker once with a frown, and then told the black to help him with the next case.

"Neither good nor bad," said the doctor, smiling.

"But I mean for the horses to draw the load?"

"There are no roads, my boy, and there will be no horses to draw the load. We have only a rough track through the bush, and our men use draught-oxen in yoke."

This was the first hint to Nic of the place being very wild. He said no more for some time, but readily set to work trying to help where he could, his father nodding approval as he noted his eagerness.

Under the master's eye and in accordance with his suggestions the loading went on better now, though from time to time little matters kept showing that the elder man lost no opportunity for finding fault with the younger, who was either weak, stupid, unwilling, or clumsy in the other's eyes. But the man worked steadily and well, and Nic began to feel annoyed and ready to tell the elder servant that if he would only work as well as his fellow the waggon would be laden much sooner.

"I dare say father will give it to him soon, though," said Nic to himself; "I've no right to interfere."

The intended short visit to the waggon lasted three hours before the doctor was satisfied to leave his men to rope everything on securely.

"And it will not be done, Nic," he said, as they walked away. "That's where I want you, my boy, to grow up into a sort of lieutenant—to act as my second pair of eyes, and see that the men do not shirk things. I'm sorry to say that they will do it if I am not looking on. Now then, I'm going to show you the horses that draw our waggon."

He led the way to a fenced-in pen, where a dozen fine, healthy-looking bullocks were grazing; and upon Nic looking up wonderingly, his father laughed.

"Yes," he said, "those are our draught animals. They are terribly slow, but very sure. By the way, though, Nic—I never thought of that—can you ride?"

"Not bullocks, father," said the lad proudly. "I'll walk."

"Rather a long walk, Nic," said the doctor quietly. "Well, I can walk part of the way, and ride on the waggon the rest. But will it take us more than a day?"

"Yes," said the doctor dilly; "it will take us more than a day. But come here."

He led the way to a rough, shed-like building, entered, and a couple of sleek, well-bred horses turned their heads from the posts to which they were haltered, and whinnied.

"Will one of these do for your lordship to ride?" said the doctor, smiling, as he went up to and patted the horses in turn.

"Yes!" cried Nic. "What beauties, father!"

"Glad you like them. I bought that sorrel nag for you. He isn't up to my weight."

"But—"

"Well, but what, boy?"

"I've never been on a horse, father," said Nic, with a shamefaced air.

"Never learned to ride? No, of course not," said the doctor. "Riding was not included in the range of studies at the Friary."

"But we boys used to catch the donkeys on the common of an evening, and mount them."

"Oh, come," cried the doctor; "then you can ride a donkey?"

"Sometimes, father," said Nic, laughing. "They often used to send us off."

"Kicking?"

"It was hardly kicking, father. One I used to try and ride would stand perfectly still till I was on and tried to make him go, and then he used to bring all his legs close together, put his head down, arch up his back, and somehow or other, when he began to dance about, we always got shot off, and came down on our backs. You never saw anything so queer."

"Oh! yes, I have," said the doctor drily, "often. Our horses here have that bad habit, and we call it buck jumping, for it is very much the action of a bounding deer. Have you been pitched off like that more than once?"

"Oh! yes, father; scores, perhaps hundreds of times," said Nic, laughing.

"Come then, you will not be afraid to mount this horse, and I dare say I can soon teach you to ride. It's too late now, or I'd give you a lesson."

He closed the door of the shed, went back to the waggon, where the younger man was on the top straining at a rope, and the elder giving orders, while the black was squatting down and looking on. Here a few words of instruction were given, and a question or two asked about the flour barrels and bacon.

These being answered satisfactorily, the doctor led the way back to the Government House, where they had just time to prepare for dinner and meet the two officers and the captain and ship's doctor, who had been asked to meet them by way of farewell.

Bed was sought early, the doctor laughingly telling his son to make much of it, for he would have to make shift for some time to come.

"It's good-bye to civilisation when we leave here in the morning," said the doctor, looking hard at his son.

"And he won't mind it a bit," said Lady O'Hara. "He's just the boy to take to a bit of rough work in the bush."

"I'm glad of it," said the doctor drily, "for we rough it in the bush, and no mistake."

Nic lay down that night in his comfortable bedroom after a long look out of his window at the beautiful moonlit harbour, with its shipping bathed in the soft, silvery light, and a feeling of melancholy came over him. He was sorry to leave frank-spoken, motherly Lady O'Hara, and the thought of going right away into the wilds, though fascinating, would inspire him with a shrinking feeling of awe.

For during the few days he had been ashore he had picked up some information, and not always of the pleasantest nature. People about had not been backward in telling him that the blacks were rather fond of spearing people who entered the bush. They had some ugly stories, too, about tiger-snakes, which lay waiting for unwary passers-by, and then struck them, the bite being so venomous that the sufferer would survive only a few hours at most, possibly only a few minutes.

There were other terrors and dangers, too, in the bush, they said; but when asked what, they shook their heads very strangely, as if the subject were not to be mentioned, for fear of ill befalling those who talked lightly. So one way and another Nic was pretty well primed, and consequently only slightly buoyed up by the knowledge that he was going to his real home, he fell asleep to dream of all kinds of mysterious horrors, among which was one that was terrible in the extreme. He was lost in the bush, and nothing was left for him to do but lie down and die; and the first part of this he had, he thought, just achieved, when a loud voice came out of the blackness and cried:

"Now, Nic, boy, it's time to get up. And I want you to see to the dogs. They know you."

Chapter Eight
To the Bush

For some moments Nic acted involuntarily as he scrambled on his clothes, feeling, as he did, in a confused way that it was his duty to dress, but why and wherefore, he had not the most remote idea.

It was cold and raw, and everything went wrong; and as he could not get himself quite dry, his shirt stuck to him and refused to go on. Those things which ought to have been in one place had got into another; and even when the cold water had thoroughly wakened him he did not get on very well, and felt ill-humoured, stupid, and out of sorts.

"It's so vexatious starting so soon," thought Nic, as lie thrust brush, comb, and nightshirt into the bag he had nearly packed over night; and at last he opened the door, just as his father called up the stairs:

"Come, Nic, my boy: they didn't teach you at school to be quick."

"Hush! you'll wake Lady O'Hara," protested the boy.

"I should be puzzled to," replied his father shortly. "Come in here."

"In here" meant the dining-room, where the first person he saw, by the light of the candles standing on the white breakfast-cloth, was their hostess.

Nic was quite awake now, and the last trace of ill-temper passed away as he shook hands.

"I did not expect to see you this morning," he said.

"And did you think I was going to let old friends start without a comfortable breakfast? Why, it will be days, boy, before you get another."

"Days?" said Nic.

"To be sure, boy. There is no stage coach for you, and you'll have to keep with your waggon. These bullocks go about two miles an hour."

This was news to Nic, who had been imbued with some kind of notion that he was going to get home that same evening, and that was why his father had started so early.

Sir John entered the room directly after, and the meal was just as if it had been nine o'clock instead of four in the morning; so that the travellers were well prepared, when the doctor rose, to say good-bye, for the cracking of a stock whip and sundry ejaculations and apostrophes to the bullocks to "come on," and "get over," and "pull," were heard outside, where a couple of horses freshly brought round were stamping and pawing the dust, impatient to be off.

The dogs were hurried round from the stables—these being the two collies intended for the doctor—and after many frantic dashes at the horses, they were taken forward toward the waggon, where the bullocks were immediately driven into a state of commotion, and faced round to lower their horns and receive their enemies.

Finally, however, the two excited animals were safely chained to the back of the waggon, which started at once with a great deal of whip cracking and shouting on the part of Brookes, his fellow, Leather, being perfectly silent, and the black nowhere to be seen.

This start having been accomplished, the doctor returned with his son to say their final farewells to the governor and his lady.

"There, good-bye, Nic," cried the latter; "it's only a little way off you live. We think nothing of a few hundred miles here, and we shall be coming to see you, or you will us before very long. Are you a good horseman? That's a spirity-looking thing I see you're to ride."

Nic was nonplussed, and his father came to his help:

"Nic hasn't had time to practise much; he'll be a better rider next time he comes down to the front."

"That's right," cried Lady O'Hara. "There: goodbye, and bless you, my boy! Give my dear love to your mother, and tell her I shall want to steal you for a visit first time I come."

"I shall not be able to spare him," said the doctor, who had mounted, and now held the rein of the second horse. "Come, Nic, boy, up with you."

Nic nervously raised his foot to the stirrup, made a desperate spring as he clung to the pommel and cantle of the saddle, and somehow came down in his seat; but the horse started, and nearly threw him on to its neck.

"Steady!" cried the doctor sharply, as he held the rein firmly; and, nervous and startled, Nic shuffled back and nipped the saddle with all the force of which his knees were capable.

"Are you all right, boy?" cried the governor.

"Yes, sir," said Nic, as firmly as he could, though he was wondering how long it would be before he was all wrong.

"Good-bye, O'Hara," cried the doctor. "You will hear from me when I get home."

"Good-bye," cried the governor; and, leaning toward his old friend, he whispered:

"I'd take care: that boy can't ride a bit."

"I know," said the doctor. "Don't let him see that you do. Good-bye."

He touched his horse's sides, and the beautiful beast started to go off at a canter, but was checked instantly, to keep it in a walk, with the result that it began to fret and dance. Nic's lighter steed followed suit, and the boy's position grew moment by moment more desperate. Now he lost one stirrup, then the other; and it was only by getting a good grip of the pommel with one hand that he was able to stay on.

Finally, though, the horses were quieted down, and paced together in a walk, when the doctor said quietly:

"Why, Nic, it's a good thing that it is still dark. I'm afraid we should have had some remarks made if people had been about."

"I—I never said I could ride, father," said Nic, in a reproachful tone.

"I'm glad you did not, boy. It's a good thing that you have no spurs."

"Is it, father?"

"Of course," cried the doctor; "if you had, Sour Sorrel would have soon pitched you off."

"I'm very sorry, father," faltered Nic, who felt very miserable as well as uncomfortable. "Had I better get down and lead him?"

"If you feel so much afraid that you dare not stop on, my boy," said the doctor drily.

The dawn was coming, and Nic turned to glance at his father's thin, cleanly cut profile, to see that he was gazing straight before him towards where the waggon could be dimly seen in front.

"Well, are you?" continued the doctor, without turning his head.

Nic was silent, and the horse stumbled through putting a foot into a deep rut of the unkept road.

"Hold up, sir—steady, steady!" cried the doctor, drawing more heavily upon the rein he still held, as well as his own; and then, after Nic had shuffled back into the seat from which he had again been shaken, "I said, are you too much alarmed to stop on?"

These words sounded very stern, and stung and hurt the boy to the quick.

"I have never learned to ride, father," he said reproachfully; "and it is all fresh to me to be mounted upon a spirited horse like this."

"Of course it is: perfectly fresh. Then you feel afraid?"

"Yes, of falling off, father. I have nearly been down three times."

"Six, Nic. Well, get off and climb on to the waggon." Nic drew a deep breath as his father checked the horses; and, stung more than ever, the boy kicked his nag with his heels and sent it forward.

"Well, why don't you get down, sir?"

"Because I'd rather keep on and ride, father," said Nic huskily.

"Do you mean that, sir?"

"Yes, father."

"Thank you, Nic," said the doctor, turning to him with a smile. "I like the boy who is not afraid to own that he is alarmed; and better still to hear you say through your teeth that you will not be beaten—metaphorically, of course. Now, then, we understand our position. This is not boasting, mind—look at me. You see me here?"

"Yes, father," said Nic, feeling envious of the easy, upright position of his father in the saddle.

"Let me tell you, then, that I feel as easy and comfortable here as if I were seated upon a cushion in a carriage. More so, for this noble beast knows me as I know him, and after a fashion we are as one together in going over the ground. Do you understand what that means, Nic?"

"Yes, father; but you have learned to ride."

"Yes, and more, boy. It means the confidence which comes of knowledge. When I came out here, years ago, I had not been on horseback for twenty years; I was a miserable invalid, and when I mounted my horse a necessity out in a wild country like this—I suffered a martyrdom of nervous dread. But I did what you have just done, made up my mind that I would master my fear and ride, and I won. It took me a whole year. As for you, it will not take you a month."

"So little time?" cried Nic excitedly.

"Or less. We have about a week's journey before us; and from what I have just learned, I shall be greatly surprised if you do not canter up to the station with me, a little stiff and sore about the knees, but good friends with Sour Sorrel there, and ready to think riding a delightful accomplishment."

Nic shook his head.

"You don't know me yet, father," said the boy sadly.

"Better than you know yourself," replied the doctor. "But don't let's waste time. You want to learn?"

"Horribly, father," cried Nic.

"Very well, then. I'll give you a lesson at once."

"Not faster, to begin with?" said Nic quickly.

"No," said the doctor, laughing. "I want to give you confidence, not destroy it. So now then, to begin with, you shall learn what danger you run. I am an experienced horseman, I have tight hold of your rein, so that your horse cannot bolt, and I have promised you not to go faster than a walk. You see, then, the utmost that could happen in that way would be that the nag might caper a little."

"Or kick and throw me off."

"He will not kick, boy. He is too well broken. Secondly, you might lose your seat and come off: If you did, how far would you have to fall?"

"About four feet, father."

"Say four. Suppose you were on a see-saw at school, would you be afraid of falling, off four or five or six feet?"

"No, father, of course not."

"Then why should you be afraid of falling that distance from the horse?"

"I don't know," said Nic. "It is because it is all so fresh, I suppose. Yes, I do: my foot might hang in the stirrup and the horse gallop away with me, kicking me every time he strode."

"When I am holding him? The stirrups, then: take your feet out."

"Out of the stirrups, father? Is it safe to do so?"

"You were alarmed lest your foot should hang in one. Quick! out with them. That's right: now draw them up, cross the leathers, and let the irons hang over on each side. Now how do you feel?"

"As if I must go off on one side or the other, father. The saddle is so dreadfully slippery."

"Take tight hold of it, then, with your knees, and keep your balance. That's not right: I said take hold with your knees, not the calves of your legs."

"That way, father?"

"Yes, that's better. Let your legs go well down, your heels too, and whatever you do don't touch the pommel with your hand."

That last order was hard, for it was very easy to make a catch at the pommel so as to hold on.

"Sit up, boy. Don't bend forward. It hurts you a little at first, but you get more and more used to it every hour. Now, then, we'll walk gently past the waggon. Don't let the men think you have never been on a horse before."

The horses' pace being so much faster than that of the bullocks, they were soon by, after the doctor had spoken in a friendly way to the dogs, given his men an order or two, and then cast a critical eye over the sleek, patient oxen, which trudged along with swinging tails and horns giving a smart rap now and then as they encountered their yoke-fellows.

The track was plainly marked, but it had no pretence of being a road as it went on and on, to be lost in the distance of the bright grey morning. Away to their left was the harbour, with its shipping, and beyond it the ocean; the town lay behind them, and on either side of the track with its lines of ruts there were plenty of green pasture and trees scattered here and there—monsters some seemed to be—and in the openings were great patches of short, scrubby growth.

All at once, as Nic was thinking how peculiar the trees looked in colour, there came a loud musical series of notes from a grove-like patch, in which the boy immediately concluded there must be a house.

"Hear that?" said the doctor.

"Yes, father, plainly."

"Well, what do you make of it?"

"Some one playing a kind of flute."

"No, Nic. That is our Australian magpie."

"Magpie?" cried Nic, forgetting his uncomfortable seat; "but magpies at home in Kent have a harsh kind of laugh."

"Like that?" said the doctor, as a loud, hoarse chuckle arose.

"No: harsher and noisier. Was that the magpie?"

"No, Nic; that was our laughing jackass."

"What! A donkey?"

"No; there he sits, on that bare limb," cried the doctor, pointing up to a big, heavy-headed, browny-grey bird, which seemed to be watching them, with its great strong beak on one side.

Nic examined the bird carefully.

"You would not think that was a kingfisher?" said the doctor.

"No," cried Nic; "though the shape is something like, all but the tail, which is so much bigger."

"But it is a kingfisher all the same, though he does not fish as his ancestors may have done. He lives on beetles, lizards, mice, and frogs, and that sort of game. There's your flute-player again."

For the sweet, melodious, whistling notes arose once more, sounding somewhat as if a person were running the notes of a chord up and down with different variations.

"It's very sweet," said Nic.

"Yes. The colonists call it the magpie, but it is the piping crow of Australia. It is one of the earliest singers, and if we'd been here at daybreak I dare say we should have heard quite a long solo."

Farther on Nic had a good look at one of the piping crows in the black-and-white jacket which had obtained for it the familiar name of magpie; but it was far from being like that handsome bird the British magpie, with its long tail glossed with metallic reflexions of golden green and purple, and with wing feathers to match.

Two or three times over, out in the open country, the horses startled Nic by their disposition to go off at a canter, but after being checked they calmly settled down to their walking pace, which was fast enough to leave the bullock team behind; consequently Dr Braydon drew rein from time to time at the summit of some hill or ridge, so that his son might have a good view of the new land which was henceforth to be his home. Here he pointed out the peculiar features of the landscape and its resemblance to an English park, save that, instead of the grassy land being dotted with oak, beech, elm, or fir, the trees were always what the doctor called "gum," with their smooth bark and knotted limbs, but gum trees of several varieties. Here and there a farmstead could be seen, but they were few and far between; still, where they did show, with the roughly built houses and their bark or shingle roofs, flocks of sheep and droves of cattle could be seen scattered widely over the plain.

"Did you say we should be about a week getting home?" said Nic, after one of these halts.

"Perhaps longer," said the doctor. "Everything depends on those crawling gentlemen behind. They have a heavy load: you see there is no road, and if rain comes, as it is sure to before long, the load will seem twice as heavy to the patient beasts, and I can't afford to hurry them and get them out of condition. Rain falls very seldom here, Nic; but when it does come there's no nonsense about it. There's a river on ahead which we shall have to cross."

"Then you have bridges," said Nic naïvely, "if you have no regular roads?"

"Bridges? No; we shall have to ford it if we were going across to-day, it would be a few inches deep; if one of our big rain storms comes, it might be forty or fifty feet. I have seen it sixty."

Nic glanced at his father.

"Simple truth, my boy," he said. "The river is in a deep trough between two ranges of hills; and if there have been rains we might be detained on the bank for days or weeks."

"And whereabouts does home lie?" asked Nic.

"Yonder," said his father, pointing toward the north-east. "The air is wonderfully clear now, and perhaps you can see what I do—that faint blue ridge that looks like a layer of cloud low down on the horizon."

"Yes, I can see it," said Nic eagerly; "but surely it won't take us a week to ride there. It looks quite close."

"Yes, in this clear atmosphere, Nic; but it is a long way off, as you will find before we get there. Of course if we could canter our thirty or forty miles a day we should soon be there, but we are an escort only. We want to take care of the waggon."

"But couldn't the men take care of that?"

"Perhaps; but a good master looks after his valuables himself. Brookes is a pretty trusty man, but the other is a new hand, whom I have lately had from my neighbour Mr Dillon, the magistrate, and I have not tried him yet sufficiently to trust. That load contains things that will be of great value to me, things Lady O'Hara bought me: seeds and implements, guns, ammunition, powder, and endless odds and ends wanted by your mother and sisters, who cannot send into the next street to buy what they want."

"But surely in this wild, open place no one would interfere with the waggon?"

"Think not? Why, Nic, we have bushrangers—escaped convicts—beside plenty of people less desperate but more dishonest, without counting the blacks."

"Are there any of them about here?" asked Nic, with a glance round.

"Perhaps. We hardly know where they may be. You see they belong to wandering tribes which roam about in search of food. They are here to-day and gone to-morrow. We never know when they may come."

"Are they dangerous?"

"Yes and no, my boy. We always have to be on our guard, especially in such a lonely place as ours."

"But why did you go and live in such a lonely spot, father?" said Nic.

"Because the place suited me, my boy. I rode over hundreds of miles of country before I pitched upon the Bluffs and took up the land. It was beautiful, the pasture was good, and there was that more than great necessary we look for in this droughty country—a good supply of water. I have known squatters out here lose hundreds of cattle and thousands of sheep in a dry summer, when everything is burnt up."

By this time the bullocks had dragged their load close by, and for the first time Nic stared at a black figure, dressed in a strip of cloth and a spear, walking behind the waggon.

"There's one of the blacks, father," whispered Nic, staring at the shock-headed fellow, who turned a little on one side, and displayed a short club with a large knob at one end.

"Only the fellow who helped to load," said the doctor.

Nic looked hard, for he had not recognised the man.

"He has got rid of his shirt and trousers, Nic, for the march home. These blacks are eager to get clothes, but it always seems a misery to them to wear anything but a bit of cloth."

"But is it never cold here?"

"Very, sometimes—frosty; but they make a bit of a shelter and a tiny fire, and linger over it till the hot sun comes out, and then forget the cold. The old people here never even built a hut, Nic—only a shelter—a rough bit of fence."

In the middle of the day, when the sun came down with tremendous power, a halt was called beneath the shade of a gigantic gum tree, and Nic for the first time realised why this name was applied to the one great family of trees peculiar to the land, for drops of gum which had oozed out were gleaming red like carbuncles in the hot sunshine.

The doctor sprang from his horse, but Nic sat quite still.

"Dawn with you, my boy," cried his father; but, instead of obeying, Nic screwed up his face into a peculiar shape.

"I don't feel as if I could, father."

"Oh! Stiff. Down with you, boy. You must work that off."

Nic set his teeth, and rolled off his horse in a most ungraceful way, to stand feeling as if the ground was unsafe and all on the move.

"Hurt?" said his father, smiling.

"Yes, father. It's as if my legs had been dragged wide apart and stretched."

"Getting in shape for your saddle, my boy. You'll soon get over this. Now look here."

Nic did look there, and was shown how to hobble his nag's fore legs to keep it from straying, and how to unbridle and take off the saddle.

"Always give your horse a good rub down where the saddle has been, Nic," said the doctor. "Horses are delicate animals. They deserve good treatment too. Your nag carries you well, and he looks to you for payment in food, rest, and good treatment. These make all the difference in the way a horse will last on a journey. Now, my lads, come along. Water."

The doctor led the way, and the horses followed like a couple of dogs. Nic was following too, with the sensation strongly upon him that he should like to go down on all-fours and follow like a dog, for walking seemed to be a mode of progress to which he was not accustomed.

"Wait a moment, Nic," said his father. "Unfasten the dogs and lead them here. They must want water too."

Nic went to where the dogs were chained to the tail of the waggon, trying to walk firmly and erect, but it was hard work, for his legs seemed to be independent of his body, and there were moments when he felt as if he had none at all.

But he tried not to show it, and while the men were unyoking the oxen, which immediately began to graze on the rich, succulent grass, Nic proceeded to unchain the dogs.

The task was not so easy as it looked, for the collies were frantic at the thought of being unfastened, and barked and leaped about wildly. To make matters worse, they had been hard at work trying to strangle one another on the way by leaping over their chains, and tying them up in an almost inseparable knot, one which refused to yield to his fingers; and after many tries Nic appealed to Brookes.

"I wish you'd come and unfasten this," he said. "I want to take the dogs to water."

"Take the dogs to water!" grumbled the man. "Why can't they take themselves? Hi! Leather! Come and untie these dogs."

The younger man left the oxen he was loosening, and approached Nic in a surly way, hardly glancing at him; but for a few moments the chain-knot baffled him, while the dogs bounded about wildly.

"Hold them by the collars for a minute," said Leather harshly.

Nic obeyed, feeling mentally lower now, for he seemed to be the servant instead of the other.

Then he felt better, for the man softened a little in his manner.

"Poor brutes!" he said: "prisoners and thirsty. Steady, my lads, steady!"

"Oh, they won't be prisoners long," said Nic. "Father's afraid that they'd run back and try and get on board the ship or to the governor's house."

"There you are," cried the man, placing the chains in his hand, when, as if scenting out the water, the two collies started off, with eyes starting and tongues hanging out of their mouths, tugging and striving to get on, and forcing Nic to follow at a trot, his legs hurting him for the first few moments horribly.

They were not long reaching the shady pool where the horses were now standing in a shallow, with the drops falling from their muzzle.

"Poor beasts! they are thirsty," cried the doctor, as Nic was literally dragged to the edge of the pool, the dogs striving to plunge right in. "Don't let them go, Nic."

"But they'll have me in, father."

"Don't let them, boy. Ah!"

Nic had not the least intention of letting them, but as the dogs had tugged at their chains the boy was forced from a hobble into a trot, and then, before the doctor could help, he caught one foot in the tough herbage, tripped, went down, and was dragged a yard or two, and then, with a rush and tremendous splash, he followed the dogs' plunge off the bank into deep water, to be towed here and there by the delighted animals, which swam about, barking, drinking, and threatening to tangle their chains in a worse knot than before—to wit, round Nic.

But after the first few moments' confusion the boy touched bottom, and began to wade back, finding it easier to master the dogs in the water than out.

"Well, that's a nice beginning, Nic!" said the doctor.

"Isn't it horrid?" cried the boy.

"Wet?" said his father laconically. "There, it might have been worse. Let them drink, and then bring them back to the waggon and tie them up. We must keep them on the chain till we get them home. Poor fellows, then!" he cried, reaching down to pat the dripping heads. "There! you've had as much as is good for you. Come along."

A tug or two at the chains brought the dogs out, to let themselves off, as it were, and scatter glistening water drops from their shaggy hides, after which they broke out into a duet of barks, and danced about on the bank, wagging their tails, evidently inviting Nic to cast sticks into the water for them to fetch, but they followed quietly enough, with the horses behind them, lowering their heads to bite playfully at the collies' waving tails.

"You can get at your portmanteau; it's on the top," said the doctor, as soon as the dogs were secured. "Get out some dry things. You can make a dressing-room behind the tree."

All this the boy proceeded to do, and by the time he had changed he felt none the worse for his involuntary bath, and hung his wrung-out garments on the scorching waggon-tilt to dry.

This done, he obeyed his father's summons, and found him seated in the shade, waiting with a basket of provisions, which Lady O'Hara had provided for their use, while the two men were seated beneath another tree eating, the black standing on one leg a short distance away, resting upon his spear and holding the sole of his right foot flat against his left knee so as to form a peculiar angle. And every now and then one of the men pitched him a piece of bread, which he caught deftly and proceeded to eat.

"Just as if he were a dog," thought Nic, as he sat down by his father and began his *al fresco* dinner.

And how good it was! He forgot all about the stiffness in his legs in the pure enjoyment of those moments. No school picnic had ever approached it, for everything was so gloriously new and fresh. The beautiful land stretched undulating right away to the blue-tinted mountains, the water-pool sparkled in the sunshine, the horses and cattle grazed in the thick rich grass, and the waggon helped to form a picture against a clump of shrubs, half-covered with yellow flowers, while a delicious scent of musk filled the air.

Never had repast tasted so delicious; and, with two exceptions, every living creature seemed to be partaking of this enjoyment in the midst of the peaceful repose in that lovely spot. The exceptions were the dogs, which kept on watching them and uttering an uneasy bark now and then, for the rich grass in which they stood was not to their taste.

Nic went on eating in silence for a few minutes, and then, breaking a loaf in two, rose and went off to the dogs, which readily attacked the bread, a long diet of biscuit on board ship having made them fairly vegetarian in their tastes.

The doctor nodded approval as Nic returned wondering whether he would receive a reproof, and the wayside meal went on till the doctor spoke.

"Well, Nic," he said, "how do you like the beginning of your rough life?"

"It's glorious, father," cried the boy eagerly.

"Humph! In spite of the first lesson in riding, the ducking, and this muddly way of eating—no table-cloth, no chairs or table?"

"Oh, I like it."

"Because it's new and the sun shines?"

"I know that the sun doesn't always shine, father," cried Nic. "I shall like it, I know."

"That's right. But look: here come some visitors that you have only seen in cages at home."

Nic had already sprung to his feet, and he walked out from beneath the tree to gaze excitedly at a flock of white birds that came sailing up, evidently to alight in the grove, but the sudden appearance of the boy made them turn off, shrieking harshly, to find a resting-place farther on, and Nic returned disappointed.

"Legs seem to be better, Nic?" said the doctor.

"Yes; I had forgotten them, father. But those birds!"

"Well, you scared them. You saw what they were?"

"Not white pigeons or gulls?" said Nic. "I could almost have fancied that they were cockatoos."

"No fancy about it, Nic. They were sulphur crests. You'll see thousands in the groves down by the river."

"Is there a river about here?"

"Your wet clothes seemed to suggest something of the kind," said the doctor, laughing.

"But that was a pond," said Nic.

"A water-hole—a deep place in the river. That depression is a river, Nic," continued the doctor, pointing; "there it runs yonder. You can trace it by the trees which cluster along its course. It is dried up now, all but a hole here and there; but after rains it is a rushing stream, and I dare say a little water is always trickling along its course from hole to hole a few feet under ground. Now then, pack up the basket. We shall want it for supper. Have a nap afterwards if you are tired. I shall not go on for an hour and a half yet."

But Nic wanted no nap—there was too much to see; and it did not seem to be long before the order was given to yoke the oxen and saddle up.

Chapter Nine
Nic's Experiences

"Now, Nic," said the doctor, as they stood ready to make a fresh start, "we shall go on, so as to reach another water-hole and camp for the night."

As he spoke the doctor rammed down the last wad and examined the priming of the new gun Nic had brought out. Then, finding the pan full of powder, he tried whether the flint was well screwed up in the hammer.

"Put these on," he said, and he handed the boy his shot-belt and powder-flask.

"Are we going to shoot anybody, father?" asked Nic eagerly.

"I hope not, boy; but it is a custom out here to go armed when you are travelling, and we are getting some distance out now away from the town. Up with your and try and mount a little better. Take hold of your reins and the mane there tightly, up with your left foot into the stirrup, and lay your hand on the cantle of the saddle; don't pull it, only support yourself by it. Now draw your off rein a little, so that the horse cannot sidle away, spring up lightly, and throw your leg over. Mount."

Nic obeyed, as he thought, to the letter, and got into the saddle somehow, making his horse fidget and wag its tail uneasily.

"Bad—very bad," cried the doctor, laughing. "I said throw your leg over. You tried to throw yourself over. Never mind; you'll soon learn. Look at me. One moment: take your gun."

Nic took the gun handed to him, and was shown how to carry it across his rein arm, and then he enviously watched his father take hold of a wisp of the horse's mane, place a foot in the stirrup, and lightly swing himself into the saddle, while his horse hung toward him a little, otherwise remained perfectly still.

"You'll soon do it, Nic. Legs feel stiff?"

"A bit cramped," replied the boy.

"Forward, then, at a walk. I shall not hold your rein now. Your nag will not leave his companion."

"Hadn't you better, father, till I get more used to it?" asked Nic uneasily.

"No," said the doctor decisively. "It was quite right this morning over your first lesson. You have learned a little already, and I don't want you, as it were, to learn to swim with corks. Come along. Steady, lad, steady."

This was to Nic's steed, which began to amble, keeping up a nice gentle motion, which would have been very pleasant if the boy had not felt a bit nervous. But as it found its stable companion continued to pace, Sour Sorrel followed its example and dropped into a walk.

The waggon was already a quarter of a mile onward, and the dogs were hanging back watching them, barking furiously till they were overtaken, and having a few encouraging words delivered to them as father and son rode on.

"I should like to set them free," said the doctor, "but I dare not yet."

The afternoon ride was almost a repetition of that in the morning, and from time to time they passed water-holes, showing that they were keeping along the course of the river, though it was not until it was pointed out to him that Nic knew he was for some distance travelling along the dry bed and was crossing it, the depression seeming little different from the surrounding country.

Weariness had something to do with it, for to Nic the country did not seem so beautiful as in the morning. He had been many hours in the saddle, and though the pace had only been a walk, the unaccustomed position told upon his muscles, and, in spite of a hint or two from his father, the boy's attitude was far from upright. He had ceased, too, for some time to keep a keen look-out for birds and kangaroos. Earlier in the afternoon he had seen some reddish, dun-coloured animals in the distance; but these had, upon nearer approach, turned out to be cattle, and a feeling of disappointment began to make itself evident as they rode on and on, till toward sunset, when the waggon was quite half a mile ahead, Nic noticed that the bright greyish white tilt was glowing and turning ruddier against the dark lines of a clump of trees, and a minute later it still seemed to be in the same position.

Nic felt disposed to draw his father's attention to the fact that the waggon was not moving, but his feeling of disinclination even to speak was growing upon him, and he was riding bent forward in silence, noticing what appeared to be a bed of whitish mist spreading among the trees, when his father startled him out of his thoughtful musings by saying laconically:

"Camp."

Nic turned and looked at him inquiringly.

"Camp, Nic," he said. "Don't you see that they've lit a fire?"

"Oh!" cried the boy, raising himself up. "I thought it was mist."

"No, Nic, smoke. That's the first thing we do out here when we halt for the night: light a fire and put on the billy."

Nic gave another inquiring look, and his father smiled.

"You'll soon learn all our colonial terms, boy," he said. "A billy is a large cross-handled saucepan to boil water in and make our tea. I'll show you how that is done—when we get there."

"I know how to make tea," said Nic.

"Yes, but not our way."

Nic looked wonderingly at his father.

"You are on the other side of the world now," said the doctor. "Now then, what do you say to a trot for the rest of the way?"

The boy winced, but he mastered his shrinking sensation.

"Very well, father," he said.

"No," said the doctor. "I'll let you off till to-morrow. You've done enough for one day."

Ten minutes after they were dismounting in just such a spot as that chosen for their mid-day halt. The cattle were unyoked, and had gone of their own accord to a water-hole about fifty yards away; the fire was burning brightly, and the kettle giving forth a few preliminary snorts, suggestive of rising steam; and the waggon was drawn close up under a huge, wide-spreading tree, among whose branches the soft cooing of pigeons could be heard. The horses were hobbled, unsaddled, and rubbed down, and when they were led off to drink, the travellers went a few yards away for a refreshing wash.

"Now, Nic," said the doctor after their return and when the provisions had been taken from the waggon, "you shall see our colonial mode of making tea."

As he spoke he poured a goodly portion into the lid of the canister, waited till the water in the billy was well on the boil, when he tossed in the whole of the tea, gave it a rapid stir round to send all the dry leaf beneath the surface, and then lifted it off the fire, let it stand for a very short time, filled the big tin mugs with which they were provided, then those of the men, after which they sat down to their evening meal.

The cattle and horses were grazing all around, and in the calm silence the *crop, crop* as they bit off the grass sounded peculiarly loud, while from a distance came the loud wailing cry of the curlew, a strange trumpet-like tone, and a note from close at hand which made Nic turn inquiring eyes upon his father.

"Curlew, crane, and the mopoke," said the doctor. "More pork the settlers call it."

"Mopoke?"

"Yes. There goes one;" and he pointed to where a dark, swift-winged bird was hovering about a tree evidently in quest of moths.

"Why it flies like the goat-sucker does at home," said Nic, pausing to watch the bird.

"To be sure it does. It is a relative, only bigger. You'll find plenty of birds that bear a resemblance to our own."

"And animals?"

"No. Birds are most plentiful, and in great variety; quadrupeds are scarce, and very peculiar. This, you know, is the land of the kangaroo, and we have varieties of that curious beast, from tiny ones we call rats, right up to the giants which stand up taller than the biggest man."

The sun had set, the great stars were shining out through the clear air, and night was coming on fast, with the cries of the birds sounding strange and even awful in that loneliness.

"Tired out, Nic?" said his father; and the boy started and stared.

"Why, you were asleep, Nic. Don't you understand me?"

"Eh? Yes. What say, father? Was I asleep?"

"Soundly, my boy. Come along; you can creep in under the tilt and go to sleep on the boxes. There are two blankets rolled up ready for you."

"But what are you going to do?" asked Nic.

"Look round for a bit, and take my turn at watching."

"But I must too," said Nic, shaking off his drowsiness.

"When I tell you, my boy. Now go to sleep, and get rested for to-morrow's work. The dogs will give warning if any one comes near."

Nic obeyed, and as he went to say "good night" to the dogs—towards which he felt no animosity for the ducking they had given him—he saw that the two men were making their bed under the waggon, while the black was sidling slowly up to the fire. There the Australian curled himself up like a great dog, while the doctor stood about a dozen yards away, searching the dimly seen landscape with a little pocket-glass.

Then Nic climbed in under the tilt, opened one blanket and doubled it, made a pillow of the other, and then—

"Yes, father—directly."

For the dawn was beginning to break, and a bright light shone up among the branches of the trees, out of which came a series of piercing bird screams.

"Look sharp: kettle nearly boils."

Nic scrambled from under the tilt, feeling now that he must be called to help keep watch, for he was convinced that he had only just lain down.

Chapter Ten
A Morning Dip

"Had a good night's rest, my boy?"

"Night's rest?" stammered Nic.

"Yes; you have been asleep eight hours, I should say."

Nic stared.

"Like a bath? Do you good. Get a towel, and have a plunge into the pool. Don't be more than a quarter of an hour gone. Can you swim?"

"Yes, father," said Nic, who felt stiff and shivery; and as he climbed up under the waggon-cover for the towel, he wished bathing had never been invented.

Getting down and making for the water-hole, he came upon Brookes, who was carrying an armful of wood for the fire, and he saluted the boy with:

"Going to have a dip?"

"Yes."

"Hope you'll like it. Don't ketch me at it."

His face was only dimly seen reflecting the light of the fire; but recalling what he had seen, Nic could not help feeling that the stock man did not use water much for outward application.

Half-way to the hole he met the black, who said something incomprehensible, to which Nic answered with "good morning," and hurried on to the bank, down in the hollow along which the river ran.

There was a thin, whitish mist just visible over the water, which looked horribly black and cold, making the boy feel as if he would have given anything to evade the morning duty.

"Why not shirk it?" he said to himself. "I might wash my face and hands, and go back."

Hurrying a dozen yards or so to where the bank was lower and the water not above eight or ten inches beneath, he prepared for a simple wash, and laid his towel on a bush; but his conscience attacked him, and, setting his teeth hard, he tore off jacket and vest in a way that was nothing less than vicious. These he placed on the bush which acted for a chair back, while the morning air struck chill to the bare skin.

"It's horrid," he thought, — "horrid. How can one go on like this?"

Ugh! how cold the black water looked in that grey dawn, for there was no sign of the sun, the stars being still faintly visible, and to keep his teeth from chattering Nic set them so hard that they began to ache.

"Pretty cowardly fool I should have looked if father had asked me at breakfast if— Bother it all. Why didn't I take off my shoes?"

Nic had got one leg half out of his trousers, but not being so clever as the black at that crane or stork-like way of standing he overbalanced, tried to save himself failed, and went down on his side, in which safer position he dragged out first one and then the other leg.

"Yes; pretty cowardly fellow I should have looked if father had asked me at breakfast if I enjoyed my swim."

He rose and hung up his trousers on the bush, thrust off shoes and stockings, and then stood on the bank white and ghostly-looking, gazing down into the deep, still water overhung by thick bushes, which made it look still more untempting. For it was big enough—there were two or three acres—to hold any number of terrible monsters. There might be water-serpents hidden under those overhanging trees, waiting amongst the roots ready to seize and pull him down; or huge alligators or crocodiles might be lurking in the deepest holes. Nic was not learned enough as to the way in which their teeth fitted between the others or into holes in the opposing jaws to know which was which. It was enough for him to remember that they were shaped like the fierce little efts which seized the worms in ponds at home when he had been out fishing.

The thoughts were horrible, and he stood shivering, and had it been broad daylight his skin would have been seen becoming covered with tiny pimples, like the cuticle of the goose plucked, and assuming a reddish, purply hue.

"Oh," he thought, "if I could only escape this bitter task!" But he was too determined to attempt that, though he could not help putting off the task as long as he could; for cold water which looks bad enough at dawn in a bath in a comfortable dressing-room seems far worse on the banks of a river; and a hundred times worse when an active brain suggests the possibility of its containing fierce, hungry reptiles in all their amphibious horror, watching and waiting, in a land of blacks, for a tender, well-fed breakfast off a delicate, well-bred white.

"It's of no use," thought Nic. "I must summon up courage and do it. He'll be waiting breakfast for me, and—Ugh! how cold!"

Nic involuntarily turned his head to gaze in the direction of the trees where the fire was blazing, uttered a faint cry of surprise and horror, and turned and dived off the bank into the hole, to feel quite an electric shock run through him, while the water thundered in his ears, and he formed a graceful arch in the depths.

Out popped his head directly, yards away from where he had taken his header, and he began to swim with a calm, vigorous stroke right away for the middle, gazing sideways the while and muttering to himself as he saw that the object which had startled him, shamefaced, into seeking the protection of the water, had walked close to the edge, taken up his favourite, crane-like attitude, and was watching him swim, with his lips drawn from his teeth and displaying them in a broad grin.

It was something after the fashion of a conjuring trick. One moment a white figure had stood there in the dawning day; the next there was a loud splash, the white figure had disappeared, and a black one stood in its place, not in the least ashamed, though almost as nude as Nic. For the black had followed, stood watching, and studied with great enjoyment the appearance of one of his white masters wearing the natural garb which he himself generally affected.

There were neither crocodiles, alligators, nor serpents in the water now, so far as Nic's fancy was concerned. After the first plunge his whole nature had awakened to a sense of vigorous vitality. The sharp touch of the electric water sent thrill after thrill of energy through him, and he swam half across the river-hole, and turned back feeling as active as an eel.

"Here, who's to get out and dress with that fellow staring at me?" thought Nic, as he neared the black. "I shall have to stop in till he goes. Hi! you, sir! Be off!"

The black's grin ceased, and he turned and fled, while Nic sprang out, had a vigorous rub, began to glow, and then dressed, to run back to the waggon as hard as he could go, finishing off his head the while.

Five minutes after his short hair had obeyed the comb, he made for the fire, where a pleasant odour saluted his nostrils, and he felt that he must have made a mistake or been deceived.

But no: it was a fact. Brookes and Leather had been busy. Hot bread was waiting, and crisp, brown slices of bacon were fizzling in the pan.

"Ready?" said the doctor; and then the boy started, for these words followed: "Have a good swim?"

"Yes, father—glorious."

"Water cold?"

"Yes; but I'm all of a glow now."

"Take your tea."

Nic took the big tin mug.

"Damper?"

"Oh no, father; I had a thorough good rub."

"I said damper."

"Yes, father, I know. Only my hair—just a little."

"He dunno what you mean, sir," said Brookes with a chuckle, as he waited to take the men's share of the breakfast away.

"Oh, I see," said the doctor, laughing. "Have some hot bread with your bacon, Nic? We call this cake damper."

Nic did not mind what they called it, and he took his portion and his rasher of hot bacon, and he repeated the action with the greatest of pleasure, sipping at intervals from the milkless contents of his big tin mug without once regretting the absence of milk or cream.

Memorandum. Ride for many hours over the luxuriant downs on a clear day, when the air is laden with the health-giving odours of the gum trees, lie down tired out, and sleep with your slumber appearing to last one minute, but enduring for eight hours; lastly, have a plunge in a clear water-hole, and after a brief swim a tremendous rub, and you will be ready to perform as satisfactorily over the *al fresco* breakfast and do it as much justice as Dominic Braydon.

"A little more, Nic?" said his father.

"Yes, please."

Nic said that twice; and a little while after, as a recollection came suddenly back:

"I say, father, are there any crocodiles or dangerous things in these rivers?"

"If there were, do you think I should have sent you to bathe?" was the reply.

"Oh no, of course."

"There are plenty, I believe, up north, where the rivers are always open right to the sea; but never here."

"But fish, father?"

"Oh yes, there are fish, principally what they call here the black-fish. You'll have to try for them by-and-by."

"Very big?" asked Nic, who was thinking of his bath.

"Oh no; small fish, but delicious eating. Now then, any more?"

"No, thanks, father."

"Then go and feed the dogs. We start in a quarter of an hour. One moment. Do you feel very stiff?"

"Stiff?—well, yes, a little, father."

"Not very bad, then. How do you feel about a trot to-day?"

"I'll—I'll try, father. Look—look!"

The boy jumped up in his excitement, for there was a whirring of wings, a burst of screaming, and a flock of birds flew over their heads, with the plumage looking in the morning light as white as snow.

"Cockatoos?" cried Nic wildly.

"Yes," said his father, smiling at the boy's enthusiasm over what was one of the commonest sights to him. "I have seen them before. Now then, breakfast for our prisoners. I shall be glad when we can let those dogs run free."

Chapter Eleven
How to Ride

"Poor old chaps!" cried Nic, as the dogs leaped and tore about when he left them, each straining at its collar with starting eyes, and uttering in unison a piteous howl which could only bear one interpretation:

"Oh, I say, it's too bad! Don't keep us tied up like this."

Nic was ready to pity them again a few minutes after, when, in obedience to a shout and the crack of a whip, the sleek oxen, which stood yoked, blinking and chewing their cuds, started for the day's march, tightening the dogs' chains. Then the collies sulkily allowed themselves to be dragged along by the neck for a few yards before, feeling that resistance was in vain, they gave up and began to start barking in protest, running forward as far as their chains would allow under the waggon, as if longing to get at the oxen's heels, and finally, after a loud yelp or two at one another, settling down to their prisoners' tramp.

The horses were bridled and saddled after Nic had taken his gun from where it had been stood against a tree. The two men were in front of the team, with Brookes talking loudly and unpleasantly to his fellow; and the black was following behind the dogs, with his spear over his shoulder, at times lowering it to stir the dogs up behind whenever they showed an inclination to hang back.

This happened a minute after the start had been made, and Nic burst out laughing.

"I say, father, look at that," he cried.

"I was looking, my boy," said the doctor. "That fellow seems to understand the dogs better than we do."

For, at the first touch of the spear, one of the collies turned round sharply, and barked; then the other received a prod—from the blunt end in both cases—and the bark uttered was exactly like a protesting "*Don't!*"

But the black, who was safe from attack as long as he kept beyond the reach of the chain, continued to administer pokes, with the result that the dogs trotted on as far as they could, looking back the while and uttering threatening barks and growls.

But the long spear followed them right under the waggon, and kept up the annoyance, till, as if moved by the same impulse, the dogs charged back together to the extent of their chains, and the black made a bound out of the animals' reach.

The result was that when, after a final look round to see that nothing had been left, the doctor gave the order to mount, the dogs were right under the waggon, with their tongues out, tugging away at their chains as sharply as if they had been born in Kamtschatka and belonged to Eskimo.

"That's better," said the doctor, as Nic landed in his saddle without making a show in imitation of vaulting ambition and seeming about to fall over on the other side. "Down again, and mount."

Nic obeyed.

"That's worse," said the doctor. "Dismount. Now again!"

Nic dismounted, and mounted once more.

"Not so good as the first time, Nic. There, take your gun. Mind: never do that! It's the worst of high treason to let your gun-muzzle point at anybody."

"I beg pardon, father."

"Granted, on condition that you are more careful for the future," said the doctor, springing into his seat in a way that excited his son's envy.

"Shall I try again, father?"

"No; it will only fidget your horse. Come along. What a glorious morning! We'll take a sweep round, and meet the waggon three or four miles on."

The sun was now up, and sending its brilliant rays horizontally beneath the great trees, making every branch and leaf glow; and, as Nic's nag paced gently along, the boy felt as if he were riding upon the glorious elastic air. He felt very little of the stiffness, only a bit sore inside the knees, where they were pressed against the saddle.

As they passed in among the trees the waggon was soon lost to sight, and Nic glanced again and again in its direction.

"Afraid we shan't find our way back to the waggon?" said his father.

"I was thinking something of the kind," avowed Nic.

"Ah, that is a great danger away in the bush, and you may as well know it; but we could not go very far now without finding a track or some station."

"A police station?"

"No, no," said the doctor, smiling. "We have police here—mounted police—to look after the convicts and mind they don't escape; but we call farmhouses-squatters' places—stations here. Our home—Blue Mountain Bluff; as we named it—is called a station by my neighbours."

"Then you have neighbours, father?"

"Oh yes, a few miles away. Mr Dillon, the magistrate, Leather's late employer, is the nearest—ten miles distant."

"Then home must be a very lonely place."

"We have never found it so, Nic," said his father drily. "Busy people are never lonely. Now then, I think I've behaved very well to you and spared your feelings. I promise that I will not laugh at you."

"What about, father?"

"Your first essay at trotting. It is of no use to keep a horse and ride at a walk. You can progress as fast as that on your own legs."

Nic drew a deep breath, and wished that he was bestriding a donkey on the common near the Friary, with his schoolmates looking on instead of his father.

"I'm ready, father," he said.

"Wait a few minutes. I want to accustom you to holding your gun on horseback. You will always have either a gun or a stock-whip, but I don't want you to begin your career as a squatter—"

"I say, father, what a horrible name that is for a sheep farmer!"

"'A rose by any other name would smell as sweet,' Nic. 'Squatter' does very well; and I say I don't want you to begin your career by shooting your father or his horse. So you shall have a shot at something. You will not be afraid to fire your gun?"

"Oh, I say, father!" said Nic reproachfully, "don't—please don't think me such a miserable coward."

"I don't, my lad—nothing of the kind. I only treat you as a raw lad who has to be trained to our ways."

"But you expect me to shoot you as soon as I begin to trot."

"I don't mean you to, Nic. But such a thing is quite possible when you fall."

"Then you think I shall fall," said Nic ruefully.

"Certainly, if you lose your balance and do not hold tight."

"But you told me not to hold!" cried Nic.

"With your hands. They are to hold your reins and gun. A horseman holds on with his knees; and I suppose yours are a bit sore?"

Nic nodded.

"Then make up your mind not to fall; but we'll have that gun empty first. You shall have a shot at something."

Nic drew rein sharply, and his horse stopped and shook its head, and champed the bit impatiently.

"Don't check your horse like that, boy!"

"I only pulled the reins, father."

"Yes, as if his mouth were made of wood. You would soon spoil him, and make him hard-mouthed, if you jerked the bit about in that fashion. A horse like this is extremely sensitive. You only need just feel his mouth with the rein, and he will stop at the slightest additional pressure, just sufficiently to make him understand what you want. Well, why are you making a face like that?"

"I shall never learn all this," cried Nic; "I'm too stupid."

"And you have ground away at algebra and Euclid! What nonsense! Come, be more ready to take a right view of things. Horses are extremely intelligent animals, and love their masters if properly treated. They are wilful at times, and then have to be punished; but I never strike or spur my horse without good reason. Now look here, Nic: this is not to show off, but to let you see what can be done with the animal, which is one of man's most valuable friends out in these wilds. Now watch!"

The doctor threw the reins on the horse's neck.

"I want to go to the left."

To Nic's astonishment the horse bore away to the left, and his own followed suit.

"Now I want to go to the right." The horse turned in that direction.

"Now I want to turn right round."

The horse turned right about.

"Now straight back."

The horses began to return upon their tracks, Nic's eyes following every motion.

"Now round again, and forward."

Once more the horse, turning right about, went straight forward, Sour Sorrel taking pace for pace.

"Why, it's wonderful, father!" cried Nic. "Australian horses must understand plain English."

"Well, they are English bred," said the doctor, laughing. "Twenty years ago there was not a horse in the country. But now, tell me, why did you check your horse?"

"To get down so as to shoot."

"Nonsense! Fire from his back when I tell you."

"But it will frighten him, and he'll gallop off, and I shall be sure to fall."

"It will not frighten him, for the horse will stand like a rock, knowing when you are going to fire. You can rest your gun between his ears if you like, only you could not get so steady an aim. It's quite true. That nag is beautifully broken. I reared him from a foal and trained him expressly for you."

"Thank you, father; but I think I would rather ride yours."

"Why?"

"He seems so much better trained."

"Not so well, boy."

"But tell me: how did you make him go any way you wished?"

"The simplest way in the world. Let your reins drop on his neck."

Nic obeyed.

"Now press the side with your right leg. That's right. Now with the left. Good. Now keep on with the pressure, and the nag will turn right round. Now press both legs together. Very well indeed. Now you see there is no magic in the matter."

Nic was astounded, for the horse had acted just in the same way as his father's.

"Let me tell you another thing. If you jump down—no, no, don't do it—but if you jump down, pass the rein over the nag's head and throw it on the ground: he will stand perfectly still."

"Without the rein being fastened to a peg or tree?"

"Yes. Try it when you get down. Now you see you are learning to ride. But I want this trot, so be ready for your shot. Cock your gun."

Nic made the lock click, and felt a thrill of anticipation run through his nerves.

"Whit shall I shoot at, father?"

"Well, you may as well practise at something running or flying."

"A bird?"

"Yes, if you see a good specimen. You may as well collect some of our beautiful birds. Wait a bit: I dare say we shall see something before long."

They paced on for about a quarter of a mile, and then a large animal was startled from out of some bushes, made a flying leap, and then went off in a series of tremendous bounds, and all the faster for the shot Nic fired and which whistled through the air over its head.

"A good miss, Nic," said his father.

"Didn't I hit it, father?"

"No, my boy—not with a single shot, even. But you see your horse did not move."

"I forgot all about that," said Nic. "I suppose that was a kangaroo, father?"

"No doubt about that, Nic. They can go pretty well, eh?"

"Tremendously. But what an enormous tail!"

"Yes, it seems to act like a balance and a support when they land, for they go almost entirely upon their hind legs. But I meant you to have tried for a shot farther on, where there is a bit of river and some low damp ground. You might perhaps have secured a goose for our supper, or had a shot at one of the snakes, which like the moisture. But come: here's a good open stretch of land. Let's have our trot. Keep your heels down, sit fairly well up, and don't think about falling. If you do come off, it is a very little way to go, and the horse's pace will take him clear of you. Now then, turn those stirrups over his back."

"Oh, father! let me keep my stirrups."

"Certainly not; they would not help you a bit, only prove a danger to a novice; and remember this: once you can ride without stirrups you can ride with. Ready?"

Nic reluctantly turned the stirrup leathers across.

"Yes, father," he said, rather hesitatingly.

"Then off!"

The horses started at the pressure given by the doctor's heels, and the next moment Nic was bumping about in the saddle, slipping first a little to one side, then to the other, making attempts to get over on to the horse's neck, and having hard work to keep his gun well across his knees.

It was hot, breathless work; and moment by moment Nic told himself that he must come off; but he did not, and went on bump, bump, bump, bump, conscious that his father was watching him from the corners of his eyes.

"I do wish he'd stop," thought Nic, as the nag trotted steadily on; and then the boy thought of the Kentish common and the games they had had with the donkeys—when, almost as soon as a boy was mounted, another came to tickle the donkey's tail with a piece of furze, with the result that the animal's head went down, its heels up, and the rider off on to his back, perhaps into a furze or bramble patch.

"But there's no one behind with a furze or bramble," thought Nic, who began to find the trot not so very bad, when, to his horror, his father cried out "Canter!" and, with the horses snorting and enjoying the motion, away they went in and out among the trees, the docile animals keeping pace together, and avoiding the dense parts by instinct.

"Now I am off," said Nic to himself; but to his surprise he kept on, finding the canter a delightfully easy pace, and that it was far less difficult to keep his seat in the saddle, the swing was so pleasant, elastic, and rhythmical.

This went on for a good quarter of a mile, until the trees grew more open and patches of scrubby bushes appeared in their way, when, before he knew it, Nic's steed, instead of avoiding a clump about three feet high, rose at it, bounded over as lightly as a kangaroo, and came to a dead stop on the other side, for it had lost its rider.

"I didn't mean that," said the doctor, pulling up and turning back.

"Here, Nic, where are you?"

"Here, father," said the boy dolefully, as he rose from where he lay—down among the thick brush.

"Hurt?"

"I—I don't know yet. No; I don't think so, father. Here, my gun's gone."

"There it is, sticking up among the bushes. I'll get it," said the doctor; and pulling his horse sidewise, he reached over and drew out the gun.

"Now then, where are you hurt?"

"Nowhere," said Nic, forcing his way out to where the nag stood, taking the reins, and after pulling down the near side stirrup, climbing into the saddle.

At that moment there was a clapping of hands, and he turned to find his father applauding him.

"Bravo! Good!" cried the doctor, with his eyes flashing. "I like that pluck, Nic. Why, boy, you did wonderfully well. You are as rough as can be in the saddle. But really, you only want confidence: you can ride."

"Can I, father?" said Nic dubiously.

"Can you? yes. You must have had some practice."

"Only playing tricks on the donkeys, father, down in Kent."

"Of course. That's it! Why, Nic, I have only got to polish you. Ready?"

"Yes, father."

"Then let's canter on."

Oddly enough—paradoxically as it may seem—that tumble on to the elastic bush took away all Nic's nervousness, and now he began to enjoy the delightful motion of the easy-paced nag, with the wind fanning his cheeks, the sun seeming to flash by him, and the soreness about the knees forgotten.

Everything about looked bright and glorious; and when, about eleven o'clock, they cantered up to the midday halting-place in a clump of gums, where the oxen had just been unyoked, Brookes and Leather stopped from their tasks to stare, and the black was so surprised that he forgot to stand on one leg, but watched the horsemen with wide-open eyes, standing upon two.

Chapter Twelve
A Black Peril

At the end of six days, though a long way from being a horseman, Nic had reached a pitch when he could mount without fear, and enjoy thoroughly a trot, canter, or gallop; and his father used laughingly to say that now he would not be ashamed to show him to his mother and sisters.

"It's a long, slow, monotonous journey, Nic," said the doctor, at the end of that sixth day; "but I don't think we've been idle."

"Idle? oh no, father," said Nic; "and I've enjoyed it thoroughly."

"In spite of the rough way of living?"

"I haven't thought of that," replied Nic. "It has all been so fresh and interesting, and there has been so much to see."

"Well, you have been well introduced to the country, my boy, and you have mastered riding—a strong part of a settler's education, for you will have to help me hunt up the sheep and cattle, and save me many a long round. Feel ready to see your mother and sisters?"

"Ready? I'm longing to see them, father. Are we getting near?"

"Yes; all being well, we shall sleep under our own roof to-morrow night, and have the waggon-load of stores and treasures under cover."

That last night in the waggon was the most uncomfortable Nic had passed. It was hot; there was a chest beneath him which had suddenly developed a hard edge and an awkward corner; the dogs, too, were uneasy, and barked a good deal at the moon. Then some kind of animal in the plural number seemed to be holding a meeting up among the branches of the huge tree under which they encamped, for there were endless squealings and skirmishes about, which woke the boy again and again, to lie and listen, and think about his new home in the great Australian wilderness, of his mother and sisters, whether they were much changed, and ending, just before dozing off again, by wondering what they would think of him.

It was, then, with a feeling of no little satisfaction that he woke again to hear the magpie piping, and hurriedly scrambled out, fully convinced that he was up first that morning, but found, as usual, that the fire was already burning brightly, and that some one had been on the watch, not one of which had he been allowed to keep.

This time it was the man Leather whom Nic joined, towel in hand, on his way for his regular morning swim.

"Morning! You're first, then?"

The man gave him a nod, and by the light of the fire his face looked surly.

"Has my father been out yet?"

"Sleep in the front of the waggon."

Nic felt disposed to go on, but he was in such high spirits that he was obliged to say a few words more.

"We shall be at the Bluff to-night."

"Oh?" said the man indifferently.

"Well, ain't you glad to get home?"

"No: I'm only a servant."

"But it's your home for the present."

The man threw a few more sticks on the fire, and said nothing.

"I say, Leather, what sort of a place is it?"

"Station's like other stations."

"Yes, but is it pretty—beautiful?"

"No."

"What? My father said it was a grand place with a glorious view."

"It's built of wood and thatched with bark, and you can see a long way."

"But the mountains?"

"There are mountains; so there are for miles."

"But the river?"

"There is a creek, but this time of the year it is mostly water-holes."

"But it's a beautiful place to live in?"

"Is it?" said the man coldly.

"Oh, I say, you want your breakfast!" said Nic laughingly.

"No; I am not hungry."

"Then what's the matter with you, Leather?"

"Nothing."

"Ah, well, I must go and have my dip."

The man gave him a sour look, and Nic ran on, passing the horses grazing together, which were ready to look up and whinny a welcome.

"There," cried, the boy, as he gave each a friendly patting and stroked their cold wet noses; "you're ever so much better companions than old Leather. Now then, finish your breakfast: to-night you will sleep in your warm stable."

The announcement made, of course, no impression upon the horses, which lowered their heads again directly, and went on cropping the succulent coarse grass, while Nic went on to the side of the pool, and began to undress, when his attention was taken by a sudden splash; and as he stood wondering he could dimly see something swimming about toward the other side.

"Must be a big water rat," muttered Nic, commencing to undress; and, confident that there was nothing likely to injure him, he plunged in, had his swim, crept out, rubbed, and was going on with his dressing again behind a clump of wattle scrub, when the splash excited his curiosity again, and turning his head cautiously, he peered down at the pool over which the pale grey light was now growing brighter.

For the first few moments he could see nothing; then a sinuous line of disturbed water showed him where something was swimming.

"'Tis a rat," he said to himself, "and those are ducks just on beyond it. No, it isn't a rat: it's one of those things with the duck's bill that father was talking about. I'll dress quickly and fetch the gun. I might get two or three ducks for supper."

The next moment he thought he would run as hard as he could to the waggon, and avoid being speared, but he did not stir, only stood in a stooping position staring wildly at' a black figure stealing along among the trees on the other side of the pool; and hardly had he realised this fact before another black appeared walking in the track of the first, and then' another and another.

Nic felt paralysed. They might be dangerous, for they were all carrying spears, and were stealing up to the water in the most cautious way.

The next minute he could see at least a dozen, and lowering his head cautiously he dropped upon his knees well out of sight, and finished dressing before softly turning his head again to watch.

The blacks were gone; and, though relieved, the boy was puzzled, for he could not make out how they could have left, as there was the open country just beyond the water-hole, and hardly a bush that could form a hiding place.

He could not have been deceived. Those must have been blacks, a strong party of them; and it was evident that they had not been seen up at the camp by Leather, or he would have warned him of their presence.

"Would he?" thought Nic. "He's a disagreeable, surly fellow, and I don't wonder, at Brookes bullying him so much. What shall I do? Perhaps after all they're gone. Oh!"

That last was a low, deep expiration of the breath, for Nic was having his first lesson in the clever cunning of the blackfellows. They were not gone, but clustered together just on the other side of the water-hole, some sixty yards away, right in sight as he peered between the thick branches of the wattle.

Nic felt fascinated for the moment, and was ready to ask himself whether it was real or a trick of his imagination. For there across the water lay about and stuck up in all kinds of gnarled and grotesque shapes what seemed to be a large clump of burned-down and blackened tree stumps; broken branches sent off awkward snag-like pieces, others presented bosses and excrescences; and but for the fact that he had seen the party of blacks creeping up, Nic never could have imagined that they were really there, thrown into these strange imitations of what was likely to be found upon the bank of a water-hole.

But there they were, either acting their part to deceive the wild fowl into coming near enough to be speared or knocked down, or trying to hide themselves from the encamping party.

Yes, dim as the light was, there could be no deception, for Nic at last made out the glint of an eye. It certainly was not a piece of gum gleaming in the dewy morning, but the eye of one of the blacks. Then it was gone.

What should he do? They were so clever that Nic knew it would be the hardest of hard work for a white to beat them with their own weapons; but the boy knew that he must act, and at once.

Dropping silently down, he lay on his breast thinking for a few moments, making his plans.

It was quite three hundred yards to the tree where the fire had been made—a long way for him to go if he were seen, for the naked blacks would be swifter of foot than he. His only course was to crawl from bush to bush;

and feeling that for the present he was out of sight, sheltered by the patch of wattle, he began to crawl slowly and as silently as he could toward the waggon.

Nic had never before realised how difficult it was to proceed over wet herbage after the fashion of a caterpillar. But this was the only way for him to get along, and he did his best, moving slowly forward where a savage would have gone on at a little run.

As he crept along it was with a strange quivering of the muscles of his back and loins, a curious kind of shrinking, in expectation moment by moment of the blacks having crept round the end of the water-pool through the dry bed of the river up the side to send a spear flying into him.

But it did not come; and at last, perspiring profusely, he passed a detached bush, curved round so as to place it between him and the blacks, and then paused to glance back.

He could not see them; but, to his horror, he found that the bush was not in a line between him and the water-hole, and he had to creep back.

Worse still, he realised now how the ground sloped upward, so that at any moment he might be in full view, and he paused, hesitating about going any farther, when only a few yards beyond he saw that there was a hollow into which he could roll, and in it creep along to the first big trees.

Nic felt that he was risking being seen by his impetuosity, but excitement urged him on, and the next moment he was in the little depression, most probably a dry rivulet bed, which ran down toward the water-hole. But whatever it was it gave him shelter till he could reach the big trees, in and out of whose trunks he threaded his way, well out of sight now, and ran panting up to the fire as his father was angrily saying to Leather:

"Surely you must have seen the black last night."

"Not him, sir," said Brookes; "he won't see nothing that he don't want. I left 'em together, and he ought to know where he is."

"Well, he has gone," said the doctor sternly; "and hullo, Nic, have you seen a snake?"

"Quick! father, the guns!" panted the boy. "Blacks! the blacks!"

"You mean our blackfellow?"

"No, father, twenty of them, just on the other side of the water-hole, hiding."

"All of you," said the doctor, in a low, firm voice, "into the waggon." Then the boy heard him mutter, as he held him tightly by the arm: "Good heavens! can they have been to the Bluff?"

Chapter Thirteen
Nic's Mission

"Father! do you think they have?" said Nic, breathlessly.

The doctor turned upon his son sharply. "Did I speak aloud?" he said. Nic nodded.

"I don't know. I cannot tell, my boy. I pray not."

By this time they were all armed, and the doctor whistled sharply, when there was a whinnying answer, and the two horses came up as fast as their hobbled fore feet would allow.

"Call in the bullocks," said the doctor to Brookes, who uttered a loud yell somewhat like the *yodel* of the Swiss peasants to their cattle on the mountain side.

The great sleek beasts responded directly, and came from where they were grazing, bellowing loudly, right up to the waggon, as if expecting to be yoked.

"To keep them from being speared," said the doctor to Nic. Then to the men: "Yoke up, and drive the waggon right out into the open. They could reach the poor beasts from behind those trees."

The men set to work leisurely enough, while at a word from his father Nic, whose hands trembled from excitement, bridled and saddled Sour Sorrel.

"Take off the hobbles, boy," said the doctor; and this was done. A few minutes later the bullocks, which had from long habit taken their places readily, were yoked, and drew out the waggon right into a clear spot away from trees, which would shelter the enemy if they made an attack.

"Hah!" ejaculated the doctor, "now we can breathe freely. Brookes, you are all right with a gun. Have you ever used a piece, Leather?"

"Not much," said the man sourly; "but I know how to load, and can keep you going."

"My son will load," said the doctor sternly. "You must do your best."

"Yes," said the man shortly; and Nic thought to himself, "Father does not want me to shoot any one."

"Now then, keep a sharp look-out," said the doctor. "If the blacks show, up at once into the front of the waggon, and we will take the back. No firing unless they try to spear the cattle. Then the blacks must accept their fate."

Incongruous ideas occur to us all, even in times of the greatest peril; and a waft of something in the air drew Nic's attention to the fire under the big gum tree, where the tea, hot cake, and bacon were ready for breakfast, and for a moment the boy felt hungry.

All was perfectly still. Then a magpie began to pipe his arpeggios, which sounded sweet and clear in the morning air; and this seemed to be the signal to start a chorus of whistling and shrieking up in the thick boughs, where a flock of paroquets were hidden; and a glow in the east made the morning grey look so opalescently beautiful that it was hard to believe there could be any danger.

"Are you sure you saw blacks, Nic?" said the doctor.

"Oh yes, father—certain."

"We ought to do some scouting, to see if they have moved and mean mischief."

"I'll go, father."

"No, boy: you are not used to the ways of these people; and I don't like to leave the waggon for fear of a rush. Brookes!"

"Yes," came from the front.

"You must go and reconnoitre. I'll cover you as well as I can. Just see if they are coming on."

"Don't see why you should send me," grumbled the man. "My wage ain't so very, high, and I've only got one life. Send Leather: he is not so much consequence as me."

The doctor uttered an angry ejaculation, and frowned fiercely; but it was no time for angry words.

"Leather, take your gun, and try if you can make out where the blacks are. Don't fire unless they see and attack you."

The man came with a heavy scowl upon his brow, shouldered his gun, and walked back in among the trees, while the doctor stood patting the butt of his gun impatiently, as his eyes searched the place in the direction of the water-hole.

"Our black must have known these fellows were in the neighbourhood," he said; "and he has either joined them or they have scared him away. Joined them, I think, or he would have warned me. They are all alike, these men: they come and work for a time, and then tire of it and go back to the bush."

"Here comes Leather," whispered Nic; and the next moment the man came back at a swift run, carrying his gun at the trail.

"Well? seen them?" said the doctor.

"Yes, over a score of them," said the man, who looked more animated now, in the excitement of the danger. "They're jabbering together this side of the water."

"Then they mean to attack. Be ready."

The man nodded, and moved toward where Brookes stood cutting himself some tobacco to chew. Then he turned back, and there was something approaching a smile upon his face, which, in spite of sun tan and the deep marks on his forehead, looked almost handsome to Nic.

"Yes: what is it?" said the doctor.

"Isn't it a pity to leave the breakfast for those blacks?"

"Never mind the food, man," began the doctor; but he checked himself. "Yes: try and get it," he said; "people must eat."

"Hold my gun, sir," said Leather, who was now, full of animation; and, handing the piece to Nic, he dashed back to the fire, while the doctor followed him slowly, scanning the trees in all directions as he kept his cocked piece ready for instant use.

Leather lost no time when he reached the fire, but, catching up the freshly made damper, he dabbed it down into the cross-handled frying-pan on the top of the bacon, placed the tin mugs in the kettle of boiling tea, carried the tea and sugar canisters under his arm, and taking pan-handle in one hand, kettle-handle in the other, he trotted back in safety, the blacks having made no sign.

"Bravo! Well done!" cried the doctor; and Nic noted that the bright, animated look passed away, to give place to a sullen scowl, which came over the man's face like a cloud.

"Help yourselves, men," continued the doctor; and Brookes came to them once again.

"Nic," said the doctor, "I am in agony. It may be all imagination, and if it is I should bitterly regret leaving the waggon. Do you see?"

"No, father; I don't quite understand. Do you mean you want to ride on to the Bluff, and yet don't want to because it may only be a scare?"

"Exactly. And if I did decide for us to ride on together, these men would take fright and leave the waggon to be plundered."

The doctor paused to search the trees again, but all was still.

"Send one of the men, father."

"I don't want to weaken my defensive force, boy."

"I'd go, father, but I don't know the way," said Nic.

"Yes: you shall go, my boy. The horse will take you straight to the station as soon as he is well away from his companion; and, look here! the track may prove faint, but do you see that notch in the mountains?"

"Where it looks as if a square piece had been cut out, and a cat's head with its ears standing up?"

"Yes: that notch is the pass through the mountains, and is just about two miles behind our house, which stands on a slope. You could not miss it."

"A wooden house: I know," said the boy; "but are the others at all like it?"

"What others? There is no other station for miles, boy. Well, will you risk it?"

"I don't see any risk, father."

"No; but blacks may be there. Well mounted, though, you could easily give them a wide berth."

"I'm not afraid," said Nic.

"That's right. You will ride straight there, then, and—"

The doctor stopped short, with his face drawn and wrinkled.

"Yes, father: and what?"

"If the station is a smoking ruin, ride back to us as hard as you can."

"Oh, don't say that."

"I have said it, boy. There—prove yourself worthy of my mission."

"Yes, father; but if all is right?"

"Stay there, and tell your mother to keep any black-fellows at a distance till I get home. You can help her defend the place for a few hours. Now: no words. Take a piece of the damper, and put a couple of rashers between, have a good deep drink of the tea—as much as you can, for you will have a thirsty ride—eat your breakfast as you go. Mind, straight as the crow flies for that notch: never mind the track. No words. Shake hands. Mount, and be off."

Nic saw that it was no time for words, and hurriedly breaking the bread-cake, he placed the bacon between the thin pieces, saw that his shot belt and powder flask were right, took a deep draught of tea, and then, gun in hand, turned to find Leather holding his horse, and looking him fixedly in the eyes.

"Yes; what is it?" said Nic hurriedly.

"Keep in the open: don't go near any of the scrub."

"Why not?" said Nic.

"Blacks," said the man, as the boy settled himself in the saddle.

"Off!" cried the doctor, pointing to the mountain gap. Nic waved his hand, pressed his nag's sides, and it bounded off; the other horse making a plunge to follow but it was tethered to a waggon wheel. But before the boy had gone fifty yards he turned, for there was a tremendous barking, and he saw that the doctor was at the back of the waggon doing something to the dogs. Then there was a shout, and he saw that they were loosened, and were tearing after him, barking loudly in their wild excitement.

"To come with me," thought Nic, and directly after, as he cantered steadily on, the two collies were racing round him, unsettling his horse as they leaped up, at its muzzle, at its legs, and then dashing on, mad with delight, but rather interfering with his comfortable seat, for they made the horse partake of their excitement and strain at the rein to join the two freed prisoners in their wild career over the tree-dotted plain.

The dogs soon settled down, though, to a more sober pace, and began to hunt in and out among the bushes and trees; finding nothing, but thoroughly enjoying their freedom.

Every now and then they came bounding back to the horse, to look up at Nic, barking loudly, their eyes flashing and tails whisking from side to side, as if telling him of their delight; and as the boy rode he gave them a word or two of encouragement.

But Nic did not speak much, for he had too much upon his mind; and as soon as he saw that there was not the slightest fear of the dogs straying away from the horse, he kept his eyes fixed upon the notch in the mountains right ahead, and rode steadily on, keeping his horse to a steady canter; and bearing Leather's laconic warning in mind, he left the track to one side or the other wherever growth seemed to be abundant, his father's order about going as the crow flies being ample warrant for this.

For the matter of that, the faint track of wheel and hoof-mark went pretty straight, only curving now and then to avoid some eminence or rugged patch of forest, which he watched with keen eyes for enemies, though, after what he had seen that morning in the grey dawn of the blacks' power of concealment, he felt doubtful about seeing them if they were in hiding to form an ambuscade.

"I wonder whether they could hit me with their spears if I was going at this rate," he said to himself, as he bore off from one dense patch which might easily have hidden a whole tribe. Then, in a state of intense excitement, he cocked his gun, trembling the while, for that there was danger at hand he felt sure, from the alarm of his horse, which suddenly cocked its ears, while the dogs lowered their heads and dashed together into the thicket.

"They'll give me warning," cried Nic aloud, as he bore off more to the right so as to skirt the little wood some fifty yards away; when out from the other side dashed half a dozen large animals, some of a ruddy hue, others of a bluish-brown colour, bounding over the ground like gigantic hares more than anything else, while the dogs gave tongue loudly and tried to head them off.

But at the end of four or five hundred yards, distanced beyond all possibility of overtaking their quarry, the collies stopped short to stand barking, and then trotted back to join the horse coming up, barking angrily, whining, and evidently thoroughly puzzled, as they looked up at Nic.

"Can't you make them out?" he cried; and the dogs barked and whined again. "Take them for sheep?" cried Nic; and in their way the dogs answered, and kept on running up the hillocks to bark at the little flock of strange beasts, that were growing smaller and smaller in the distance.

Onward again in a bee line, and an hour passed, with the notch in the mountains apparently at exactly the same distance as it was when they started on their journey.

Then came another little scene. On Nic's right the meandering line of bush and tree suggested where there was the course of a river, and the dogs suddenly, from where they were some distance ahead, scented out an occupier in a clump of rough growth low down in a swampy patch of thick grass.

Nic swung round his gun once more; but this time the dogs did not drive out a herd of kangaroo, for they stopped short, with the thick coat of hair about their necks bristling up while they charged in and retreated again and again.

"Can't be blacks," thought Nic, and he checked his nag slightly, but found the horse began to show signs of uneasiness, sidling away as he approached, carefully watching for the point of a spear or some shock head.

"There they are," he said to himself the next moment, as he made his horse bound away, for some distance farther on he saw both—the rough spears and long-haired heads dotted here and there.

The next moment, though, he was annoyed with himself for his needless alarm, the objects he saw being only the native grass trees with their peculiar growth of tufted heads bearing some resemblance to a rough shock of hair, the long bare flower spike standing up above suggesting at a distance the native spear.

There, too, in an open patch, was the cause of the dogs' uneasiness, in the shape of a snake richly marked with brown, and apparently six or eight feet long, as it lay in close curves, with head erect, playing about and seeking an opportunity to strike at the first dog which came within reach.

Nic felt plenty of inclination to have a shot at what was probably, from its appearance, the venomous tiger-snake of which he had heard the men speak. But the urgent duty forced him on, and he cantered forward for another hour, to where the track, now on his *left*, passed close by a pool of water, toward which the dogs set off, barking loudly; and the horse followed straight for the spot.

As usual, it was well wooded all about, but after seeing the dogs reach it first and career through and, through it without so much as a yelp, Nic had no hesitation in riding up, loosening his nag's girths, and then, while it drank a little, taking out his own breakfast, a part of which he ate with poor appetite, sharing the rest between the dogs as soon as they had had a good drink and swim.

The halt was very short, and while the horse was refreshing itself with a few mouthfuls of the rich grass, its master stood gazing through the clear sunny air at the notch in the mountains, which looked to him just as far off as it did when he rode off that morning—just as near.

He tried to calculate how many hours he had been riding, how many miles he had come, but gave up in despair. All he could feel was that the sun was getting very high, and that the heat would be very great for the rest of the way, and he knew that he must deal gently with his horse, and keep to the pace he had ridden through the morning: to go faster might mean a break-down.

"Now, Sour Sorrel," he said suddenly; and the horse left off grazing, and stood gazing at him with its great deer-like eyes.

It stood quietly enough while he gave it a good rub with some natural hay where the saddle covered its satin coat, then clapped the saddle back, tightened the girths and mounted, while the dogs careered round him with their ears up and brushes waving, barking with delight, and once more leaping up at the horse's muzzle.

Then forward once more—out of the shade and into the scorching sun.

Nic started his horse at a walk, and noted that it needed no guiding, but took to the faint track at once, steering straight for the notch, and making for a thick patch of wooded country, till a pressure from the rider's leg turned it off to a more open part, from which he bore away, so as to pass round to the west of the woodland.

As soon as it was on the springy green grass, the nag broke at once into a canter, and the dogs now settled into a steady pace, keeping one on either side, while Nic found it hard to believe that he was riding over wild land, the ground bearing so strongly the appearance of forming part of some park devoted to grazing; but now he saw no trace of beast or sheep, little of wild creatures, save where there were signs of water, and then only a few birds, generally a kind of plover, or ducks.

The heat was now intense. Nic had only enjoyed a week's training, and he was in poor condition for so much exertion, so that before long he was soaked with perspiration, and growing weary as he gazed at that terrible notch which seemed to come no nearer, he began to lose heart and wonder whether he would be able to accomplish his task.

The horse, too, was showing signs of exertion, and the dogs, as they trotted on, lolled out their tongues and displayed no disposition to break out of their steady pace to investigate anything to right or left.

"Phew! It is hot!" muttered Nic, as his horse cantered on, with the sun dazzling his eyes like molten silver, and biting his neck, while the whole of the atmosphere was quivering as it rose from the moister parts of the earth. Then, in the regular rhythmic motion of that canter, there were moments when the traveller began to feel drowsy. But he shook off the feeling, nipped the horse's sides more tightly, and felt how the beast responded by increasing its pace.

On still, and on, over the rich green flower-decked earth; past groves of trees whose names he did not know,—some bearing the thin foliage of grey or sage green, with delicate shades of pink and blue, others like a coarse-leaved spiky-looking fir, whose boughs touched the ground, and densely clustered upward in a pyramid of dark glistening growth that would have hidden a dozen men from a traveller's gaze.

There were the mountains, too, in a long ridge, stretching away to right and left, and always of a delicious amethystine blue, that looked as transparent as water, but always as far off as ever.

A grand, a lovely ride, but a terrible one in that heat; for this was the time when the doctor always had a midday halt by water and in the shade of trees. But there was no stopping for hours at a time like this. Nic felt that he must get on as fast as he could, and with his eyes fixed upon the notch he rode forward to the regular beat of his horse's hoofs.

Hotter and hotter grew the day, and as Nic glanced from side to side he saw that he was not the only sufferer, for the dogs were trotting along with their heads down, and they gazed up at him and whined. His horse, too, began to look more distressed, but it did not flag, keeping up that steady canter toward the blue mountains that never seemed to grow any nearer.

For a few moments the idea lingered in Nic's brain, that he must draw rein in the shade of the next clump of trees, but the thought evoked the face of his father, back there at the waggon, anxious about those dear to him, wondering how all had sped at the Bluff, and he felt that he could not halt even for an hour—that he must go on and on.

Then he began wondering how he would find the place—whether the blacks had been during his father's absence, and attacked it when it was only defended by women and the servants, who might have escaped for their lives.

This idea of the place having been attacked sent such a thrill through Nic that he felt ready for any amount more exertion, and instead of halting he urged his willing steed on, shouted to the dogs and made them leap forward, while his eyes wandered about in search of enemies, but only to see something moving in the distance which, resembled the ostrich of his old picture-books. There was no sign of man, no house, flock, herd, or water, while his tongue was beginning to feel swollen and dry, and a peculiar thickness as of a mist began to obstruct the distant view.

"How much farther is it?" thought Nic; and he shaded his eyes by holding the hand which bore the gun across his forehead.

But he saw no better, and he winced from the touch, of the gun-lock, for it was hot.

Then on, still trusting to the horse more than to himself, for the air had grown thicker, and the mist hot, strange, and dazzling for a time. There were singing noises, too, in his ears, and as he gave his head a shake in his effort to get rid of them, he suddenly found that the dazzling mist had gone, and he could see right away to the notch—that dent in the mountains which seemed to lead him on and on, but only to recede as he advanced.

That clearness of vision did nut last, for the mist closed in again, lifted, and he saw a bright lake of beautiful silvery water, stretching out as far as he could see, and toward which with throbbing temples he urged on the horse. The next minute it had disappeared, and some one was calling him; the thickening of the air was not from mist, but as of smoke. He must, he felt, with a terrible sense of depression, have neared his devastated home, which was burning, and the light breeze was wafting the dense smoke all over the plain.

"What news to take back to his father!" he thought, in his despair, and this made his senses reel; something struck him heavily, and then he was looking up at the blue sky, as a dark object came between him and it.

For a few moments he must have been quite unconscious, while the next thing he saw was the horse's muzzle close to his face.

He started up into a sitting position, for a dismal howl rang in his ears, followed by a loud joyous barking, which brought him to his feet, guessing the truth.

For the heat had produced that dimness of sight, tortured him with the sight of that imaginary lake, and finally brought on a bad attack of giddiness, which had made him reel in the saddle and fall heavily to the ground.

The shock had helped to revive him; and feeling better, he picked up his gun from where it lay beneath the horse, managed to climb back into the saddle, and the brave beast started on at once straight for a clump of trees about a mile away, while, before they were two-thirds of the distance, the dogs began to bark, and seemed to recover their strength, for they bounded on, and the horse broke into a gallop, following in their track.

A minute or two later Nic knew why, for there was a flash of light from amongst the trees, and soon after he had thrown himself from his horse's back, and was upon his chest in the shade, drinking draughts that seemed to quench the fire in his throat, bathing his face, and listening to the gentle, sucking noise made by the horse where it stood knee deep, and to the barking and splashing of the two dogs as they revelled in the refreshing coolness of the great water-hole.

Nearly half an hour passed before Nic resumed his place in the saddle; the horse broke into a canter at once, the dogs ran barking by his side, and, refreshed and clear of vision, it seemed now that the notch in the blue mountains was not quite so far away, while, in spite of the heat, the country on all sides was growing as beautiful as it had seemed at his early start.

On still, but no sign of the station. The ground had ceased to be so level, there was hardly any track, and their course was among clumps of trees, rocks, and rugged hillocks, and there were times when the view was cut off by their descent into some deep gully.

But his father had said that if he kept straight for the notch he would be sure to see the house the only one; and no house was in view. He must be near it now: was it still in existence? or had some horrible catastrophe befallen it?

The heat was growing insufferable again and the giddiness returning: he could not go much farther. He had been trusting the horse too much: it had evidently brought him astray far down in that suffocating gully,— the growth was different. He was riding amongst ferns—ferns like those he saw at home, and ferns that spread green lacework fronds right overhead. He must be dreaming again and going to fall from his horse, which was ascending the rapid slope the farther side of the gully. They were soon at the top, and the breeze came pure and sweet again; and a wild cry of exultation burst from the boy's parched throat, for, not a mile away, standing high upon the slope beyond another gully, there was a long, low, white house, with a cluster of wooden buildings near. Beyond it a rising ground was dotted with sheep; there were cattle, too, farther away, and, as in response to his cry, the dogs burst out into a loud barking, Nic pressed his horse's sides, the spirited animal breaking into a swift gallop and racing on.

For there was no sign of fire or smoke: a glorious picture of a bright oasis in the great wilderness was before him, and his former fears were vain; for, yes—no—yes, out there in the clear air stood a group of watching figures, and the next moment the boy's eyes grew dim—not so dim, though, that he was unable to see white handkerchiefs waving him a welcome—a welcome to his long-wished-for home.

Chapter Fourteen
"Sweet, Sweet Home"

Sour Sorrel wanted no reining in, but stopped short at the foot of the great hillock, down which two bonny-looking, sun-browned maidens had run, followed by a tall, grey, graceful-looking lady.

"It is Dominic, isn't it?" cried one of the girls.

"Yes, it is!" cried the other. "Oh, Nic, how you have grown!"

"And oh!" cried the other, "how you have distressed poor Sorrel! You shouldn't have ridden him so hard."

This was in the intervals between kisses, as the lad was embraced by first one and then the other. But as soon as he could free himself, Nic ran to meet his mother, who was descending more slowly.

"My dear boy!" she cried.

"Mother!" and they were locked in each other's arms.

Mrs Braydon could say no more for some minutes, but stood with the tears streaming down her handsome face, clinging tightly to her son, while the two dogs looked on uneasily, whining and giving short, half-angry barks, as if they did not quite understand whether the attentions of the three ladies were friendly toward their young master.

The tears stood in the eyes of the two girls as well, but they were tears of joy, and in a merry, laughing way the elder cried:

"Oh, mother, you must not keep him all to yourself!"

"No, no, of course not," cried Mrs Braydon, locking one arm now in Nic's. "Poor boy! how hot and weary he is, Janet!"

"Yes; and he has nearly ridden poor Sorrel to death," cried the second girl.

"In his eagerness to get home," said Mrs Braydon, clinging to her son affectionately. "At last—at last! Oh, my boy, it has seemed so long! But your father, is he just beyond the gully?"

"No, no!" cried Nic excitedly. "A day's journey away."

"And you have come alone?"

"Yes; but tell me," cried Nic. "The blacks: have they attacked you?"

"No, no," cried Janet quickly; "are they out?"

"Yes; we saw a large party this morning coming to attack the waggon. Father was afraid that they might have been here, and he sent me on for news."

"No," said Mrs Braydon, "they have not been near us. But your father?"

"I left him with the two men and the waggon."

"They'll be all right, mother," said the second girl, squeezing up to Nic's side and giving him a quick kiss on the cheek. "Oh! how wet and hot you are. Sticky boy!"

"Yes, mother dear," said Janet. "Hil is quite right. There's nothing to mind."

"But he said the blacks were going to attack the waggon, my dear," cried Mrs Braydon anxiously. "We had better send over to Mr Dillon for a party to go and meet them."

"Oh, nonsense, mother!" said Hilda, giving her dark brown curls a toss; "father would laugh at the idea. He'll fire a few shots over their heads and send them scrambling away."

"Yes, of course," said Janet calmly enough. "Mamma is a little nervous sometimes, Nic. We don't mind a few blackfellows about here. They are only like big children."

"But what ought I to do?" cried Nic anxiously. "Shall I ride somewhere and get help?"

"Perhaps it is not necessary," said Mrs Braydon, smiling rather piteously. "The girls are right. But, my dear boy, how did you find your way?"

"Father pointed out that gap in the mountain over there, and told me to ride straight for it."

"What place was it where you left your father?"

Nic described it as well as he was able.

"I know: it must be the third water-hole from here; five-and-thirty miles away."

"And he has ridden all that way since morning!" cried Mrs Braydon. "My poor boy! It is dreadful!"

"There," cried Hilda saucily; "it's all over, Jan. I knew mamma would spoil him as soon as he came. Go and have your face washed, Nic; you're not fit to touch ladies. *Cooey—cooey!*"

Nic stared to see his pretty young sister, a year older than he, suddenly put her hands to her mouth and utter a peculiar cry.

"She's calling one of the men."

"*Cooey!*" came in response, and a shock-headed black in shirt and trousers came running down from one of the sheds.

"White Mary want er?"

"No, no: where's Samson?"

"White Mary want er—Sam," said the black aloud, as if telling himself; and he trotted off with a queer gait, his legs very far apart, as if he found trousers awkward to walk in; and he then burst into a sharp run, for the dogs, which had been smelling his heels, began to bark and rush after him.

"Here, here, here!" shouted Nic, for the black uttered a yell; and the dogs turned back obediently, and came to his side wagging their tails, and, apparently satisfied in their minds, were ready to respond to the friendly advances of the two girls.

"Hi! Sam!" cried Hilda, as a diminutive grey old man came hurrying down, smiling and touching his hat. "Take Sorrel, and give him a feed of corn and a good rub down. Hardly any water."

"All right, miss. So this is young master? How do, sir? Glad to see you. Master close home?"

"No, no, Samson," said Mrs Braydon anxiously. "What do you think? My son was sent on to see if we were safe here. The blacks are out, and a party surprised them by the waggon."

To Nic's annoyance the man showed a few very old yellow teeth in an ugly laugh.

"Master'll surprise some o' them if they don't take to their legs mighty sharp, missus."

"Then you don't think there's any danger?"

"Yes, I do—for them," said the man. "Some on 'em'll be howling while t'others picks shot-corns out o' their black hides with a pynted stone."

"Yes, of course," said Hilda coolly.

"Then you don't think I ought to send over to Mr Dillon to get help for him?"

"Help? Tchah! Don't you be so narvous, missus. They blackfellows don't know no better. They comes out with some streaks of white chalk on their black carcadges, and they goes up to a waggon flourishing their hop-poles and making faces, and frightens some people, and then they steal flour and stores; but if they've gone to our waggon, I 'magine they've gone to the wrong un. Take a precious ugly face to scare the doctor. Tell you what he'll do, ladies all. He'll shoot over their heads *first*."

"Yes, of course," said Hilda.

"That's right, Miss Hil. Then if that don't do no good, he'll give 'em a dose o' number six. And then, missus, if that don't do, he'll try swan shot; but don't you be frecken. Master knows how to manage strange blackfellows. Come along, my lad. Say, young master, you have give him a sweating, and no mistake."

The horse went and placed its muzzle over the little old man's shoulder, and gave a puff like a deep sigh of satisfaction.

"Knows me, young master," said the man, grinning. "Ay, nussed you, Sorrel, when you was on'y a babby, didn't I?" he continued, patting the arched neck and carefully turning a few strands of the mane back in their place.

"There, mother dear," said Janet affectionately; "you see it is not necessary."

"But I feel as if, now I know you are all safe, I ought to go back," said Nic.

"You couldn't do it, sir," said the old man. "Why, you don't s'pose I should be talking like this if I thought the doctor was in trouble! There's allus blacks about; and it's on'y missus as is so scared about 'em. It's all right, sir. Where did you say you left the master?"

"By the third water-hole."

"By Bangoony," said the old man. "Day's trot, and the bullocks'll want a three-hour rest half-way. They'll be here twelve o'clock to-night, for master'll make it one day for the last. Don't you fret, missus; the doctor knows what he's about. Blacks ain't lifers. He'll be here all right. Come along, my bairn!"

This last was to the horse, which followed him toward one of the sheds; and the dogs went after, one of them uttering a low growl as the man gave the nag a sounding slap.

Samson stood still, and then turned to the dog. "Now then: none o' that. It ain't your horse." The dog growled, and its companion joined in. "Oh, that's it, is it? I say, Mr Dominic, sir, hadn't you better interrajuice us? They say they don't know me, and I'm too useful to your father to feed dogs."

"They won't bite," said Nic, going up, but walking very stiff and lame.

"That's what folks allus says," grumbled the old man; "but 'dogs do bark and bite, for 'tis their nature to.' Just you tell 'em to make friends."

"Yes. Look here: friends! friends!" cried Nic. "Shake hands, Samson."

"Sure I will, sir," said the old man, grinning, as he rubbed a hard blackened hand down one leg of his trousers. "That ain't dirt, sir. I've been tarring some o' the sheep. On'y a bit sticky."

"I don't mind," cried the boy, holding out his hand, which was taken in a firm grip, and proved to be more than a bit sticky, for it was held tightly as the man stared hard at him.

"And the master to'd me, he did, as you was on'y a bit of a sickly slip of a lad as he left in London or elsewhere when he come out here—a poor, thin, weak, wankle sort o' gentleman, not what he is now."

Nic wanted to loose his hand and get back, but it was held fast, and the old man went on:

"Why, you'll grow into a *big*, strong man, sir, bigger than the doctor. Ay, I 'gaged with him arter he'd nussed me for my broken leg, as the ship doctor down at Botany Bay said must come off. 'Nay,' says your father, and him all the time suff'rin' from a norful corf,—'nay,' he says, 'don't you have it took off, my man,' he says; and I says I wouldn't, for o' course I didn't want to go about like a pegtop; and he sets to and makes it right. This here's the leg, stronger than t'other. I call it the doctor's leg, and I said I'd come up country with him if he'd have me, and he said he would, and I helped him make this place. We cut the wood and knocked in the nails, and I've bred horses and sheep and cows for him, and I'm going to stick to him to the end, and then he's promised to dig a hole hisself under yan big gum tree with my name placed over me, and that's where I'm goin' to sleep. Now you wants to go back to your mar. She's been a-frettin' arter you for years while you was being taught to read and write, so be a good boy to her. But, I say, you couldn't ha' rid another five-and-thirty mile to-day."

"No," said Nic. "Take care of the horse."

"Ay, and the dogs too. Here, give's your paw."

The dog he spoke to growled and showed its teeth.

"Ah, friends! Give him your paw," cried Nic.

The dog held out its right paw, but threw up its head and drew back its muzzle, as it looked at Nic protestingly, as much as to say, "He's only a stranger, and I don't know anything about him."

"Now you," growled Samson; and the same business was gone through, with the dog whining uneasily.

"Hullo! what's the matter?" said Samson, lifting the leg. "There—don't make that row. It's on'y a thorn. You'll get lots o' them in your toes if you behave yourself. Dogs ought to wear boots in some o' these parts. That's it. Big un too. See it?"

He made an offer as if to prick the dog's nose, after drawing out a long, sharp thorn, making the beast yelp; but as soon as it was out it gave the place a lick, and then barked loudly and danced about the old man, both dogs following him readily now as he went off grinning to the stable.

Mrs Braydon and the girls were waiting, and Nic was led limping toward the house.

"Only a bit stiff with riding," said the boy. "Then we are to be comfortable about father?"

"I suppose so, my dear," said Mrs Braydon. "Janet, my love, see to the tea."

"Everything is ready, mother dear," said the girl affectionately; "and really I don't think we need fidget. Nic cannot go back. He must stay and take care of us and the station."

"Yes," said Mrs Braydon sadly, as if she thought it would be of more consequence to take care of the doctor; and Nic was led into the house, after passing through a neatly kept, well fenced-in garden, full of trees, shrubs, and flowers new to him, though beyond a hedge there was a broad spread of homely old friends of a useful kind, growing luxuriantly.

He was ushered at once into a pleasant room, made bright, in spite of its extremely simple furnishing, by white dimity curtains and home-made mats, the bed in the corner looking white as snow; and, left to himself, the boy luxuriated in a comfortable wash, though in place of ewer and basin he had but a bucket and tub.

Before he had finished, his mother was back with a cup of refreshing tea, this time with cream.

"You'll find everything very rough, my son; but every time the waggon goes on its journey to the port it brings back same more domestic comforts."

"Never mind the roughness, mother," cried Nic, kissing her, and bringing a smile of joy playing about her lips; "it's home, and I'm along with you all again."

"Yes, my son; and I can be quite happy now," said Mrs Braydon, clinging to him fondly. "There, drink your tea," she said quickly, "finish dressing, and there's a brush by the window, and I've brought you my glass. How brown and blistered your poor face is!"

"Oh, that's nothing, mother," cried Nic. "Hah! delicious!" he sighed, as he finished the tea, making his mother smile her satisfaction.

"Be quick. We have a tea-dinner ready, for we felt that you might come at any time. You will not have to come downstairs, dear; we are all on one floor. We only had one room and the waggon and a tent first; but others have been added, one at a time. I ought to go now, but it is so hard to leave you, my dear."

She kissed him lovingly again—they were the first kisses she had pressed upon his lips for over five years—and then she hurried out.

"Hah!" sighed Nic; "I wish I knew that father was safe." Then, stiff and with his hand trembling from his long ride, he took up the comb to smooth his hair.

"Might as well sit down," he said; and he sank back on the bed. "How soft! Feathers! And the pillow—how cool! Cheeks burn so," he muttered, as he subsided on the restful couch to gaze sidewise at the window with its little sill and flowers growing in a box, all fresh, bright and fragrant.

"I like flowers," he said softly, and then—"Hah!"

He was breathing softly.

The bow strained tightly for so many hours was now unstrung. Every nerve and muscle were relaxed, and the soft, pure air which came through the open window played upon his scorched cheeks.

The horse was swinging along in that easy canter out of the burning sunshine into the shade—a soft, cool, delicious, restful shade—on and on and on toward the Bluff; and Nic felt that there was no more care and trouble in the world. There was nothing to trouble him. He had felt his mother's kisses on his cheeks and lips, and the horse was not rushing, only swinging along in that glorious canter, for the shade had grown darker, into a soft, sweet obscurity, and everything was so still.

Chapter Fifteen
After Nature's Remedy

Nic opened his eyes slowly, to gaze at a bright patch shining upon the floor, and he lay for some minutes gazing at it, thinking it very beautiful.

He knew it was the moon shining through flowers—a soft, mellow moonlight which came through a small window.

Then the full rush of thought came, and he started up.

"Awake, dear?"

"Mother!" cried Nic. "Why, have I been to sleep?"

"Yes, my darling, a long time."

"And the tea—dinner?"

"It's quite ready, my dear."

"But but what time is it?"

"The clock has just struck one, my boy."

"Oh, what a shame!"

"No, my dear; it was nature's great need."

"But I slept like that! What news of father?"

"None, my love," said Mrs Braydon, with a piteous tremor in her voice.

"I ought to have gone," cried the boy angrily.

Bang! crash! like blows on the wooden sides of the house.

"What's that?" cried Nic, starting to his feet.

"Hi! missus!" came in a harsh voice. "Here they are. What did I say?"

"Come?" cried Mrs Braydon wildly.

"Ay, missus. Our black's just run in to where I was watching beyond the gully. I heard the cracking of Brookes's whip, too, in the still. There! hear that?" he continued, as there was a faint distant report. "Master's yonder."

Nic stepped to the corner of the room, where he had stood his gun when he entered, went to the window, cocked the piece, thrust it out with its barrel pointing upward, and fired, in answer to his father's signal.

"He'll know what that means. All right," said the boy. "Oh, mother, I feel so guilty; but he did tell me to stay and take care of you, for if I did not return he said he should know that all was right."

"My word, young squire, you made me jump," cried Samson, coming to the window. "Was that to siggernal the master?"

"Yes, of course."

"I'm a-goin' to meet him now. Too tired to come with me?"

"Oh no," cried Nic; and the next minute he was trudging along beside the old man, leaving the house with its windows lit up and the fire shining through the open door as a welcome home to the master.

"You ought to go first, young gentleman," said Samson, "but you won't know the way in the dark; and as I'm going along by the sheep track, there won't be room for you alongside me, so you'd better come behind. Keep close, for it's dark under the green stuff and a bit awkward, but it cuts off a quarter of a mile. Come on."

Nic followed the old man across a fenced-in enclosure, over the fence, and then down a steep slope into a gully, where their path soon resembled silvery lacework on velvet, for they were going beneath arching ferns of the most delicate nature. Then they had to leap dark roaring water, that flashed and sparkled where the moonbeams touched a broad glassy curve before it plunged down into some dark mysterious depth.

"Pretty place this by daylight, sir," said the old man. "Mind how you come across here. Give me your hand to steady you, for it's pretty tidy dark."

"What is it—water?" asked Nic.

"Yes; it's a deep bit of a pool as the master dammed up, and this here's a tree felled to lie acrost it like a bridge. You won't like it by daylight p'raps, but it's quite safe, and you can't see how deep it is in the dark."

Nic hesitated for a moment, then lightly grasped the man's hand, but only for a moment. The next the bony hand had clutched his wrist like a vice.

"That's better," said the old man. "Now you can slip if you like, and I can hold you if you do."

There was nothing else for Nic to hold but his tongue and his breath, as he stepped on to the rugged wood in the black darkness, for the moonbeams were shut out now by the rocks, overhead, and then, as he took step for step behind his companion, so close to him that he kept kicking his heels, he felt the difference underfoot for a few paces and the tree trunk yield and give a little in an elastic way. Then all at once the character of the path was changed, and Nic felt the hard rock beneath his feet.

"Is that deep?" he said, rather huskily.

"Well, with what we've got not far away we don't call that deep. It's on'y a sort o' crack like. 'Bout hundred and fifty foot, say."

"A hundred and fifty feet!" cried Nic, with an involuntary shiver.

"Somewheres about that," said Samson coolly. "But you wouldn't hurt yourself if you went down, for there's a good depth o' water in the pool. But you'd get strange and wet."

Nic drew in a deep breath.

"There—it's all good going now, sir: a bit downwards and then up hill."

The old man strode on, leading his companion up and down for a while and then beginning a steady ascent.

"This is the bit as the sheep made going to and from the folds. 'Nother five minutes and we shall be atop o' the side o' the gully. You come along a bit higher up. There we are," he said, at last. "Now look straight ahead and tell me what you see."

"A light swinging to and fro, and up and down."

"That's it, sir; and that light's the master's waggon lantern. Know why it dances about like that?"

"Somebody seems to be swinging it."

"Yes," said the old man with a chuckle; "and some, body's that big bullock with the white spot on his for'd. Know how he carries the lantern?"

"Tied round his neck."

"Nay; it's been hooked on to his horn," said the old man with a chuckle. "I showed master how to do that, and you wouldn't think it was in a big stupid-looking hox; but it's my belief as old Cheery likes carrying that there light, and is quite proud of it."

"Nonsense!" said Nic, as he watched the faint star down below them on the level.

"No, I dunno as it's nonsense, sir. I think he do, because if he didn't he'd on'y have to give his head a cant on one side and send that there lantern a-flying; and he never do. Now steady: it's a bit steeper here. See your way better, can't you?"

"Yes, it's so much more open; and how beautiful it looks in the moonlight!"

"Ay, it do, sir; but it looks better by day a deal. Now hold hard."

Nic stopped, and the old man gave the Australian cry, which was answered hoarsely from the darkness round the swaying lantern. Then there were several sharp cracks of a whip and the rattle of chains.

"That's old Brookes. He can slash a whip. Good workman, Brookes, on'y he hayve got too much tongue. There now, we're down on the level, and you can make out the waggon. Leastwise I can."

"Father!" shouted Nic excitedly. "All well?"

"All well?" came back.

"Yes!" and a minute later the boy was walking by his father's side, holding on by the horse's mane, answering questions and asking others.

"Oh yes," said the doctor; "they came out at last and made a show of attacking us; but I sent a charge of shot spattering among the leaves over their heads, and they turned and ran."

Half an hour after, while the oxen were still laboriously tugging the heavy waggon up the slope leading to the station, Nic and his father reached one illuminated door, where the doctor sprang down to embrace wife and daughters, after which he handed his horse's rein to old Samson and waited till the wain was drawn up into the enclosure and the bullocks were turned loose to graze.

"Our task to-morrow, Nic,—to see to the unloading."

"But will the things be safe there?" said the boy.

"Safe? yes, unless the blacks come down upon us. But I have no fear. Now, Nic, I'm not like you: I haven't been fed and pampered by the women for hours. I'm starving for a good meal."

"So am I, father."

"What, again?" said the doctor, as he reached the door, just as Brookes and Leather carried the lantern into the kitchen, where a meal was spread for them. "Here, my dear, this boy says he's hungry again."

"Again, father?" cried Hilda; "why, he has had nothing but a cup of tea!"

"Why? Not well?"

"Oh yes, father, quite," cried Nic. "I've only been asleep."

Chapter Sixteen
Life at the Station

The late supper in the plain, homely room—where the table was on trestles, the chairs were stools, and the arm-chairs ingeniously cut out of casks, the carpet sacking, and the hearthrug skins—and the performance in the way of sleep on his arrival, interfered sadly with Nic's night's rest.

It was an hour after his father's return before they all retired; and as soon as Nic was in his room he felt not the slightest inclination for bed. Everything was so new and fresh; the brilliant moonlight lit up the tract outside with such grand effects that the first thing he did was to take the home-made tallow candle out of its socket and hold it upside down till it was extinct, and then put it back.

The room was now all bright in one part, black shadow in the others; and he was going to the open window to look out, but just then an idea struck him, and he took up his gun, closed the pan, drew the flint hammer to half-cock, and proceeded to load. He carefully measured his charge of powder in the top of the copper flask, and poured it into the barrel, in happy unconsciousness that in the future ingenious people would contrive not only guns that would open at the breech for a cartridge containing in itself powder, shot, and explosive cap, to be thrust in with one movement, but magazine rifles that could be loaded for many shots at once.

Then on the top of the powder he rammed down a neatly cut-out disk of felt, the ramrod, drawn from its loops and reversed, compressing the air in the barrel, driving the powder out through the touch-hole into the pan, and making a peculiar sound running in a kind of gamut: pash—pesh—pish—posh—poosh—push—pud—pod—por—with the wind all out and the powder compressed hard down by the wad. Next a little cylindrical shovel full of shot was extracted from the belt, whose spring closed as the measure was drawn out, and the shot trickled gently into the barrel, glistening in the moonlight like globules of quicksilver. Another wad was rammed down; the pan opened and found full of the black grains, and the ramrod replaced in its loops behind the barrel, the gun being stood in the corner beside the bed ready for emergencies in that rough land.

Nic's next proceeding was to listen and find that the murmur of voices heard beyond the partition had ceased, and he slipped off his shoes and stepped softly to the open window.

The flowers smelt deliciously in the cool, soft night air, and he looked out, leaning his arms on the sill to realise more thoroughly that he was in the place he had so often longed to see when he did a similar thing at the Friary in far-off Kent.

It seemed impossible, but it was true enough. His old schoolfellows might be looking out of the window now over the Kentish hills, but he was divided from them by the whole thickness of the great globe. They were in the northern portion of the temperate zone; he, as he leaned out, was in the southern. They would be looking at the hills; he was gazing at the rugged mountains. Then, too, it was just the opposite season to theirs—summer to their winter, winter to their summer.

"It's like a big puzzle," thought Nic. "I shan't understand it all till I've made a globe. I wish I'd studied the big one at the Friary more. How strange it all seems!"

As he looked out, the place appeared very different. He had seen it in the full sunshine; now, in the silence of the night, the trees glistened in the moonlight as if frosted, and the shadows cast stood out black, sharp, and as if solid.

And how still and awful it all seemed! Not a sound,—yes, there was: an impatient stamp from somewhere on the other side of the house. He knew what that was, though: the horses were troubled by some night insect. There was another sound, too, as he listened—and another—and another.

He was wrong: there was no awful silence; the night, as his ears grew accustomed to the sounds, was full of noises, which impressed him strangely or the reverse as he was able to make them out or they remained mysteries.

As he tried to pierce the distance, and his eyes wandered through the network of light among the trees on the slopes which ran up toward the mountains, his first thoughts were of blacks coming stealing along from shelter to shelter, till close enough to rush forward to the attack upon the station; and over and over again his excited imagination suggested dark figures creeping slowly from bush to bush or from tree to tree.

Once or twice he felt certain that he saw a tall figure standing out in the moonlight watching the house, but common sense soon suggested that a savage would not stand in so exposed a position, but would be in hiding. Then, too, as minutes passed on and he was able to see that the objects did not move, he became convinced that they were stumps of trees.

That sound, though, was peculiar, and it was repeated. It was a cough, and that was startling, just in the neighbourhood of the house. But again he was able to explain it, for he had heard that cough in the fields of Kent, and the feeling of awe and dread passed off; for he knew it was the very human cough of a sheep.

But that was no sheep—that peculiar croaking cry that was heard now here, now there, as if the utterer were dashing in all directions. That was followed by a hollow trumpeting, and a short, harsh whistle, and a strange clanging sound from far away, while close at hand there was a soft, plaintive whistling and a subdued croak.

By degrees, though, as he listened, he was able to approximate to the origin of these calls. Night-hawks, cranes, curlews, and frogs might, any of them, or all, be guilty; and some kind of cricket undoubtedly produced that regular stridulation, as of a piece of ivory drawn along the teeth of a metal comb.

Then there was a heavy booming buzz, as some great beetle swung by; and beneath all, like a monotonous bass, came a deep roar, which could only be produced by falling water plunging down from on high into some rocky basin.

"What a place! what a wonderful place!" thought Nic, as he gazed out— perfectly sleepless now; and as he thought, the idea of wild beasts came into his head, for there was a deep-toned, bellowing roar, very suggestive of tiger or lion, till it was answered by a distant lowing, and he knew that the first was the bellow of some huge bull, the latter the distant cry of a bullock far up in the hills.

The time glided on. The white bed was no longer inviting, and he could not tear himself away from the window. At last, though, thinking that he had better lie down for fear of being very tired next day, he reached out his hand to draw in the casement, but kept it there, for a very familiar sound now struck upon his ear: *Clap, clap, clap, clap* of wings, and then a thoroughly hearty old English cock-a-doodle-doo! and the boy burst into a merry laugh.

"Go to sleep, you muddle-headed thing," he muttered. "Don't make that noise in the middle of the night.—They always do that at home when the moon shines."

But the cock-crow was answered from a distance, and there was the lowing of cows; chirping came from the trees, there was the piping of the magpie, and soon after the deep chuckle of a great kingfisher, followed by burst of; shrieks and jarring calls from a great tree; and it suddenly struck the watcher that there was a pallid light shed from somewhere behind him.

"Why," he said half aloud, in a regular Hibernian spirit, "it's to-morrow morning!"

Morning it was, coming on fast; and all thought of bed being now given over, Nic began to put on his shoes.

"Lady O'Hara said things were all upside down here," he muttered; "but I didn't know I was going to sleep in the daylight and sit up all night."

A few minutes' thought, however, took away his surprise at the apparently sudden advent of the dawn, for it was well on toward morning when the family had left the dining-room—that name being maintained; and now, feeling bright, cheery, and full of anticipations of what he had to see in his new home, Nic had a wash and brush and hurried out, to find that the business of the day had begun.

The first he encountered was Leather, who responded to his cheery good morning with a keen look and a surly nod, as he passed on, and went off from the shed he had left for the open field.

The next minute, as Nic went round the house, there was a tremendous burst of barking, and the two dogs charged at him so excitedly that one went right over the other in collision; but they were up again directly, leaping at him, careering round, snapping playfully at each other, and madly showing their delight at meeting a familiar face in the strange home.

"Hullo, old fellows!—good dogs, then!" cried Nic, lavishing his caresses on the excited beasts. "Down there! steady there! I'm not for breakfast: don't eat me." The dogs sobered down and trotted beside him, each trying to walk with its sharp-pointed muzzle thrust into one of his hands.

"Chuckle, chuckle, chuckle," came from a great tree which sheltered one side of the house, and the dogs looked up and barked.

"'Morning, young master," came in a harsh, cracked voice: "smart morning. Here, you two: I'm just going to feed old Nibbler, and I'll give you a share."

There was the rattle of a chain hard by, and a heavy bark, as a great dog like a greyhound that had grown stout, came out of a kennel formed of a barrel laid on its side. The great beast looked at the two collies and growled, while the latter set up the dense frills of hair about their necks and showed their teeth.

"None o' that, now!" cried old Samson. "You three have got to be friends. You don't know Nibbler, Master Nicklas."

"Dominic," cried the boy.

"Ah, I allus forget. Missus has told me your name times enough, too. I can allus recklect that there's a Nic in it. Hi, you, Nib, this here's the young master—young master! d'yer hear?"

The dog growled, but wagged its tail.

"We calls him Nibbler, sir; but he's a biter, and no mistake, ain't yer, old man? You ought to ha' had him with yer when them blacks come yesterday. He don't mind spears and boomerangs, do you, Nib?"

The dog growled and showed its teeth.

"Pst, lad!—blackfellow."

The dog made a bound to the full extent of its chain, and uttered a deep bay.

"All right, Nib. Gone!" cried Samson, showing his yellow teeth. "Breakfast."

The dog's manner changed directly.

"Come and pat him, Master Nico-de—Dick-o-me—I say, sir, hadn't I better keep to Nic?"

"Yes, if you like," replied the boy, approaching the great dog, but only to be received with a low growl.

"Ah!" shouted Samson, "didn't I tell you this was young master come home? Down!"

The dog threw itself on its side, blinked at him with one eye and raised one paw deprecatingly, as it slowly rapped the ground with its long thin tail.

"Now come and put your foot on his neck, sir, and pat his head. Don't you be afraid."

"I'm not going to be," said Nic; though he felt a little nervous, and thought of the consequences of a snap from those steel-trap jaws.

"That's right, sir. There—you'll be friends enough after this, Nibbler knows."

But Nibbler shook his head and growled, for the collies, after protesting, whining jealously at Nic's favours being bestowed upon a stranger instead of upon them, barked again and came on steadily, as if to attack the stranger.

"Down, down!" cried Nic; and they stopped.

"It's all right now; they shan't fight. Here, I'll show you. You ketch hold of this, sir."

Samson took an old pitchfork from where it stood in a corner, handed it to Nic, and then, somewhat to the boy's dismay, took hold of the big dog's collar with both hands, and set it free by dragging the strap over its ears.

Then for a moment there were threatenings of a fight, but a shout from Samson checked the turbulent spirit.

"Give Nib a rap over the head with that fork shaft if he don't mind you, sir. He's hard as iron, so you may hit sharp. Couldn't break you, Nib, eh?"

The dog looked up and uttered a short bark. "Here, Master Nic," whispered the old man with a grin: "go closely to him and say sharply, 'Kangaroo!'"

Nic did as he was told, and the dog gave a tremendous bound and stood looking wildly round, ending by running back with a deep-toned bark, looking up at him as much as to say, "Where?"

"Gone, Nib!" cried Samson. "Now follow the young master, and he'll give you some breakfast."

The little old fellow led the way, Nic followed, and the three dogs came behind, Nibbler with a collie on either side, keeping up a low muttering growl, which sounded like threats of what they would do if the big dog interfered with their master. To which Nibbler responded by some language of his own, and leering looks to either side, as if in search of spots where there was not so much hair when he began to nibble.

Samson stopped at the far end of the farthest shed, where there was a little lean-to; and on raising a wooden latch and throwing open the door, there within hung half a sheep, with the skin on a peg, and a chopping-block and a hatchet in the middle.

"Slaughterhouse, sir," said Samson, with a grin. "'Bliged to be our own butchers out here,—fishermen too. S'pose you'll ketch our fish now? Mind chopping off some o' that sheep while I hold it on the block?"

"I? No," said Nic.

"That's your sort!" said the man, lifting the half sheep from a hook fastened in the beam overhead. "Emmygrunts does anything. I want you to chop off that lyne, and then cut it in three bits for the dogs."

"Then you don't only give them bones?" said Nic.

"Gives dogs what we've got plenty on. It's mutton now. We don't want this to spyle. It was alive and well yes'day, but a couple o' dingoes hunted the pore thing down. Hi! Nib, what come o' them dingoes?"

"R–r–r–r–ur," snarled the big dog fiercely.

"Ay, you did, mate. He gave them dingo, sir. These wild dogs is one of our biggest noosances after the sheep. Now, please chop straight. Well done, sir! There's three. Take care. That chopper's very sharp. Now through there and there. That's right. Three bits. I was going to bury half on it, for it won't keep mor'n two nights; but your two sheep, dogs'll help him. We'll feed 'em up a bit for two or three days, and then starve 'em for two or three more to put it straight. Now then, sir, you stick the fork into they three bits, and you shall feed 'em, that'll clinch old Nibbler's making friends with you. See?"

Nic nodded.

"Look," said Samson: "he knows what I've been saying."

The dog, which was sitting watching, with a collie on either side—the latter evidently in doubt as to whether the joints were intended for the house—gave a deep bark.

"Now give him the biggest bit, sir."

Nic stuck the fork in the piece of loin and held it out to the big dog, and it came and took it with a low muttering sound, wagging its tail slowly from side to side, while the collies grew excited, growled, and tossed up their heads to utter a protesting whine.

"Here, you, Nib, wait," cried Samson. "Give t'other two their bits, sir."

Nic served each collie, and then stared at what followed.

"Now then!" cried Samson, "take it out in the back and eat it. Show your chums the way. Right off. No messing about nigh the house. Off with you!"

The big dog uttered a low growl, and went off with its breakfast, the collies following; all three looking decidedly comic with their jaws distended.

"There you are, sir," said the old man, wiping the chopper very carefully and then sticking it into the big clean block. "Seems a pity. Beautiful mutton. The brutes had only just pulled it down when Nib was on to 'em. Leather called me to see. It was half-hour's walk, and there he was sitting by the sheep, and the two dead dingoes close by."

"Didn't he begin worrying it?" asked Nic.

"Him, sir? Nibbler worry a sheep? Not him. Why, I've seen him lie down and let the lambs play about him. I should like to ketch him at it. Not him, sir: I eddicated that dog. There ain't his like nowhere. Coming along o' me, Master Nic?"

"Yes: I want to see all about the place."

"That's right. Ah, you're a lucky one: it's all ready for you. When me and master come there was just nothing; and now see what it is. Look what a garden we're getting. Here, Brooky! Did you bring in the cows?"

"Yes.—'Mornin', sir," said the man.

"'Morning. Tired after your journey?"

"Wonder if I warn't!" said the man. "I had everything to do. Look ye here, Sam: next time waggon goes up to town you'll come too, and so I tell the master."

"What's the matter, matey?"

"Heverything. That there Leather's no good at all. I have to do all the work, and I won't stand it."

"Why, I thought Leather did more than you," cried Nic. "I noticed it as we came; but you always grumbled at him."

Samson showed his yellow teeth and chuckled.

"Don't you be sarcy, sir," growled Brookes; "and what are you crowin' at, old Sam? You needn't begin makin' a noise like a laughin' jackass. Something's going to be changed, or I goes to another station."

"Goin' now?" shouted Samson, as the man strode off angrily.

"Never you mind," growled Brookes; and he disappeared round a barn-like structure.

"He's got his knife into Leather," said Samson, chuckling. "Strange, disagreeable sort o' chap, Brookes, sir. Leather's sour as Devon crabs; but I will say this on him: he do work, and work well. But yah! a hangel couldn't satisfy Bill Brookes. Reg'lar curds-and-whey sort o' fellow. But don't you stand none o' that, sir," continued the old man seriously. "You're young master: you let him have it for telling you not to be sarcy. He wouldn't ha' said it to me; and if you don't check him I shall tell the master. Bill Brookes wants to play first fiddle here; but he can't and won't. I'm foreman; and if I've on'y got a little body, Master Nic, I've got a will as big as Bill Brookes's, and bigger too. Now I'll go and feed the pigs."

This highly interesting piece of business was gone through, Samson mixing up some meal and water, pouring it into the troughs, and belabouring the greedy animals with the mealy stick.

"Take your feet out o' the stuff, will yer?" he roared. "They do make good pork and bacon and ham, Master Nic, but they are about the savagest, fiercest things I know. Fine pigs, though, ain't they? Come on: I want to see if that chap's getting on with the milking."

Sam led the way to a shed with open side, where the black whom Nic had seen on the previous day was busy milking; the thick, rich milk given by one of half a dozen beautifully clean cows descending in its double stream, *quisk—whish*, and frothing up in the white pail.

"Take some in to White Mary soon," said Samson, and the man raised his shining black face and grinned.

"I say, why do you say White Mary?" asked Nic, as they left the cow-shed. "Who's she?"

"Because you've got to talk to them blackfellows so's they can understand you, sir. White Mary's white woman to them. He's going to take the pails as he fills 'em in to Miss Janet: she sees to the dairy. And Miss Hilda, she's White Mary too, and so's your mar."

"Oh," said Nic thoughtfully. "Now then, I want to see the horses."

"Which? those on the run or in the stable?"

"On the run?"

"Yes. They're miles away, and you'd want to ride."

"Well, in the stable."

"This way, then; but won't you come and see my garden first? I've got real apple trees a-growing."

"I'll see the garden after. I want to look how Sour Sorrel is."

"Fresh as a daisy, sir."

"I want to feed him."

"You should have got up sooner, Mister Nic. I fed the horses more'n hour ago, and rubbed 'em down. Do you like Sorrel?" said Samson, showing his teeth.

"Like him!" cried Nic, with a voice intense in its appreciation.

"That's right, sir. I bred him speshly for you, Master Nic. He was to be for you, and you won't ride him too hard, will you?"

"Why, it would be a sin!" cried Nic.

"Sin ain't half bad enough word for it, sir," cried the old man. "Any one as'd hurt a horse with a temper like Sorrel, and such a willin' heart, ud do anything wicked, I don't care what it is. Why, I don't believe even a lifer ud do that."

"What's a lifer?" asked Nic.

"Transported for life, sir."

"Oh yes, I remember now," said Nic, as they turned into the long wooden stable. "Ah, father! you up already?"

"'Morning, Nic, my boy. Oh yes, we are early birds here. Been round the farm?"

"Yes, some of it. He has been showing me."

"Well, do you think you can be content with our rough life?"

"Oh, I say, father!" cried Nic protestingly, "don't talk to me like that! Like it? Everything seems too good. Why, I love it already."

"Don't be too enthusiastic, my boy," said the doctor, clapping him on the shoulder. "It is not all bliss. See what a journey it is to civilisation."

"Bother civilisation!" cried Nic. "That means me being away from home with people who don't care for me."

"You should make people care for you," said the doctor gravely. "Our friendships depend much upon ourselves."

"But I wanted to come out, father."

"And you've come to where nearly all our neighbours are blacks— savages, and many of the others convicts, who are not merely blacks on the surface, Nic. Well, we shall see how you get on. You may alter your tone, my boy."

Nic said nothing, and the horses—six—were inspected.

"Janet and Hilda ride those two little mares, Nic," said the doctor; "and sometimes I get your mother to mount this old favourite, but not often. The others are away grazing."

"You have plenty of horses, then?"

"Yes. They are a necessity here, where so many miles have to be covered a day. You think you will be contented here?"

"Of course, father."

"But you'll have to work, Nic."

"To be sure, father. I'm sure I shall like it."

"A great change from school, my boy."

"Yes, father; but it was a great change for you to come from your London practice."

"So it was, Nic," said the doctor: "a greater change, perhaps, for I was no longer young and sanguine. Greatest of all was the change for your mother and sisters—leaving, as they did, all the pleasant comforts of life, to be their own servants and stoop to all kinds of work. But they were very good. They saw health was the great thing. Nic, boy, for once let me refer to this seriously. I came out believing that I might prolong my poor weary life a year. At the end of that year I thought I could prolong it two more; and at the end of those three years I began to be hopeful of living with those dear to me another three."

"And now, father, you are going to live to be a fine, healthy, hearty old man."

"Please God, Nic," said the doctor, reverently raising his hat,—"for the sake of your mother and the girls."

"He might have said, 'and for your sake too,'" thought Nic, as the doctor walked away to pat one of the horses, returning directly after to talk in a bright cheery way.

"I'm glad you like the horses and the place, Nic," he said. "Your mother and I were a little nervous about it being dull for you."

"Oh, I shan't be dull, father," cried the boy. "Not if you have a boy's healthy appreciation of nature, Nic; and that I hope you have. No, you can't be dull; there is too much to take your attention. It will be a rougher education, but it is a grand healthy life—one like this out in a new land, to make a good simple natural home. People fear to come to some of these places, because they say there's no doctor. I am a doctor, Nic."

"Yes, father; and I've heard say that you were a very clever one."

"I did my best, boy. But I was going to say I am a doctor, and saving for an occasional accident, which nature would heal, I am like a fish out of water."

"Break-fast!" cried a merry, girlish voice; and Hilda, looking bright and eager, looked in at the stable door.

"Ah! here you are, Nic!" she cried. "What a shame! your first morning, and not been to say 'how are you?' to mamma!"

Nic rushed by her before she had finished, and ran into the house, where Mrs Braydon was eagerly waiting to welcome him to the board.

"I needn't have been so apologetic," said the doctor drily, as he came in a minute later and took his place. "Here have I been preaching to this boy about the hardships of our life, and our rough fare, and—humph! French ham, new-laid eggs, coffee, cream, honey, jam, hot bread-cakes, and—tut—tut—tut! My poor boy, I am so sorry there are no fried rolls. Can you make shift?"

"Yes, father," said Nic, laughing, as he thought of school fare. "I'm going to try."

He did.

Chapter Seventeen
A Strange Encounter

"Don't go too far, Nic," said Dr Braydon, a few mornings after the boy's arrival at the Bluff.

"Oh no, father; only I must see what the place is like all round."

"Of course; I have no time to-day, or I'd take you for a ride round."

"But ought he to go alone?" said Mrs Braydon.

"He must learn to run alone, my dear," said the doctor. "We can't chain him up like a dog."

"No," said Mrs Braydon, rather piteously; "but there are the precipices."

"Nic has eyes in his head, and will not go and jump down there. He can't very well fall by accident."

"The snakes, my dear."

"He must learn at once to keep a sharp look-out for them. I suppose there were plenty of adders on the common at school?"

"Plenty, father."

"But the blacks, my dear. I have not got over that scare."

"They're gone, my dear. That man came back last night and said that he saw them, and hid because he was afraid. The party hung about after the waggon for about an hour, and then went right off across the river."

"But they may come back."

"Oh yes," said the doctor tenderly; "but don't be afraid. Nic will not go very far—eh, boy?"

"Oh no, father; I'll really take care."

"And you will be very careful, my dear?"

"Of course he will," said the doctor.

"I will really, mother," said Nic. "I'll only go to-day and have a look round."

"Shall we go with him and take care of him?" said Janet mischievously.

"Yes, I'll come," cried Hilda, exchanging glances with her sister, while the doctor looked on quite amused, and waited for his son's reply.

"No, that you won't," cried Nic indignantly. "Just as if I were a little boy! I know: you want to take me for a walk and each hold a hand. I don't want to hurt your feelings, but I begin to feel at home in the place."

"Of course," said his father. "There, Nic, I'm going to trust to your discretion. Of course the snakes are dangerous, and you must keep a sharp look-out. You can take your gun with you."

Mrs Braydon started.

"Don't be alarmed, mamma. Nic can be trusted to carry a gun. It's of no use to wince, my dear. Nic has come out here to grow into a man, and he must begin to act like one. You'll be careful with the piece, of course?"

"Yes, father: very."

"That's right. Now then, I'll tell you the great danger—one, however, that you are not likely to fall into now, because you will not go far enough—the danger is, being bushed."

"Being bushed, father? what's that?"

"Wandering into the bush and losing your way."

"But I'm not likely to do that, father."

"Old experienced colonists have been lost, Nic. I have myself."

"You have, my dear!" cried Mrs Braydon. "I never knew."

"No, I did not wish to alarm you," said the doctor quietly. "It was on that occasion when I was a week away searching for stray cattle. You remember now?"

"Yes, I remember now," said Mrs Braydon, turning pale. "There, don't be alarmed now. Nic is not going anything like so far as the bush—not much out of sight of the house. The danger is this, Nic: once a man wanders into the scrub the trees and shrubs are all so much alike, the hills and mountains so much the same, that the mind gets deceived and at last confused. Then the country is so vast that, once he goes wrong, he may wander on and on till he frightens his mother out of her wits and makes his sisters cry," said the doctor merrily. "Now do you understand?"

"Yes, quite, father. But I've got a pocket compass."

"Good! Learn to use it well."

"And I promise you, mother dear, that I will not go into the bush, or anywhere to-day far from home."

"That's right, my boy," said the doctor. "Be off, then, and we shall have a big meal at sundown. You are free till then."

"Thank you, father," cried Nic, whose veins throbbed with eager anticipation of the pleasures to be enjoyed in what seemed to be the first real holiday he had ever had. "You'll trust me too, mother, won't you?"

"Yes, yes, my boy," cried Mrs Braydon.

"Of course she will," said the doctor. "Mamma has grown quite nervous since she has had a fresh chicken to take care of: she makes more fuss over you than she does over the girls."

"But they know the place better, my dear," pleaded Mrs Braydon.

"Nic will know it ten times better in a fortnight," said the doctor. "Eh, Nic?"

"I'll try, father," cried the boy, laughing. "I'm not going to be beaten by a couple of girls."

"Off with you, then!"

"Shall I take the dogs, father?"

"Yes. No: not to-day. I shall keep them chained up for another week, to get them more used to the place. They may do what you will not do—go astray."

Five minutes later Nic was waving his hand to his mother at the window as he strode off, proud and elate, with his gun over his shoulder and his shot belt across his breast, the powder flask peeping out of his breast pocket—for in those days men had not dreamed of even percussion guns, let alone breech-loaders and cart ridges ready to slip into the piece.

"Nic!"

The boy turned to see his father mounted on his chestnut, and with a stock whip in his hand.

"Which way are you going?"

"I want to try and find my way to the edge of the precipice, father, and look down from the Bluff into the great gully."

"Very well. Straight away for a mile—north-west. Shoot any snakes you see. They alarm your mother and sisters, and they are dangerous to the dogs."

The doctor pressed his horse's sides, turned his head, and went off at a canter, looking as if he had grown to its back, and Nic watched him in admiration for a few minutes.

"I wish I could ride like that," he said to himself as he strode off taking great breaths of the elastic air. "Well, father was a boy once, and could not ride any better than I can. I shall try hard."

"Hah! how beautiful it all is!" he said softly, as he paused at the end of a few minutes, to gaze right away; for he had reached an eminence in the park-like land from which he could see, fold upon fold, wave upon wave, the far stretching range of the Blue Mountains.

"And they are blue," he cried aloud, "and blue and lavender and amethyst; but I suppose when one got up to them they would look green and grey and gravelly red. It's the distance, I suppose."

He was quite right: the lovely hues came from seeing the mountains in the distance through the layers of pure air; and after satiating himself for the moment, he strode on, keeping a sharp look-out for snakes and for the animals he was most anxious to see—kangaroos.

But he could only see sheep dotted about in plenty, and farther afield ruddy-looking oxen grazing on the rich grass, and after a time he began to feel a little disappointed, for, let alone wild animals, he did not see so much as a bird.

He kept on, though, with his eyes wandering in all directions, calling to mind all the different creatures which inhabited the land, and making up his mind that his next walk should be along the riverside.

"There'll be birds in plenty there, and fish; and I may see the curious otter rat sort of thing, with its duck-like bill. If I could only find its nest of eggs!"

He laughed at the absurdity, as it seemed to him, of an animal having so strange a nature, and then began noting how different the trees were from those at home, so many being covered with a greyish-green and pinky foliage, while others seemed to have their leaves stuck on edgewise instead of lying flat, the consequence being that the shade they gave was rather thin.

"A mile north-west," he thought: "I must have come as far as that, but I can see no precipices—only a hill or two yonder. There are some sheep grazing, though, over there. Father's, of course. What a lot he must have!"

He went on in the supposed direction for another five minutes, noticing that the trees were closer together, and that there was more undergrowth, amongst which the creamy-fleeced sheep were wandering; and before entering this undergrowth he took a look round and behind to see that his way home was unmistakable.

"That can't be the bush," he said, with a laugh, as he threaded his way among the trees, and directly after caught sight of a man walking slowly along, evidently inspecting the sheep.

"Hi! Ahoy!" cried Nic; and the man turned. "Why, it's Leather!"

He started off at a trot to join the man, who stood stock still awaiting his approach.

"'Morning, Mr Leather," he cried, as he joined the man, who faced him with his brows knit, and a bitter, sour look in his countenance, as he said morosely:

"'Morning, sir. My name's not Leather."

"Oh! I beg your pardon."

The man laughed unpleasantly, and Nic felt an involuntary dislike to him.

"But I heard them call you Leather."

"Leatherhead generally," said the man roughly: "because I'm such a fool."

"Then it's a nickname," cried the boy, thinking instantly of his own annoyance at school. "I say, I'm very sorry: I didn't know. What is your name?"

"Call me the same as the others do," said the man roughly. "Leather will do."

"Oh, but I should be sorry to say anything to hurt you."

"I'm used to it, young gentleman. Well, what is it? Does your father want me?"

"Oh no: I'm having a walk to see the country. I want to find the Bluff."

"You are on the Bluff," said the man, in his surly tones.

"Oh yes, I know. The whole place is called the Bluff. But I mean where you can stand on the edge and look down into a great gap thousands of feet deep."

"Look round."

Nic looked about him, and then back at the bitter-countenanced man.

"What am I to look at?"

"Can't you see the edge of the Bluff?"

The man took a few paces, winding among the low growth, and Nic followed him, to start back directly in alarm.

"Nothing to mind," said the man; but Nic did not see the freedom from danger, and he involuntarily caught hold of a handful of twigs at the top of the nearest bush to steady himself, as he gazed away down into a mighty valley whose sides looked to be sheer and whose bottom was thousands of feet below. It was like looking down into an open country shut in by a perpendicular wall of mountains where a glittering river ran, and the trees were dwarfed into tiny shrubs, while patches of forest looked like tufts of grass. The colours were glorious; but for the moment the boy felt nothing but that breathless, shrinking sensation which attacks some people upon a height; and he said huskily:

"How horrible!"

"Yes," said the man gloomily. "Right: how horrible!" and he scowled down at the vast depression.

"No, no," cried Nic excitedly. "How lovely—glorious—grand!"

"No," said the man, without turning his head; "how horrible!"

"Oh no," cried Nic again. "I did not mean it. I was startled. It looks so deep. How do you get down?"

"Step over the edge and fall," said the man bitterly.

"What?"

"One good step and down you would go, and be out of your misery."

"Oh, nonsense," cried Nic. "It's wonderful. Show me the way to go down."

"What, go first?"

"Yes."

The man uttered a strange laugh which made Nic shudder; but he mastered his shrinking and said: "Tell me: which is the proper way down?"

"They say there is no way down."

"What! is it so dangerous?"

"Yes."

"Do you mean to tell me that we could not get down to that beautiful place below?"

"The regular way is to go as the sheep and cattle do sometimes. They get grazing too close, and slip and fall. Most of them are killed, but some fall from shelf to shelf and get over it. Look!"

He caught Nic by the shoulder, roughly pressed him nearer the edge, and pointed with one hand.

Nic's heart began to beat heavily, but he drew a deep breath and would not shrink.

"Well?" he said, after a pause. "I'm looking. What at?"

"Can't you see sheep down below, and quite a drove of bullocks?"

"No," said Nic: "my eyes are not used to it—yours are."

"Yes, mine are," said the man. "Those were your father's cattle and sheep, and some of Dillon's from the next station, and other people's from farther still; and now they belong to nature. Don't you think your father is a fool to come and live where he loses his stock down a trap like that?"

"No, I don't," said Nic haughtily, for the man repelled him. "I think he was very wise to come and live in the most beautiful place I ever saw."

"I don't," said the man, laughing curiously, as if it hurt him and gave him pain. "I think the place hideous. Well, you want to go down," he continued, tightening his grip and showing his teeth as he thrust Nic forward. "There, I have only to give you one push and down you go; but you wouldn't see anything when you got down."

"Because it would kill me," said Nic quietly.

"Yes; and your old man would set us all to hunt for you, and one of the blacks would make you out at last, lying right at the bottom."

"And fetch me up," said Nic, without flinching, but with the cold perspiration standing out on his forehead and in the palms of his hands.

"No, even they couldn't get down to you; and your father would come every day with his glass to watch you till the birds and the ants had left nothing but your bones to whiten there, as the bones of bullocks have before now. Well, shall I throw you down? You asked me to show you the way."

"No, thank you," said Nic quietly.

"Why shouldn't I?"

"Because you, a strong man, wouldn't be so murderous. And because I never did you any harm."

"No," said the man, drawing him back from the brink, and looking him full in the eyes, with the half-savage glare passing out of his own to give place to an air of profound melancholy. "No, I wouldn't do you any harm, sir. You're a brave lad."

"No, I'm not," said Nic, letting himself sink back on the sunny herbage, for he felt sick and giddy. "It was horrible: it made me turn faint. Why did you do that?"

He spoke now in indignant anger.

"Because I was a brute," said the man hoarsely. "They've made me a brute. I thought I would try you and see what was in you. There, go back home and tell them," he cried, with his voice growing intensely bitter; "and you can have the pleasure of seeing me flogged."

"What!" cried Nic, forgetting his own feelings in seeing the way the man was moved. "You—flogged—for playing that foolish trick!"

"Yes; foolish trick, my lad. But there, now you've come home, keep away from me. You've a deal to learn yet."

"Well, you own it was foolish," said Nic, for want of something better to say.

"Yes, a piece of madness, my lad. You said you begged my pardon a bit ago. I beg yours now."

"Of course. There, it's all right," cried Nic. "But don't you think I should go and tell tales. My father would, of course, be put out,—but flog you! He doesn't look the sort of man to flog his people, does he?"

The man looked at him curiously. Then, drawing back sharply, his manner changed, and he began to look sullen, as he said in a morose voice:

"Didn't your father say anything to you about me?"

"No."

"Didn't he tell you what I was, sir?"

"No," said Nic, with's suspicion now dawning on his mind. "You are his stock man, are you not?"

"Stock man? No: Brookes is his stock man. There—keep away from me, my lad."

"Why?" said Nic.

"Because I'm only a sort of two-legged animal, a machine to do your father's work. I thought you knew."

"That you are—"

Nic stopped short.

"Yes, my lad—a convict, sent out of my country for my country's good."

"I know now," cried Nic eagerly. "I've heard—I was told on board. You are sent up the country for good behaviour. Then you are my father's assigned servant?"

The man stood looking down at him for a moment or two with his face full of wrinkles. Then he turned quickly and walked hurriedly away, never once looking back as Nic watched him till he was out of sight.

Then the boy shuddered.

"How horrible!" he thought. "He might have thrown me down. No, it was only a mad trick. But what a man to have about the place! I ought to have bullied him well; but I can't go near him again. I wish I had not shown the white feather so."

Ten minutes later Nic had forgotten his adventure, as he lay there upon his chest close to the edge, gazing down from the Bluff into the tremendous gully, rapt in amazement by its wonders, fascinated by its beauties. He stayed for hours tracing the river, and as his eyes grew more accustomed to the depth he made out the animals grazing below and looking like ants.

"Yes, it is glorious!" he said at last; and he turned his head to look around and rest his eyes upon the green on the other side, when he felt as if turned to stone. He had escaped one danger, and another seemed to have sprung up, for peering out at him from a dense patch of grass was a black face with glittering eyes and a surrounding of shaggy hair, while the gun was lying between them, and just beyond his reach.

Chapter Eighteen
A Fright

The position was startling in the extreme, and all the tales he had heard on shipboard and at home, as well as in the letters he had received from his sisters, respecting the blacks, flashed into his mind. He knew how dangerous they were, and the enmity some of them bore toward the white invaders of their shores; and though he could see nothing but the man's face, he felt certain that, hidden by the grass, the black would have his spear with its hardened point—a weapon these men could throw as unerringly as the peculiar boomerang which would be stuck in his waistband to balance the deadly nulla-nulla—the melon-shaped club carved from a hard-wood root, whose stem formed the handle.

And as these thoughts ran through Nic's mind he kept his eyes fixed upon the bright dark eyes of the black, every nerve upon the strain, every muscle strung, and ready for action. For in those painful moments Nic had determined to "die game," as he called it in schoolboy parlance, living as he did in days when a brutal sport was popular. At the first movement made by the black Nic meant to spring upon his gun, and have one shot for his life; but he remained motionless, trying to stare the man down, and in the faint hope that Leather might come back, and the black shrink from attacking one who faced him.

"Wild beasts shrink away, so why should not wild men?" thought Nic.

And so they lay there each upon his chest, watching one another, Nic having a fine opportunity for studying the native's rugged features and shaggy hair and beard. Every now and then there was a rapid winking of the eyes; but their fierce stare seemed to be uninterrupted, and caused a peculiar kind of aching and twitching at the back of Nic's eyeballs, as moment by moment he expected the man would attack.

At last the strain began to be greater than the boy could bear. He had developed an intense friendship all at once for Leather, and looked vainly again for his presence there; he would have shouted for him, but he felt that in the immense space around his feeble cry would not be heard, and that out there in that savage land he was, early as it seemed, to have his first lesson in the settler's duty—namely, to fend for himself.

For Nic could bear the horrible state of suspense no longer. He felt that he must fight for his life, and that after all the odds were fair. His enemy was a full-grown, sturdy savage, doubtless well armed, while he was only a boy, but he had the help of one of civilised man's most deadly weapons to balance matters.

Then he felt that there was no balance in the matters for the black had his weapons ready, while he had left his gun out of his reach.

"Only let me escape this time," thought Nic, in a despairing way, "and I'll never do such a foolish thing again."

The sun beat down upon him, the air around quivered in the heat, and the locusts kept up a loud chirruping, jarring note which grew maddening. Then from far away there came faintly the melancholy *baa* of a sheep calling plaintively to its missing companions, and directly after what Nic took to be the call of some wild bird in the distance—*coo-way*—*coo-way*—and this was answered faintly from farther off.

The next moment Nic had grasped the fact that it was no bird-call; for the black's face was puckered up, his eyes nearly closed as his mouth opened, and he repeated the cry in a wild, shrill, ringing tone twice more, and then his mouth shut with an audible snap, and he remained perfectly still again, watching the boy.

But Nic could bear no more. This brought matters to a crisis. It was the savage's *cooey*, and it meant that others were coming to join this man. So the boy felt that he must either attack or retreat.

To retreat meant to invite attack, and in his desperation Nic determined that the braver plan and the one more likely to prove successful was to take the initiative, and to do this he began slowly and cautiously to stretch out one hand towards his gun.

In an instant the black's eyes twinkled, and there was a movement in the grass as of some animal gliding through it.

"Getting his spear," thought Nic, with his heart beating frantically, as he drew himself sidewise toward the piece.

As he expected, the black moved too, but only as shown by the motion of the herbage. In fact, there were moments before the boy began to exert himself when it seemed to him that there was that fierce black head before him and nothing more, and that the whole scene was nightmare-like and unreal.

But with the action all became terribly substantial. He was reaching for his deadly weapon, so was the black, or to get himself into a better position for assault. And as Nic with throbbing breast drew slowly nearer, never once taking his eyes from those of his foe, the knitted brows and shining black face seemed to approach.

But he knew it was only an optical illusion caused by the intense strain upon his eyes; and feeling that quick action was necessary, he made a sudden spring to his right and grasped the gun, with which he leaped to his feet, just as the black also bounded up with a long, quivering spear in his hand, while there, plainly seen in the narrow band about his waist, were the boomerang and club.

Click went Nic's gun trigger, as a thrill of confidence ran through him, and, holding the piece at the ready, he presented it at the black's breast.

At this the man made a bound backward, and throwing himself into an attitude, he levelled his spear, as if about to hurl it and pierce Nic through.

"I wish I knew nigger," thought Nic, getting more confident; "I'd tell him if he'd go away I would not fire."

But no word was spoken on either side, white and black standing motionless in their attitudes of menace, eye fixed on eye, as if each were ready to shoot or hurl spear at the slightest movement made by the other.

The situation at last became so irksome that Nic could bear it no longer, and in a hoarse voice he cried:

"Now then, be off, and I won't shoot."

To his surprise the black shouldered his spear, and then obeyed a sign Nic made with the barrel of his gun, turning round and beginning to march away, slowly followed by the boy, who felt that if driven to extremities he could easily hit the broad, shiny back before him, with the muscles playing elastically at every step the man took.

"He understood the sign I made," thought Nic, who determined to keep near the black for fear of treachery, as the man strode on in and out among the trees, while a fresh idea now struck Nic. Suppose the man was going on to join his companions who had cooeyed to him. It was like walking into additional danger. Still the boy did not flinch, for fear of receiving a spear in the back if he turned away.

But he was master for the moment; and growing more and more confident, he strode on behind the black, heedless of the direction in which they went, and leaving the end of the case to fate. All he hoped was that, sooner or later, the savage would suddenly make a dash for his liberty, when the boy fully determined to scare him by firing over his head, to make him run the harder.

Nic had some idea that they were bearing toward his home, but he could see nothing but park-like trees and low wattle bushes; and after this strange procession had continued for some time he began to grow uneasy, and to think of taking out his pocket compass to try and make out his bearings, before stopping short in the first open place to let the black go on out of sight, covered meanwhile by the gun, when, just as the sufficiently open place was reached, there came a hoarse cooey from somewhere close at hand.

Nic stopped short, feeling that he had walked right into the lion's mouth; and standing ready, with his eyes wandering round, waiting for the enemy, he listened to the black's reply.

The next minute the black faced round, and the rustling of bushes was followed by the appearance of a second figure thirty yards away.

Nic threw up his gun, not to his shoulder, but over it; for the figure was that of the stock man, Brookes, who shouted:

"Oh, there you are, young gentleman. Your mar's getting in a orful way. She sent Bungarolo to look after you, and then, as he didn't come back, she sent me."

"Oh!" groaned Nic, in a tone of disgust; for all his bravery, as he thought it, had been thrown away, and a peculiar sensation of self-humiliation and shame came ever him.

"Yes, here I am, Brookes," he said. "Then this is a tame black?"

"Tame un?" said the man, with a chuckle. "Oh no, he's wild enough; I never see one on 'em yet as you could tame. No tame man would go about without trousers when he's had two pair give him to my sartain knowledge. He's one as hangs about sometimes."

"But I mean he is not one of the more dangerous blacks?"

"Oh no, I think not, sir—so long as you treat him well, and he gets treated right enough with soft tack and mutton. He comes to see our other two as you know."

"But does his tribe live about here?"

"I dunno, sir. Nobody does know. These chaps is like the cockatoos: they swarm about the place one day, and next day there isn't one, and you might go for a hundred miles and never see one of their blessed heads. He's wild enough. Hangs about the place, and does a bit of work if he likes it. If he don't, he goes. These blacks is, to my mind, the only real gents as there is.

Look at him now. He don't want no clothes nor no house, only a hut, as he makes out of a few bits o' bark and calls a gunyah, perhaps only a mia-mia."

"What's a mia-mia?" said Nic.

"Sort of a hurdle thing as he puts up for shelter, and to keep the wind from blowing his fire away. Then as to clothes—look at him now."

Nic turned to look, but the black had disappeared, and ten minutes later he passed out of the thick growth to come in sight of the house, outside which Mrs Braydon was standing, watching anxiously for the return of her son.

"I wish he had been a real savage though, after all," thought Nic. "It would have been far better fun."

Perhaps!

Chapter Nineteen
Nic Shows His Teeth

Nic did not say anything about his adventure with Leather, and was perfectly silent about his fright with Bungarolo, who showed his teeth next time they met, pointed to the lad's gun, and shook his head, the fact being that he was as much startled as Nic.

During the days which followed the boy had long rides with his father to see cattle on distant ranges, to visit flocks grazing nearer home, and gradually grew acquainted with the pleasant, patriarchal life the doctor lived.

The weather was glorious, for there had been rain in abundance a month earlier, and the consequence was shown in the rich pasture and abundance of flowers flourishing in the bright sunshine. The air, too, was deliciously invigorating, and Nic never knew that he was tired, even when he had been a whole day in the saddle, until suddenly about bedtime he discovered that he could not keep his eyes open. Then he would sleep soundly till the piping crows and the poultry awoke him at daybreak for another busy, happy day.

Nic determined that he would have no mare to do with Leather, who went stolidly about his work. He was a convict, and the boy felt that the man was a sullen, ill-tempered fellow, who, instead of trying to make up for the past, now that the opportunity had been given him to amend and begin a new life, evidently looked upon himself as ill-used, and avoided everybody.

There were a certain number of slips printed from copperplate and pasted upon cardboard at Dr Dunham's, all consisting of good, sterling advice to the young, which the boys had had to copy over and over again, so as to get in the habit of writing a good, clear, round hand, with fine upstrokes and good, firm downstrokes; and one of them which Nic had well in mind was, "Judge not rashly." But Nic did judge rashly all the same.

One day he took his gun with the intention of shooting a specimen of the lovely Blue Mountain parrot or lory, and this he meant to skin and preserve. He had seen the birds in flocks when out without his gun, and stood entranced at the beauty of the little creatures, with their breasts gleaming with scarlet, crimson, orange, and purple mingled in the most wonderful way, while their heads were of a peachy blue, and wings and backs, right to the end of their long tails, of a lovely green.

He had taken some of the smallest shot, so as not to damage the plumage; and after a warning from Mrs Braydon to be careful, he was crossing the enclosure beyond the garden toward a field where he could hear Brookes's voice raised in a loud, bullying tone.

Directly after he came upon old Samson, who was wheeling manure in a barrow made of half a barrel cut lengthwise, and furnished with a couple of good sound poles, nailed on so that two ends formed the widely apart handles the other two being fitted with iron, which drew them together and secured the wheel, which was a round cut with a saw from a tree trunk, bound with iron hooping, and looking like a single Gloucester cheese.

"Heavy," said the old man, stopping to rest.

"What's that for?" asked Nic, who liked the old, keen, but thoroughly amiable factotum.

"Garden, sir. Good, strong, fat stuff as'll grow anything. I'm making a cowcumber bed."

"Not much of a barrow, Sam," said Nic.

"Well, it ain't, Master Nic, and I'd ha' made another afore now, on'y I can't get a wheel. The master's going to get me one first chance, for the wheel bothers me. I could make the box, but wheels want practice. I did try to make one, and I forged a pretty good tire down yonder but the wood part! My word, it was a rickety, wobbly one, and broke down second day. Didn't teach you to make barrow wheels at school, I suppose?"

"No," said Nic, laughing. "Wheel-making's an accomplishment."

"Then they ought to ha' taught you. Been strange and useful to you as a squatter, sir. Didn't teach you to shoe horses nayther, I'll be bound."

"No, nor blacksmithing either."

"Then it's a shame, sir, for I know the master paid a lot o' money for you to be well taught. I wish they'd teached you to make wheels, for you see these here soon warps in the hot sun and cracks. But there," cried the old man, grinning, "there's hard, sound trees enough to cut down and saw into thousands and thousands of barrow wheels; and as to horseshoeing, I can teach you that, my lad. I shoe all ours, and the master likes my shoes better than those he makes."

"Does father make horseshoes?"

"Does he make horseshoes?" cried Sam. "Why, I should think he does, and trims a hoof, and nails splendid. He beats me hollow. There he goes—at it again," muttered the old man, as Brookes's voice rose. "I wish he'd leave the poor chap alone."

"Is he bullying Leather again?"

"Ay, my lad; and he'd like to tan Leather too, on'y he daren't do that. I 'most wish the poor chap'd give him one for his not, and then p'r'aps he'd be quiet with his tongue. Brooky's never satisfied. He's like lots of 'em: he thinks, because a chap's a 'signed servant, he's to be bullied and kicked. They forgets as a convict is a man arter all."

"Of course," said Nic, frowning.

"The free men settlers is jealous of the government chaps, and hates 'em. I don't doubt Leather's a reg'lar crab, but set him to do a job and he does it. I never know'd him skulk or flinch anything. The master'll ketch old Brooky at it some day, and then there'll be a row. I do wonder, though, as Leatherhead don't give him one between the eyes."

"Perhaps he will some day, if Brookes goes too far."

"Nay, nay, my lad, he won't do that. That wouldn't do. 'Signed servant's got to take what he gets, and be thankful. Why, do you know what'd happen if Leather turned on Brooky?"

"Brooky would complain to the master, and Leather would be fetched over to Mr Dillon's—magistrate, you know. He'd have the cat, and a warning that if he didn't behave he'd go back to the chain gang, and it would be a bad mark agin him."

"Then it would be very unfair," said Nic sharply.

"Yes, sir, it would; but the world don't allus play quite fair, and, you see, government has to be very strict with 'signed servants, for some on 'em's been shocking bad uns, and if they weren't kep' down with what they calls a hiron han', honest people wouldn't come to live out here. 'Bliged to be very strict; if they weren't, the convicts might get the better of us all. Well, this ain't making cowcumber beds, is it? Going shooting?"

"Yes; I want to get some specimens to stuff."

"That's right, sir. You do? There's some very pretty birds about these parts; but if I was you, my lad, I'd get one o' the blackfellows to go with you. He'd carry what you shot—when you happened to hit anything."

"All right. You needn't grin, Sam. I can hold the gun straight sometimes."

"'Course you can, my lad. Why not? You'll shoot and ride and do everything soon, and I'll teach you all I know 'bout shoeing and forging and gardening. But as I was a-saying, you get Bungarolo or Rigar or Damper. No, I can't spare Damper 'cause of the cows, and Rigar's handy with the bullocks. You have Bung; he'll take you to places where the birds are. These blacks know all that sort o' thing; and as to getting bushed, you'll never get bushed so long as he's with you."

"What's bushed?"

"What's bushed, sir? My word, they did take your poor father in over your education. Don't know what being bushed is? Why, being lost, my lad. There, you're a-romancing me, Master Nic. You're a-making me a reg'lar old ruck-a-tongue. I've got to do my work, and my work to-day's cowcumbers."

Samson lifted the handles of his rough barrow, and went off without looking back, while Nic made off with his gun on his shoulder, bearing a little to his left, so as to pass round a shed, beyond which Brookes's voice could be heard.

As Nic reached the fence he saw that about fifty sheep were shut behind hurdles, and Leather was catching them by the wool, turning them on their sides, and then carrying them to where Brookes knelt, with a brush and a tub and a sheep before him, dividing the wool and applying some tarry mixture to sore places caused by the attacks of virulent flies—a cruel-looking process, but one which saved the poor animals' lives.

Brookes's back was towards Nic, and Leather's eyes on his work, over which he bent frowning, and using his great strength to master the struggling animals, and carry them to his companion, who went on loudly, as Leather slaved away, dripping with perspiration, in the hot sun.

"Government's mad, that's what government is, to let loose such a set o' scum to mix with honest men. I dunno what things is coming to. If I had my way, I'd soon have yer again in the chain gang, and scratch yer back every day with the warder's cat—that's what I'd do with you. There,"—to the sheep—"off you go. Now, then, how much longer am I to wait for that next sheep? Of all the lazy, idle, skulking hands that ever came about a place you're the worst. Now, then, don't kill the poor beast, and don't keep me waiting all day for the next."

The sheep had made a sudden bound and nearly escaped; but Leather, bending low the while, flung his arm round it, hugged it to his breast, and bore it to Brookes.

"Yah! you clumsy, lazy brute; you're not fit to handle a sheep. Don't kill it, thick-head. Hang yer, you're not worth your salt."

This was too much for Nic.

"Then why don't you go and fetch the sheep, and let him have a turn with the tar?" roared the boy, with his face scarlet.

"What?" cried Brookes, swinging himself round, and dropping the brush.

"Say 'sir' when you speak to me," cried Nic. "You heard what I said. You're always bullying and insulting people. It's abominable. The man's working like a slave, and you're kneeling there and doing hardly anything."

"I'm blest!" panted out Brookes, with rings of white round the irises of his eyes.

Leather was panting too. His face looked corrugated, and he stood there bent down, frowning hard at the ground.

"It's shameful!" cried Nic. "I'm sure my father does not know you speak to your fellow-servants like that."

"My what?" roared Brookes furiously. "Do you know he's only a convict?"

"Yes, I do. But what's that got to do with it, sir? As long as he works and does his duty to my father, he's to be properly treated. You're always bullying him. I've heard you ever since I've been home."

"Here! Where's your father?" cried Brookes, rising to his feet, and advancing toward the fence with a threatening look, while Leather bent lower.

"Gone on one of his rounds," said Nic, springing over the fence, and facing him. "I wish he were here."

"And so do I," roared Brookes. "Look here, young gentleman; don't you think because you've come home that you're to lord it over me. I'll have to know that you've got to beg my pardon, insulting me before that lazy, lying, idle convict, you miserable young whippersnapper!"

"What!" said Nic, beside himself now with passion. "How dare you! How dare you speak to me like that! Insult you—you common, foul-mouthed bully. Go on with your work, sir. I'm your master's son, and if I'd a horsewhip here instead of this gun, I'd lay it across your back."

Brookes stooped, picked up the brush viciously, and rolled up his sleeves.

"Oh," he cried; "that's it, is it? Horsewhip me, eh? We'll soon see about that. Here, you convict."

"Do you want me to strike you?" cried Nic.

"Yes; you'd better," growled the man, dropping on his knees. "We'll soon see about that. Here, you, bring me another sheep."

"No. Stop!" cried Nic, turning to Leather, who was bringing on the sheep; "let him fetch them for himself. While my father's away I'm master here. Go away. You shall not be bullied like that, whatever you have done. Go and find some other work amongst the sheep."

Leather looked at him strangely.

"You heard what I said," cried Nic.

"Yes, sir," said the man, in a husky voice.

"Then go at once. Nic was treating you worse than he would dare to treat a dog."

Brookes banged down the brush and rose to go.

"You stop," cried Nic. "My father said those sheep must be dressed to-day, and you know it. Finish them, every one."

Brookes dropped upon his knees again.

"I beg your pardon, sir," said Leather quietly. "It is very hard work for one man. I'm used to this sort of thing. Hadn't I better stay?"

"No," said Nic firmly. "You heard my orders. Go." He pointed across the enclosure, and Leather went without a word.

"Now," said Nic, "finish those sheep."

Brookes muttered low threat after threat of what he would do, but he went on dressing the sheep; and Nic turned, walked back to the house, altered his mind, and went right away toward the bush, but his nerves were all of a quiver, as he thought over the meeting to come with his father, and he did not fire his gun that day.

Chapter Twenty
Leather's Other Side

"Well, Nic, what does all this mean?" said the doctor on the following day. "Brookes has been complaining to me that he was busy yesterday dressing those sheep, when he found Leather, as they call him, my assigned servant, lazy, careless, and insolent. He was speaking to him rather sharply, when you suddenly appeared from behind the fence, flew in a passion, abused him, defended the other man, talked in a way that would make Leather disobedient in the future, and finally ordered the man to go away and leave Brookes to do all the work himself. Now then, my boy, is this true?"

"Well, about half of it, father."

"I'm sorry to hear it, Nic, though I'm glad you are so frank," said the doctor, rather sternly. "You own to half. Now how much of the other half would be true if judged by an impartial observer?"

"I don't think any of it, father."

"Humph!" ejaculated the doctor. "This is a great pity, my boy. I cannot have dissension here at the station. Brookes is a valuable servant to me, where men with a character are very scarce. He is, I know, firm and severe to the blacks and to the convict labourers I have had from time to time, and I must warn you these assigned servants are not men of good character. Has this Leather been making advances toward you, and telling you some pitiful tale of his innocency to excite your compassion?"

"Oh no, father," cried Nic. "He has been as distant and surly to me as could be."

"Ah! There you see! The man is not well behaved."

"He works well, father, and was doing his best; but Brookes does nothing but bully and find fault, and he went on so yesterday at the poor fellow that at last I felt as if I couldn't bear it, and—and I'm afraid I got in a terrible passion and talked as if I were the master."

"I repeat what I said, Nic. I am very sorry, and I must ask you to be more careful. You say you played the master?"

"Yes, father."

"Very badly, my lad. He is a poor master who cannot govern his temper. Men under you always respect quiet firmness, and it will do more in ruling or governing than any amount of noisy bullying. There, I am not going to say any more."

"But you don't know, father, how cruelly he uses Leather."

"Neither do you, Nic, I'm afraid. You are young and chivalrous, and naturally, from your age, ready to magnify and resist what you look upon as oppression. There, be careful, my lad. I shall keep an eye on Leather and take notice for myself. As to Brookes, I shall leave matters to you. I do not ask you to apologise to him, but I should like you to run over yesterday's business in your own mind, and where you feel conscientiously that you were in the wrong I should like you to show Brookes that you regret that portion of what you said. One moment, and I've done. I want you to recollect that he is a man of fifty, while you are only about sixteen. Do we understand each other?"

"Oh yes, father," cried the boy, earnestly.

"Then that unpleasant business is at an end. Did you get your specimens yesterday?"

"No," cried Nic; "the quarrel yesterday upset me, and I could only go and wander about in the bush thinking about it. I did not shoot a bird."

"Then go and make up for it to-day," said the doctors smiling.

"But," said Nic, hesitating, "don't you want me, father—to begin work?"

"Yes, by-and-by; not yet. I should like you to have your run about the place for a week or two more—or a month, say. It will not be waste time. You cannot see what is going on about a station like this without learning a great deal that will be invaluable by-and-by. Of course I shall take you with me for a few runs or rides. By the way, did they finish emptying the waggon?"

"Oh yes, father; I saw that done, and kept account of the packages that came over in the *Northumbrian*. I didn't know the rest."

"That was businesslike, and the more so for its being done unasked."

"But Brookes didn't like my being there, father."

"Indeed!" said the doctor slowly. "And the other man—Samson?"

"He liked it, father. We're capital friends. I like him: he's such a rum old fellow."

"Well, you must get to like Brookes too. Now have your run."

Nic felt better, for the previous day's trouble had sat upon him like a nightmare. Hurrying to his room he took his gun, and leaving it at the door was guided by the voices to the big store-room, where Mrs Braydon and the girls were busy unpacking and arranging some of the stores brought by the waggon.

Here he was soon dismissed by his sisters, and after promising to be back in good time, he went off across the home part of the station, catching sight of Samson, Brookes, and a couple of the blacks busy over some task in an open shed, which task looked like the stacking up of bundles of wool rolled neatly together.

"I can't go and tell Brookes I'm sorry before them," thought Nic; "and I'm afraid I don't feel sorry. I suppose, though, I was a bit in the wrong. Father knows best; but he wouldn't have let Brookes speak like that. Brookes wouldn't have dared to do it."

The boy had got about a mile away from the station and into a part of the doctor's land which looked as if it had been carefully planted with trees, but his common sense told him that it must be in precisely the same condition as when he took up that part of the country; and after stopping to look round and admire the beauty of the place in every direction, he began to wish that he had brought the two dogs for a run.

"Father says that they are better at home, though, for a bit," he muttered, as he trudged on again, looking for birds or other game, but seeing nothing whatever, not so much as a snake.

His direction this time was parallel with the tremendous gorge whose edge he had stood upon to gaze down; and as in comparison the present part of the huge estate was, though beautiful, somewhat monotonous in its constant succession of large ornamental trees and grassy glades, he was beginning to wish that he had gone in the other direction, to explore the gully down into which Samson had guided him on the way to meet the waggon.

"I want to see that tree bridge, too, that we crossed. Never mind: that will do for another time."

Nic kept on in and out among the trees, glancing at his pocket compass from time to time, but satisfied of his ability to retrace his steps, for he was convinced that the huge gorge must be away to his left, so that if he kept it upon his right in returning he would be certain to come out correctly.

Every now and then he obtained a grand view of the mountains, with their prevailing tint of blue in the distance gradually becoming grey, yellowish brown, red, and of many delicious greens, as the great spurs, bluffs, and chasms came nearer and nearer till they plunged down into the gorge.

It looked to be a very fairyland of tempting mystery, waiting to be explored; and till the trees hid the towering eminences from his sight, he went on planning endless excursions for the future.

"But it does seem so strange," he said to himself at last, as he wiped his streaming forehead and stood in the shade of a great green tree, gazing up in its forest of boughs. "One would think that such an out-of-the-way place would swarm with birds and wild creatures; while except flies and beetles nothing seems to live here. Ah!" he cried at last.

For he had caught sight of something moving among the low scrubby bushes beyond the next tree, and softly cocking his gun he began to stalk it. But the next minute he had made up his mind not to fire at what would in all probability be a kangaroo.

"And I don't want kangaroos," he said; "I want birds." But he wanted to get as close as he could to the animal, and he stole on and on slowly for about fifty yards, till, as nearly as he could judge, whatever it was must be just beyond the next bushes.

Toward these he was creeping, when he started round with a quick jump, for some one had spoken.

"Are you looking for me, sir?"

There stood Leather bending over a sheep, whose fleece he was relieving of a strange growth of burrs and prickly, brambly strands with which the creature was tangled.

"No," said Nic, as soon as he had recovered from his surprise. "I did not know you were this way. What are you doing?"

"Shepherding, sir," said the man, with a sad, weary-looking smile, which half fascinated Nic, and he stared at one who seemed to be quite a different man. "The poor brutes get terribly tangled by these wild growths, and sheep are not very wise, sir. They're poor, helpless sort of creatures. As soon as they are helped out of one difficulty they get into another."

"Yes, I suppose so," said Nic, speaking as if he thoroughly understood sheep; though his knowledge of the popular old useful animal consisted in the facts that when they were young they were lambs, that they grew wool, and that when they were killed they became mutton.

They have so many diseases, too, sir, and so many enemies.

"What, the dingoes?" said Nic.

"Yes, they play the part of the wolf in Europe. It's astonishing how they have overrun the country."

Nic stared again, but averted his eyes for fear the man should notice it. This did not seem the Leather he had seen so much of on his way home and since.

"Are there no wolves, then, here?" he asked.

"No, sir, fortunately for the squatters; and it's a pity they introduced these dogs."

"They? Who did?"

"Impossible to say, sir. The captain of some ship, I suppose—perhaps of more than one ship; and they increased and multiplied till they run wild all over the land."

"Oh no; surely they must always have been here?" said Nic.

Leather shook his head.

"This is a land of surprises, sir," he said quietly. "There were hardly any, if any, animals here but the kangaroos and the like, when the place was first settled. Haven't you read all this?"

"No," said Nic; "I have only just left school. But there doesn't seem to be many even of them."

"Millions," said Leather, smiling, "if you know where to look for them."

"But I haven't seen one since I left home this morning."

"And perhaps passed dozens, sir, from large ones, bigger than I am, down to the kangaroo rats and mice, not much bigger than those at—in England."

Nic noticed the man's hesitation, but appeared not to heed it.

"But could you show me any of them?"

"Oh yes, sir, if you wish. They want looking for, but I spend so much time alone here in the bush that I get to know their habits. Some of the small ones are pretty little long-legged creatures. Wonderful jumpers too."

"And you call them all kangaroos?"

"Some people do, sir."

"Kangaroo! Why, that must be a native name."

"Haven't you heard about that, sir?"

"Heard what?"

"About their name, sir?"

"No—nothing."

"They say that when the first people met the blackfellows they asked them what they called the leaping creatures they saw hopping along so far on two legs, like animal grasshoppers; and the blacks said 'Kangaroo.'"

"Yes, I thought it would be a native name."

Leather smiled.

"No, sir; 'kangaroo' is the blackfellows' way of saying 'I don't know what you mean.'"

"Could you show me where I could shoot one of those Blue Mountain parrots, Leather?" said Nic, after a pause, during which the boy stood thoughtful and wondering at his companion's change of manner.

"Oh yes, I think so, sir. There are plenty about."

"I haven't seen one for days; when I did I had no gun; and besides, I was not ready to stuff it."

"This is not a good time of day to look after them, sir; but I dare say you have passed plenty."

"No—not one."

Leather smiled faintly.

"They are very quiet, like most birds in the heat of the day, and are sitting up among the leaves, huddled up and with their feathers all loose, so that you don't see the bright underpart, and their backs and sides are all green like the leaves. It wants practice to see them."

"When is the best time, then?"

"Early in the morning, when it is cool and fresh, and they are just off to feed. You hear them whistling and shrieking to each other then."

"But do you think you could show me one now?"

"I'll try if you like, sir," said Leather quietly. "One of the blacks would soon show you, but my eyes are not so well trained as theirs."

The man led on, and Nic followed on tiptoe, thinking of how different he was, and wondering why so strong a feeling of dislike to him had sprung up: why, too, a man of bad character and a convict should be able to speak so well and take so much interest in the things about him.

"You need not walk so carefully, sir," he said; "and you can talk. The birds will not fly off. They trust to their colours keeping them hidden. These sheep look well, sir."

"Yes," replied Nic, without glancing at the white-fleeced creatures feeding about, for he was thinking of the scene of the day before and felt afraid that Leather would allude to it.

But he did not, for he seemed disposed to talk quietly and respectfully of the different things about them as they went on through the openly wooded region for about a mile.

"Like honey, sir?" he said.

"Oh yes. Do people keep bees out here?"

"Well, sir," said Leather, smiling pleasantly, "Dame Nature does. There are plenty of wild bees. There's a nest up just above that fork."

He pointed to a spot about forty feet from the ground, where what appeared to be some flies were darting about a hole.

"Those are not bees," said Nic, gazing up at the place where the bark appeared to be split and a portion of the tree decayed.

"Yes, sir—Australian wild bees. They make plenty of delicious honey."

"Where you can't get at it!"

"Oh yes; a man who can climb would get it. The bark of these trees is soft and easily cut through."

"But the bees would sting him to death while he was doing it."

"If they could, sir; but these bees out here are harmless. I've seen the naked blacks climb up, with a piece of smouldering, smoking wood to drive the insects away, and then rob a nest. They would not have much protection from the insects if they were attacked."

"Well, no, not much," said Nic, laughing. "But the nests must be hard to find. You won't know that place again."

"Oh yes, sir," said Leather quietly, as he stood glancing up in the tree. "You see I brought you straight here. Besides, after seeing one of the blacks track the bees home it is very easy, for the country is so open. It is not like being in the dense scrub."

"How do they track them?" asked Nic.

"Catch a bee when it is busy in a flower, touch its back with a tiny speck of gum from one of the trees, and touch the gum with a tuft of that white silky wool—"; and he picked a scrap from the seed-vessel of one of the trees.

"And what good does that do?" asked Nic.

"Good, sir? The white cotton is easily seen when the bee flies homeward, the black chasing it till perhaps he loses it. But he has got nearer to the nest, and he will do this again with other bees, till he comes at last to the place where the nest is."

"And did you find that nest so?"

"Yes," said Leather quietly. "I lost sight of the first bee about forty yards away; the next bee I missed too, but the last showed me the way at once. Now, then: look straight up there."

"Oh, I can see them flying in and out plainly enough," replied Nic.

"I was not talking about the bees then, sir. I mean away to the right a little, and a good fifty feet higher."

"Don't see anything, only the sun coming through like silver rain."

"To the right of that, sir, where the leaves are thickest. Now can you see?"

"I can see where the leaves are thickest, that's all. What am I to look at?"

"The paroquets."

"What?" cried Nic excitedly, as he gave himself an aching sensation in the back of the neck from the awkward position he assumed: "I can't see anything."

"Look again, sir. They are hard to see. I can count six together, and one which seems to be a handsome cock bird, quite by itself."

"That's the one I want," said Nic in a whisper, as he cocked his gun and stood peering up in the part indicated, but only to have his eyes dazzled by the rays which shot down from above.

"You see it now, sir?" said Leather quietly.

"Nor; nothing but leaves and twigs—nothing else. Are you sure you can see the birds?"

"Yes, sir, quite. My eyes are more used to this sort of thing than yours. I have been so much alone in the bush, often with no companions but the sheep or the blacks."

"And are they friendly to you?"

"Oh yes; in their way, sir."

"But look here: are you really sure that you can see some of those parrots now?"

"Certain, sir," said Leather, smiling. "Try and follow my finger. There: now you can see them."

Nic had a long look, and then shook his head in despair.

"I'm sorry you cannot see them, sir. Would you like me to shoot that bird for you?"

"Yes," cried Nic, holding out his gun. "No!" he said, drawing it sharply back.

"Because you think, sir, it is a ruse on my part to get possession of your gun and then go off as a bushranger," said Leather bitterly.

Nic coloured deeply as a girl, but he tossed up his head.

"Well," he said sharply, "that's true; I could not help thinking it."

"I suppose not," said the man sadly. And he turned away.

"You know you got hold of me out there by the precipice and talked about dropping me over."

"Yes," said Leather, starting. "It was the act of a fool; but I felt very bitter that day, sir."

"And how do I know that you don't feel bitter to-day?"

"Hah! How indeed!" cried the man.

Nic hesitated a moment, and then, ashamed of his suspicions, he held out the gun.

"Shoot the bird for me," he said.

Leather looked at him keenly.

"I don't think so now," said Nic, as the man drew back frowning. "I want the bird. I can't see it. I know you wouldn't trick me."

The man snatched the gun almost fiercely, examining the priming; and it was hard work for Nic to stand fast and force himself not to believe that he had done a foolish thing. But he did stand firm and met Leather's flashing eyes.

He was not long kept in suspense, for, without a moment's hesitation, Leather took aim. There was a flash, a puff of smoke and loud report, and a bird came rustling down through the twigs and boughs.

"A fact—not a ruse, sir," said Leather bitterly, as he handed back the gun.

"I beg your pardon," said the boy excitedly; and the man looked at him in wonder.

"People do not beg pardon of convicts," he said very shortly; and, bending down over the spot where the bird had fallen, he carefully parted the low growth into which the specimen had dived head first, and then, taking the beautifully coloured little creature by the hooked beak, he tenderly drew it out with the feathers falling back into their places, and hardly showing a mark.

"That is about as perfect as one can be, I think, sir," said Leather quietly.

"Lovely!" cried Nic enthusiastically. "How am I to get it home safely?"

"Take hold of it by the beak, sir, a moment," replied Leather; and, being relieved of the bird, he looked round till his eyes lit upon a peculiar-looking grass, one of the waving strands of which he picked, drew through his hand, and then passed it through the bird's nostrils, twisted the ends together lightly, and handed the loop to Nic.

"That grass is nearly as tough as wire, sir," he said. "Carry it by that, letting it swing. Are you going to collect bird-skins, sir?"

"I'm going to try, Leather. I shall want to get a good white cockatoo," said Nic, eagerly plunging into the subject, so as to try and make up for the suspicion he had displayed.

"Oh yes, sir," said the man, who now showed not the slightest resentment. "There will be plenty of work for you in that way. You can get the sulphur crests, and those with orange crests, and the rose-coloured, and the pretty grey creamy-yellowish-cheeked birds which have the cockatoo's crest and the long tail of the paroquet."

"I don't know of these," said Nic eagerly.

"The country swarms with beautiful birds, sir, especially with those of the parrot tribe. There is the black cockatoo, for instance—not that you'll care for it."

"Why?" said Nic.

"Because it is ugly," said Leather, smiling, as if he enjoyed the boy's enthusiasm. "It is wanting in bright feathers, but it is a curious bird, with a tremendously strong beak."

"I must have a specimen, though," said Nic. "What others are there?"

"I can hardly tell you, sir. The parrots are in great variety. Stop: there are two grass parrots that I know of. One is a green bird striped all over across with a darker green, like the breast of a cuckoo or a hawk, and it has fairly long legs, which enable it to go about actively on the ground. Other parrots have, as you know, very short legs, only suitable for clinging and climbing in the trees."

"And the other—grass parrot you called it?"

"A lovely little creature, cross-barred like the ground parrot; but its colours are brilliant, and it is one of the most graceful-looking little birds of the kind."

"Why, Leather," cried Nic, "you are quite a naturalist! How do you know all this?"

"How could I help knowing, sir—spending days and weeks and months alone, out here in this great wild country, watching sheep or helping to hunt our stray cattle? What should I have done in a solitary bit of a hut without speaking to a fellow-creature perhaps for a month?"

"But you have not been like this?"

"Not since I have been at the Bluff, sir. When I came up the country to be Mr Dillon's servant I was almost constantly alone. They used to send me my rations now and then. It was a very solitary life."

"How lonely!"

"Yes, sir—lonely," said the man, with a tinge of bitterness in his tones; "but it had its advantages. There was no Brookes."

Nic started and looked keenly in the man's face; but he frowned and turned hastily away, as if angry at what he had said.

"I must be getting back to the sheep, sir," he said hurriedly. "They are terribly weak, foolish things, always catching some disease. I hope you will get your bird home safely, sir. I should skin it directly. Things so soon go bad out in this hot place."

He turned away in among the trees; and Nic walked off with his gun over his shoulder, very thoughtful as he picked his way in and out among the bushes, till, feeling hot, he rested his gun against a bough, and sat down in the shade of one of the thick-foliaged, huge-trunked trees which seemed an exception to the rest—so many being thin-leaved and casting very little shade.

He had laid his specimen carefully down upon the grass, and was gazing at it without seeing any of its beauties, when a sudden thought struck him, and he sprang up to carefully reload his gun and place it before him.

"Mustn't forget that," he muttered. "Never know what may happen."

He sat down again in the pleasant shade to inspect his trophy; but once more he did not see it, for the convict's face filled his mind's eye, that lowering, sun-browned, fierce countenance which lit up at times with a smile that was sad and full of pain, and at others was so bright that the deep lines in the man's face faded, and he became attractive.

"It's queer," said Nic to himself. "One minute you regularly hate the fellow, and feel half afraid of him; the next you quite like and feel as if it would be nice to know more about him. No, it wouldn't: he's a convict, and they warned me about him."

Nic became very thoughtful, and though his lovely Blue Mountain parrot, the object of his morning's walk, was close to his side, he did not glance at it, and the beautiful birds the convict had mentioned were for the time forgotten. For he found himself wondering what Leather had done, and why he had done it; whether he was a very bad man; and gradually found his head getting into quite a muddle of conflicting surmises.

"I wish I hadn't let him think I was suspicious," he said to himself. "He jumped at it directly. I suppose I showed it pretty plainly. But no wonder! Any one would have felt as I did. To hand over one's gun to a convict, and give him a chance to point it at you and say, 'Now then, hand over that powder flask and that belt and all your wads.' Of course, so that he could go off—bush-ranging, don't they call it? Why, it seemed a mad thing to do.

"And yet I did it," said Nic to himself, after a thoughtful pause; "and he didn't run off. Why, he acted just as a gentleman would under the circumstances. I did feel sorry for him. There, I don't care: he can't be such a bad fellow as old Brookes wants to make out. Brookes is an old beast! I'd tell him so for two pins."

Nic's thoughts were flowing very freely, and feeling quite excited he went on:

"He must have done something very bad, and he has been severely punished; then they let him come out from the gang to be an assigned servant, and he's trying hard to make up for the past, and when he gets bullied and ill-used it makes him look savage and fierce, of course.

"Well," said Nic, after a thoughtful pause, "I can keep him in his place and yet be civil to him. I'm not going to jump on a man because he has done wrong; and I don't see why he shouldn't be forgiven—if he deserves it, of course, and—somehow, though I don't like him, I seem to like him a good deal, and that's about as big a puzzle as some of the things in mathematics, and—" This next was aloud:

"Oh, murder! Needles and pins! Wasps and hornets! Oh!"

Nic had jumped up, to begin dancing about, slapping his legs, shaking his trousers, pulling off his shoes, and trying hard to get rid of something that was giving him intense pain.

"It's those bees!" he cried. "They've got up the legs of my trousers; and he said they had no stings. No! ants!—You nasty, miserable, abominable little wretches—no, big wretches," he muttered, as he picked off and crushed one by one the virulent creatures, which had made a lodgment upon his legs and evidently come to the conclusion that they were good to eat.

He soon freed himself; but the tingling, poisonous nature of their bites was still very evident, and excited an intense desire to rub and scratch.

"Why, there's quite a regiment of the little vicious wretches!" cried the boy as he was going back to where his gun stood by the tree. "I suppose they smelt me."

It seemed so for the moment, for a long line of the ants could be traced through the grass on and on; and then Nic uttered an exclamation, sprang forward and caught up his specimen, to hold it at arm's length and begin shaking it.

"Why, it's covered with them," he cried, as he swept them off, got them on his hands, saw them racing up his arms, and found them so quick and so tight-clinging that the task grew painful in the extreme before he could get rid of them, and when he did he tossed the rumpled, disfigured bird back amongst his enemies.

"There!" he cried: "eat it then. It's completely spoiled. What a pity I did not let it live!"

"Never mind, Nic," said his father that evening, as he sat at home, giving himself from time to time a vicious rub. "Take it as a lesson. We all have to go through that sort of thing, and you'll know better next time. But it was a fine specimen, you say?"

"Lovely," replied Nic eagerly; but he did not say a word about who shot the bird, for he felt that if he did his father would be annoyed.

Chapter Twenty One
A Day's Fishing

Nic felt uncomfortable. There was something fascinating about being in company with a man who knew so much of the wild nature of his country; but then the man was a convict—he had been warned against him—and a companion that the doctor would not approve. But still, somehow or other, the boy was constantly finding himself in Leather's company, for the man was as much drawn to Nic as he was to the convict.

The consequence was that they were often together out in the wilder parts of the doctor's great estate.

One day, after a hint from his father, consequent upon his saying that he was going to explore the gully by the waterfall, he had taken the old fishing-rod and line from where it hung upon two hooks in the kitchen—a rod the doctor had used in old trout and salmon-fishing days, and had brought over on the chance of wanting, but had never found time to use.

"That gully is very beautiful higher up, Nic, and I have seen plenty of fish in the deep parts, gliding about among the tree roots and old trunks that have been washed down in the floods and got wedged in. I should certainly take the rod. The men tell me they are capital eating, but I have never tried."

"We had a dish one day, father, when you were out," said Janet.

"How did you get them?" asked the doctor.

"Samson brought them in—a basketful," cried Hilda.

"Then you had better ask old Sam what he baited with, and take your bait accordingly."

"Yes, father," said the boy.

"Take the biggest basket, Nic," said Hilda mischievously.

"Ah, you think I shan't catch any," said her brother, nodding his head; "but you'll see."

The rod was dusty, but good and strong, and in the bag the doctor pointed out there were plenty of good new hooks and lines; so leaving them ready, Nic went down the garden to where he expected to find old Sam.

Sure enough there he was hoeing away, and he stopped and wiped his perspiring face upon his arm as the boy came up.

"That's right, sir," he cried. "Glad to see you here. I want you to take a bit more hinterest in my garden. See they taters: ain't they getting on? Look at my peas and beans too. I calls they a sight, I do. Make some o' they gardeners in Old England skretch their wigs and wish they could grow things like 'em."

"Beautiful, Sam; but—"

"There's cauliflowers too, sir: ain't they splendid?"

"Couldn't be better, Sam; but—"

"Try my peas, sir." *Pop!* "There's a pod. Dozen fine uns, just as if they was a row o' green teeth laughing at you."

"Deliciously tender, Sam; but—"

"It's the sun, Master Nic; it's the sun," said the old man, who was too much wrapped up in his subject to heed the boy's remarks. "Sun's a scarce article at home, but here you gets it all day long, and it's the clouds is scarce. Why, you know summer at home, where the skies seem all like so much sopping wet flannel being squeezed; and not a sign o' sunshine for six weeks. What's to grow then?"

"Nothing, I suppose, Sam; but—"

"Of course you wants the water, sir. More sun you gets more water you wants, and that's why I tiddles it all along through the garden from up above yonder, just ketching it above where it comes over the waterfall."

"Yes, waterfall, Sam," cried Nic heartily. "I say, didn't you catch a lot of fish up there somewhere and bring home one day when my father was out?"

"To be sure I did," said the old man, now beginning to lend an ear.

"That's right. I want to catch some too."

"You'd ketch 'em then, my lad. There's lots on 'em."

"Tell me how you caught them. What did you use for bait?"

"Shovel," said the old man, grinning.

"What?"

"And peckaxe."

"I don't understand you."

"Why, it's plain enough, sir. It was when I was turning a hole into a sort o' ressywar to supply the garden—irrigglygate it, the master said, but I calls it watering."

"But I was talking about the fish, Sam."

"I know, sir; so was I. 'How did you ketch 'em?' says you. 'Shovel,' says I. I was making a place beyond the waterfall, and they swimmed in a hole there, where they'd got and couldn't get out again. So I makes a dyke with the peck and turns the water off and then ladles the fish out with the shovel. Two basketsful there was. One I took indoors for the ladies, and t'other we ate; and Brooky put away so many they made him queer for some days. But they didn't hurt me."

"But I wanted to fish for them with a rod and line."

"Oh–h–oh!" cried the old man. "You won't get many that-a-way. P'r'aps it would be best for you though. It's nation hard work pecking and digging, making dams and gullies among the rocks when the sun's hot."

"But I want some bait."

"Ay, you'll want some bait. We used to ketch eels at home with a big wum. There's lots here—whackers, some on 'em. Shall I get you a few?"

"Yes, do, please."

"So I will, Master Nic—barrowload if you like. You get me an old canister. There'll be some nice fat uns down aside where I grows my cowcumbers. Ah! I never thought, when I got digging 'em out o' the side of the cowcumber beds at home, I should ever get making on 'em out here, t'other side o' the world."

Nic fetched a bag instead of a canister, and soon after stood ready to start.

"You go same way as I took yer that night, Master Nic, and then work your way up for a hour or so, and all under they tree-ferns you'll find pools and pools with lots o' fish in 'em; but I don't know how you're going to get on with that long thin clothes-prop of a thing. But, there, you're a gen'leman, and I s'pose you knows best."

"Well, I shall try with it, Sam," said Nic, laughing.

"Ay, sir, do, and good luck to you. Now I'll get back to my hoeing."

Nic shouldered his rod, and with his basket in his hand he left the garden, went round by the wooden building set apart for the men, and then struck across the open ground for the gully, where he soon came upon the tree-bridge he had crossed that moonlight night in company with old Sam; and he could not help hesitating for a few moments as he looked down into the narrow, dark rift, along which the water was rushing far below, while the noise of the waterfall was hollow, reverberating, and strange.

Nic took a long breath, and looked at the tree, which had been felled so that it tumbled right across the rift, and then worked with an adze so as to make a level surface about as wide as an ordinary plank, the lower branches being left on at the sides of the trunk and beneath.

He drew another deep breath, and noted that if he fell, unless he caught at one of these hanging branches, checked himself and managed to climb back, he must drop all that tremendous depth into the black-looking pool of water below.

He drew a third deep breath, and thought that if he had known what the place was like, old Sam would never have got him across, that first night of his coming.

Then he took another long, deeper breath than ever, and said to himself:

"If that were a plank laid flat upon the ground I could hop along it upon one leg, so it is only cowardice to hesitate."

The next minute he was across, and walking along the other side of the ferny gully, to stop by the waterfall and admire the beauty of the glassy water as it glided over the rocks and fell down into the thick mist, which rose like a cloud toward the overhanging mosses and ferns.

But though the place was attractive enough to have kept him there for hours, and he wondered why he had not come to have a good look at it sooner, he felt that if he meant to catch any fish that day he must be stirring.

There was a well-trodden path along by the river, which beyond the waterfall ran on in a continuation of the gully but here the walls opened out rapidly, till a few hundred yards above it became a lovely little sunny valley, with rocky masses piled near the bed of the little river, made beautiful by the abundant growth. The ferns were much bigger than any he had yet seen, and the path wound in and out in many a zigzag, now toward the sloping sides of the ravine, now toward the sparkling, torrent-like stream, over which drooped many a bough, as if for the sunshine to rain through in a silver shower upon the water beneath, which flashed gloriously where the bright rays fell.

"I don't wonder at father choosing this place," thought Nic. "It grows more beautiful every way one goes."

He must have wandered and climbed in and out for a couple of miles before he grasped why it was that the path was so well beaten. A moist spot in a shady part, where the river was just upon his right, showed this, for the narrow track was printed all over by the hoofs of sheep, and he knew now that the footpath was their work, made when in hot weather they had selected the moist shades for grazing; while at a turn a few hundred yards farther on he had an indorsement of his surmise, for the slopes of the valley had grown less abrupt, and as far as he could see one side was dotted with creamy-white fleeces.

And now in the more level ground the torrent had become a swift, bright stream, bubbling and rippling here, swirling round in eddies there, and again becoming dark and deep-looking.

He gazed down into the transparent water, but his research was not rewarded by the sight of dark, gliding forms with sinuous, waving tails. Still, though no scaly prizes offered themselves for capture, there were plenty of other objects to attract him. Every now and then some beautiful butterfly flitted across the water, and twice had he paused to gaze with pleasant vexation at a lovely streak of wavy blue, as a kingfisher darted from its perch to fly up the stream.

"Well, I do call this tiresome," he cried, taking his fishing-rod from one shoulder to change it to the other. "If this had been my gun, you wouldn't have shown yourselves."

This was addressed to a little flock of small green birds which flew whistling and chattering more than chirping up the slope toward the level land above.

"I dare say those are the little green parrots Leather talked about."

Twice more he had capital chances to obtain specimens,—one being at some half-dozen birds, which seemed to be all pink except their snowy heads; the next time at a couple more in a tree. These did not fly till he was close enough to see that they were bright with bronze and green and red.

"Why, they must be pigeons," he said, as they darted off. "Well, I suppose one may see birds of any colour now."

At last!

He had reached an ideal spot, where one side of the river was dammed by a tangled mass of tree trunks which must have been brought down by some flood, to get jammed, and then gradually be stripped by the action of the water, till only the stems and larger branches were left; while on his side there was a dark, tempting-looking pool of water, which he approached cautiously, after laying down his rod, and then crawling toward it, gradually looked over the sharp, rocky edge of the river into the sunlit depths, to see dark bodies in slow motion some feet below sailing here and there to capture the tit-bits brought down by the stream.

Nic's eyes glistened as he drew back as cautiously as he had approached.

"This looks like real fishing," he said to himself, as he thought of the unsatisfactory sport he had had at home at the various ponds in the neighbourhood of the Friary, when a farmer gave them leave to go. "Wouldn't some of the boys like to be here. I shouldn't be surprised if this place has never been fished before. My word! they ought to bite."

Such uneducated fish certainly ought to have bitten; but though Nic approached the side again cautiously, keeping well back out of sight, and after carefully covering his hook with a worm, dropped it without a splash in a likely place, and then in a more likely one, and again and again into other spots which seemed each of them more likely than the last, not a bite did he get!

He was patient, too. He put on fresh baits, tried all over the pool, dropped in his worm so that it might be washed from the stream into the still, dark water, and sink among the fish.

Still there was not the sign of a bite.

"They must all have gone away," thought Nic, just as there was a burst of sharp screams from a flock of cockatoos, which, like the other birds, seemed wilder here in the moist shades than he had found them high up on the park-like downs near the great mountain gorge.

He crept upon his chest cautiously once more to get his eyes just over the sharp rock edge of the pool, to look down into the depths, fully convinced that he would not see a fish; but to his surprise there was quite a shoal of a goodly size slowly sailing about, and after a few moments he was able to make out that they were close by the bait, which lay at the bottom, moving slowly, while one of the largest fish was certainly looking at it.

"Bother!" muttered Nic, as he looked round about and thought of old Sam's style of fishing. "Well, one can't catch these with a shovel and a pickaxe. No one could bale out this pool."

"Having bad luck, sir?" said a deep voice; and Nic started up to find Leather standing close behind.

Chapter Twenty Two
A Woolly Patient and a Scare

The man had approached over the soft moss unheard, though Nic had had warning of his coming from the cockatoos, which had shrieked out their alarm notes as he came down from among the sheep.

"Why, Leather, I did not hear you coming," said Nic, half annoyed by the interruption.

"I suppose not, sir. You were too intent. Don't they bite?"

"No, not a bit," said Nic gruffly; and to himself, "I wish he'd go."

"What are you fishing with, sir?"

"Worms."

"They will only take worms after a flood, when the water's thick."

Then without a word the man walked away, and Nic drew his line sharply from the water.

"Might have told me what bait they would take," muttered the boy. "Perhaps he doesn't know. Wish I had brought some paste. I don't care; that's good enough bait for anything. Now, here, some of you—bite."

But they did not, and Nic sat upon a great stone, feeling rather ill-used. He was glad the convict had gone, and at the same time sorry.

"I suppose I answered him very gruffly, and that sent him off," thought Nic.

"Now, sir. I've caught a few of these."

Nic jumped again, for once more the man had approached in silence.

"Eh! what have you got?"

"Locusts, or grasshoppers, sir. Have you a nice-sized new hook?"

"Oh yes, plenty," cried Nic eagerly, opening a flat box from which the man took one he thought suitable.

The next minute the hook bearing the great worm had been removed and one good-sized shot only left on the line.

"Now,—sir," said Leather, "these grasshoppers are tender, so drop the bait gently on the surface, right over yonder where the stream comes round that end of the tree root.—Well done. Couldn't be better. Now be on the look-out, sir."

The running water carried the great insect several feet into the still water before the weight of the shot began to act. Then very slowly it was drawn down beneath the surface, and they saw it descend and disappear in the obscurity, the line being slowly drawn after it.

"They won't take that ugly, crooked-legged thing," said Nic. "Why, it would choke any fish that ever breathed."

"Watch," said Leather quietly. "It takes some time to sink, for you have only one shot on; but it looks more natural, and it has not yet reached the fish. I think I'd draw in my slack line now, sir, and be ready to strike gently."

"No good," said Nic, who, however, took the advice.

"If you do hook one, don't let it run in among the old tree trunks, sir. If you do, the fish is lost. Directly you feel one, strike and lead it to the other end of the pool, and get it out in the shallows, where I can land it for you."

"Handle it carefully, Leather," said Nic, with a grim smile. "You see your grasshoppers are no better than my worms. These fish don't understand biting."

"No, sir, or they wouldn't have taken that locust. Steady, sir, steady. That's a heavy one. Well done; you'll master it. Your tackle's strong, and you must get it away from those roots and branches. That's the way. I'll go on and wait."

For, quivering with excitement, his pliable rod bent into a bow, and the line running sharply here and there through the water, Nic was following a fish which had taken the bait with a rush deep down in the pool.

A minute later he had it near the surface, and had drawn it into the stream which ran out of the deep hole, into the shallowest part of which the convict had waded, and as soon as line and current had brought it near enough, he gave one deft scoop with his joined hands and threw it out on to the bank.

"I say! is it true?" cried Nic. "I can't hardly believe it."

"It looks true enough, sir," replied the man. "Shall I take it off the hook?"

"Oh yes, please," cried Nic excitedly. "You've got some more of those grasshoppers?"

"Three, sir," said Leather, as he laid the fish at the boy's feet, "and I can soon get some more. You'll find these fish very good eating, but you must catch a dishful."

"Why, Leather, you seem to know everything about the country."

"I have had a long training, sir. You will know more than I do when you have been here two or three years. Now, then, throw in again."

"Here, hi! Do you know one of them sheep's falled down into a hole? I'm sure master don't mean you to be wasting all your time out there, and idling about like a schoolboy."

This was yelled hoarsely from some fifty yards away, and Nic saw that his companion started as if he had been stung.

An angry speech was on Nic's lips at this interruption, but he checked it, for he knew that he had no right to keep the man from his work.

"Coming directly," he said in loud tones. Then to. Leather: "Stop a minute while I catch another, and then you shall go. You must land it for me."

Brookes was not kept long waiting, for another fish was hooked and landed in the same way; but before Leather had scooped it out Brookes was shouting again furiously.

"Must go, sir," said the convict.

"Stop and I'll come with you," cried Nic, laying down his rod as soon as the fish was unhooked, and he hurried with the man to where Brookes stood talking, though half he said was inaudible.

"Here, Master Nic," he said, as they approached, "I dunno what your father'll say. Here's one of his best sheep o' that new breed down in a hole. You've no business to let that fellow leave his work."

"Where is it?" said Leather anxiously.

"Where is it? Where d'yer s'pose it is?" said Brookes fiercely. "Down in the narrer."

"The sheep were all safe a few minutes ago," said Leather; and he ran off.

"Oh, yes," said Brookes, in a sneering tone; "'course they were."

"Is it badly hurt?"

"Badly hurt? I s'pose so. It'll have to be killed."

He trudged on, muttering surlily, and Nic followed up on to the level ground, where they could see the convict lowering himself down, only his head and shoulders being visible.

The next minute they were standing at the edge of a narrow rift some six feet wide and as many deep—a rift that ran on down into the valley they had just quitted, and at the bottom of which lay a sheep bleating piteously as Leather bestrode its woolly carcass.

"Why didn't you pull it out instead of coming sneaking after us?" cried Nic.

"Eh? What?" cried Brookes, staring. "'Tain't my place to look after they sheep. Leatherhead was set to do it, and he goes on neglecting his work. Ah! here comes the master. Now we shall see."

For the doctor was coming cantering toward them over the level ground from about a quarter of a mile away, and Nic felt vexed and in dread of what was to follow.

"Is it hurt, Leather?" he said.

"Yes, sir, badly—its leg's broken," replied the man; and bending down, he placed his arms round the poor animal, raised it up on to his shoulder, and began to climb with difficulty out of the rift. As he reached the edge he nearly slipped back.

"Why don't you help?" cried Nic angrily; but Brookes did not stir; and if the boy had not darted forward and got a good pull of the wool, man and sheep would have toppled backward to the bottom.

"Thank you, sir," said the convict. "There's no foothold, and I lost my balance. One moment. That's it;" and the sheep was rolled off his shoulder on to the grass.

"What's the matter?" cried the doctor, cantering up, leaping down, and throwing the reins over his horse's head on to the grass, when the beautiful animal stood still.

"One o' the best ewes down in that grip. I come and found it just now."

"Yes, but you didn't try to get it out," said Nic.

"It warn't in my charge," growled Brookes.

"How was this, my man?" said the doctor. "You were set to look after them."

"Yes, sir," said the convict respectfully. "The sheep were all right a quarter of an hour ago."

"Yes, and they'd ha' been all right now if you'd looked arter them 'stead o' wasting your time fishing," growled Brookes. "I'm glad master's here to know."

"Were you fishing, sir?" said the doctor sternly; but before Leather could answer Nic cried quickly:

"No, father, he wasn't. He came down to the river to get me a few baits. I wanted him there. Why didn't Brookes help the sheep out?"

"Because it was the other man's duty, sir," said the doctor quickly; and Leather gave the boy a sharp look, as much as to say, "Don't speak, sir; you'll make things worse."

"Ah, you needn't signal the young master to take yer part," cried Brookes. "It's true enough; you ain't worth your salt on the station."

"That will do, Brookes," said the doctor.

"Oh, I don't want to say nothing, sir. I was only looking arter your property."

"Tut, tut, tut!" cried the doctor, as he felt the sheep's leg. "One of my choicest ewes. The leg's broken. That active sheep couldn't have broken its leg through falling down there. It would have jumped it like a goat. Why, Leather, the poor brute has been savagely kicked."

"It looks like it, sir," said the convict quietly.

"Why, so it do," chimed in Brookes, as he bent over the helpless sheep.

"Do you know anything of it, sir?" cried the doctor, eyeing the convict keenly.

The man shook his head.

"It's very strange," said the doctor, looking at Brookes, who took off his hat, scratched his head, and looked round at the convict, while Nic glanced at Brookes's boots and then at the poor sandal-like shoes the convict wore, which were evidently a piece of his own work.

"Like me to kill the poor thing out of its misery, sir," said Brookes, "and take off its skin?"

"No," said the doctor shortly.

"Won't be nothin' the matter with the meat, sir."

"Nic," said his father, "jump on the horse and ride home. Ask your mother to give you a roll of bandage, and bring it back here."

"Yes, father."

"Why, you ain't going to bind that 'ere leg up, are yer?" said Brookes.

"Will you be good enough not to interrupt?" said the doctor. "Here, hi, Nic, my boy. Tell Samson to give you a sack and an axe. You can throw the sack across the horse."

"Yes, father," cried the boy; and he cantered off, obtained the bandage and sack, and was back in less than an hour, to find that Leather had, under the doctor's directions, cut some pieces of wood from a tree, and with these for splints the doctor cleverly bandaged the broken leg.

"There, Nic," he said, "I should not do that in a regular way, but this is a very valuable sheep, brought out to me by one of the last ships. Now one of you cut a good stout pole, say twelve feet long."

Brookes looked at Leather, who caught up the axe and ran off.

While he was gone the doctor opened a part of the bottom of the sack, and cut four slits in the side; and this being done, Nic looked on in surprise while the sack was drawn over the struggling sheep's head, its head pulled out of the bottom, and the legs put through the four slits.

"Now gather the sack together so that the poor brute cannot struggle out, Brookes," said the doctor; and this was easily effected, as the animal was upon its side.

Then the doctor made holes and laced up the mouth of the sack securely, all but a few inches; and by this time Leather was back with a stout, neatly trimmed pole.

"Do you see what I mean?" said the doctor.

"Yes, sir," replied the convict, and he slipped the pole through the sack above the sheep's back, leaving about four feet out at each end.

"Now, Brookes, take the other end," said the doctor; "lift together, and get the pole on your shoulders, both of you."

"What, and carry that lame sheep home?" said Brookes.

"Yes; and its legs must not touch the ground."

"But hadn't you better let us chuck it across the back of the horse?"

"No. Now, together. Lift," cried the doctor; and as this was done the sheep gave a dismal bleat, and hung from the pole, with its head and legs out,—a ridiculous-looking object, which made Nic smile, but Brookes's face made the smile expand, so soured and puckered did it become, for the sheep was heavy, the farm buildings were some distance away, and the sun was coming down hot as the two men strode away, Leather looking heavy and stern, but apparently ready to undertake any amount of work.

"You can ride, Nic," said the doctor, as the boy fetched up the horse.

"But my fishing-rod and line, father?"

"Where are they?"

"Down yonder, by one of the pools."

"Oh, then you must go that way home."

"Yes, father, and I have two fish."

"Well done."

"I say, father, I feel sure that Leather did not kick that sheep."

"Who did then?" said the doctor.

"I don't like to say, father."

"That is suggesting your belief that it was Brookes, a man whom I have always found to work well in my interests, Nic. He has no spite against me."

"Do you think the other man has?"

"I don't know, boy. There, go on your way, and I'll go home. One word, Nic. I want you to enjoy yourself, but I cannot have my men taken away from their work, mind that."

The doctor cantered after the men bearing the sheep, and as Nic stood for a few minutes watching them, he heard the sheep give a piteous baa, as if protesting against its treatment, after which the men halted and changed shoulders.

Nic was too far off to see the expression of the men's faces, but he felt pretty certain that Brookes's was anything but pleasant, and he felt glad.

"I believe he did that out of spite against Leather," thought Nic, "so as to make it seem as if it was through neglect. I don't know, though, a man could hardly be such a brute."

Nic descended into the little valley once more, and made his way along by the stream to the pool where he had left his rod.

"There's one more locust," he said to himself; "and I'll try and catch another fish. Three will make a much better show. I dare say one would bite directly;" and determined to spend a few minutes in adding to his brace, he hurried on, thinking how beautiful the great, dense clump of trees on the other side of the stream appeared, many of them drooping gracefully over the water.

"The beauty of a place like this is," he thought, "that you can leave things about and there is no one to take them."

He smiled as he picked up his rod, drew the line through his fingers, and baited the hook with the great insect ready to cast right over into the stream so that the locust might be washed naturally into the sunlit pool.

"Now, if I can catch another as big as the— Hullo! where are those fish?"

Nic did not cast the locust, but stared hard at the spot where the fish had been laid down upon some fern leaves; but though the latter were still glistening with slime, the prizes were gone.

"They must have flopped their way back into the water," said Nic to himself; "they went that way because it was all on a slope. Well, of all the tiresome nuisances I ever knew, this is about the worst. I wouldn't have lost those fish for anything. They must have flopped to and fro down here and over that soft place."

Nic's thoughts stood still. The soft place he alluded to was close down to the shallow where Leather had waded in, and the water which had dripped from his legs lay upon the herbage and soft, dank, moist earth; but there was something else—footprints! Not Leather's, made by broad shoe-soles, but newly impressed marks with wide-spreading toes, the big toe in each case being rather thumb-like in its separation from the others.

For some two or three minutes Nic did not stir, but bent down staring at those footprints. Then he glanced sharply over the shallows at the thick foliage, fully expecting to see a spear come flying at him.

"That's the way my fish went," he muttered as he turned and fled, feeling a sudden check the next minute, as if some one had seized the rod which hung over his shoulder, and a thrill of fear ran through him as he turned sharply round, when snap went the line, and he saw that the hook and locust were sticking in an overhanging bough, and about a yard of the line was hanging down.

That was enough to drive away some of his fear, but not all.

"One can't fight blacks with fishing-rods," muttered the boy as he again began to run, and he made his way homeward more quickly than he had come, and did not pause once to look back, though if he had it was doubtful whether he would have seen the cunning black face peering from out of the wattle scrub, watching him as he ran in and out through the trees, and then disappearing as soon as Nic was out of sight.

The fugitive did not pause till he reached home bathed in perspiration, just as his father rode slowly in side by side with the laden men, they having taken a shorter cut while he had followed the wanderings of the stream.

"Ah, Nic," cried his father, "you shouldn't run and overheat yourself like that, boy. Now, men, carry the poor beast into the stable and rest the pole on the rails; its hoofs will then be about five inches from the ground.— What?"

"Blackfellows, father," said Nic, as soon as he could get his breath; "I saw their footmarks, and they have carried off my fish."

Chapter Twenty Three
A Squatter's Life

Nic's announcement caused a little panic. The three blacks who came and went about the place were summoned and sent out searching, the house was placed in a state of defence, and Samson, Brookes, and Leather all furnished with guns and ammunition to stand ready for any emergency, taking it in turns though to keep watch, while horses and cattle were driven into the south enclosures by the house, and everything possible done to secure their safety.

Knowing his mother's nervousness, Nic could not help staring in wonder at the calm way in which she and her daughters behaved at what might, for aught they could tell, be a dangerous time, for neither showed the slightest trace of fear.

In a couple of hours, though, the black known as Bungarolo came back to announce that, "Blackfellow all agone," and he pointed away toward the dense bush, miles from where they were standing.

The explanation of the other two blacks when they returned cleared away the rest of the alarm, the doctor concluding that a few of the many wanderers had been near and gone away again, blacks probably belonging to a friendly tribe.

Consequently the next day matters went on as usual, save that Nic had to mount with his father, and, accompanied by two of their blacks, made a wide circuit about the station, touching the edge of the great gorge at one point and then riding round for miles.

Twice over the men, who trotted along easily enough step for step with the horses, pointed out tracks going and coming; and as the party was made out to be three only it was felt that there was no cause for alarm, and toward evening they rode back to the station with the glad news.

"But wouldn't it have been very awkward for them if the blacks had come while we were away, father?" Nic ventured to ask on their way back.

"Yes, but they would have shut themselves in at once," said the doctor; "two of the men would have been with them, and the other would have followed us, firing signals as he came. If the danger had been imminent, he would have seized the first horse and galloped over to Mr Dillon's station."

"I see," said Nic.

"It's mutual help out here, Nic. If one station is in danger, those nearest are always ready to gallop to its help."

Then came days and weeks of busy life, with Nic finding little time for amusement, but enjoying the novelty of his new career. There were long rides to drive in cattle; visits to be paid to flocks miles away from the station; messages to be taken to Samson, Brookes, or Leather, who in turn were far away with the roaming sheep or oxen; and the boy was joked at home by mother and sisters for the way he ate, slept, and seemed to expand.

During this period he saw little of Leather, and the incident of the injured sheep and Brookes's apparent enmity toward the convict was for the time forgotten, these two rarely being together.

Still, at different times Nic could not help noticing what a rooted dislike there was in the regular men against their convict fellow-servant, even old Samson shaking his head and expressing his belief that the station would be far better without "such as he."

"I don't want to be hard on anything 'cept blight, Master Nic," said the old man one day; "but it comes nat'ral to a man to feel shy of a gaol bird who may rise agen you at any time and take to the bush."

"Oh, but Leather is not that sort of man, Sam," said Nic.

"Ah, that's very nice, young gentleman; but you don't know, and I don't know. All I say is if there's a bull about on that side o' the fence it's best to walk on this."

"But the bull may not mean to do you harm, Sam."

"P'r'aps not, sir; but bulls have mad fits now and then, so does convicts. I've know'd two stations 'tacked and every one killed, and they said it was the blacks; but they very soon found that it warn't, for in each case a lot had escaped from the chain gang, took to the bush, and every 'signed servant as they come across jyned 'em."

"That's very horrible," said Nic. "And what became of them?"

"Ah, you may well say that, sir: some was shot down by the soldiers, some was killed by the natives, some was lost in the bush and died o' hunger and thirst, while the blacks speared the rest all but one, and he gave himself up. They do a lot o' mischief, these chaps, when they take to the bush, sir; but, fortunately for honest folk, they all come to a bad end."

Then came a more leisure time, when old Samson took a holiday, as he called it—that is to say, he worked from daylight to darkness over his rather neglected garden; while Nic had leisure to think again of his natural history specimens, and went out with his gun; but he did not feel at all keen about sitting down in a woody place near the river to fish and offer himself as a mark for any black who meant to practise hurling his spear. It was so much more satisfactory to mount Sour Sorrel and ride off, gun in hand, through the open woodland with the soft breeze sweeping by his cheek, and pick up a beautifully feathered bird from time to time.

The injured sheep had grown quite well, and, save that it limped as it grazed, its leg was as strong as ever; "and that lameness does not interfere with its promising to be a good mother," said the doctor, smiling, as he pointed to the pair of white lambs gambolling by the lame sheep's side.

"Did you ever satisfy yourself as to how its leg was broken?" said Nic.

"No, my boy; and I did not want to. I have my suspicions, but I let them rest. It is the same at most of the stations—the free men dislike the bond. It is natural. And now that things are going on peaceably, we will let them rest."

One day, quite by accident, the boy found himself thrown in contact again with Leather, whose brown, deeply lined countenance always brightened when Nic came across him somewhere with his sheep.

"I say, Leather," he said, as he sat on his nag watching the man busily carving a stick he had cut: "you remember telling me about how the blacks followed the bees?"

"Yes, sir."

"Can you show me?"

"Yes," said Leather, smiling sadly; and he looked about till he found a tree with some of its seed-vessels full of fine silky cotton, smeared one end of a twig with a bead of gum from another tree, and then walked on, followed by Nic, till they came to a patch of bushes, whose fragrant blossoms had attracted the bees by the dozen.

One pollen-laden fellow was soon caught, the gum stick touched its back, the white cotton was brought in contact, and the uninjured insect set free.

Up in the air it went at once, regardless of the yellow flowers among which it had been buzzing, and then flew away in a straight line, with its white patch on its back, to be traced some forty or fifty yards, before it disappeared among the trees.

"Gone!" said Nic, who was in advance, for he had followed the insect on horseback. "Think there's a tree here?"

"No; these are not the kind of trees they nest in. They do not go hollow."

"What will you do, then?"

"Repeat the process, sir."

And this was done four times, till the last bee was traced to a quarter of a mile from where they started, and a tiny hole was made out sixty feet from the ground, about which scores of little dark insects could be seen darting.

"Now how to get the honey?" said Nic.

"Send or bring Bungarolo here to-morrow with an axe and a bucket, and you shall have plenty."

Eager to see the taking of the spoil, Nic was over in good time next morning, the black trotting by his side; and upon reaching the tree the Australian savage took the axe from his waistcloth, while Leather lit a great piece of touchwood by means of a burning glass. This wood began to burn, emitting a dense white smoke, and as the convict waved it about, the black took off his waistcloth, passed it through the handle of the bucket, and tied it again about his middle, so that the bucket hung behind. Then, axe in hand, he began to chop notches in the soft bark, to make steps for his active feet, and climbed steadily up and up, Nic watching him the while.

"It looks very dangerous," said the boy. "Think he is likely to fall?"

"Not in the least, sir. They begin doing these things when children, and they don't seem to have any nerves."

It seemed indeed as if the black did not know fear, for he went on up and up till he was fully sixty feet from the ground, and here he held on with his legs while he undid his waistcloth once more and tied it now to a branch, so that the bucket hung close to the hole where the bees buzzed in and out, as if feeling in no wise incommoded by the black face so near.

And now Bungarolo stuck the axe into the soft bark and rapidly descended, grinning hugely at his success. Leather handed him the smoking torch, and he went up again, holding the end of the soft wood in his teeth.

On reaching the hole, the smoke which had accompanied him in his ascent became thicker, and being held just below the entrance, scared away the bees coming back, and those coming out into pouring forth faster and faster, till there was quite a cloud darting about above that of the blinding wood smoke.

Then a few cleverly directed strokes of the axe made a big opening through the bark, the axe was thrown down, and the black's arm thrust in right up to the shoulder, and his hand drawn out bearing a great cake of honeycomb.

This he deposited in the bucket, pausing now and then to give the smoking wood a wave, or to hold it inside the opening, to drive out the bees before bringing out more and more comb, till the bucket was pretty well full.

And now the most difficult task seemed to await the black; but he held on again with his legs, untied the waist cloth, rested the bucket on his chest, while he knotted the cloth ends together again, and slipped it over his head. Then, taking the smoking wood from where he had placed it inside the hole, he threw it down and descended safe and triumphant, to begin cleaning his sticky hands after the fashion of a cat, before bearing the bucket back to the station, where Mrs Braydon gave him a lump of damper for a reward.

Chapter Twenty Four
Leather Speaks Out

Another day, it seemed as if Sorrel felt with his master, and took him straight to a fresh part of the great sheep run, near where the vast gorge was fenced at its edge with mighty trees, beneath one of which Leather was seated, looking hard and stern.

Nic was very thoughtful that day. There was something he wanted to ask the convict, but he always shrank from satisfying his curiosity; and this time he showed that he had something upon his mind so plainly, that Leather after their abrupt salutations had passed, said:

"Not well, sir?"

"Yes, quite well. Why?"

"Looked queer, sir."

"Oh, nothing," said Nic hastily, for he had made up his mind to question the man, and now the opportunity had come he felt that he could not speak.

"I was thinking about you a little while ago, sir."

"About me? Why?"

"You were saying the other day that you had seen so few snakes. I've seen four this morning. Two of them are poisonous; you may as well have a shot at them."

"How do you know that they are poisonous?"

"Partly from the bad character they have, sir, partly from the shape of the head."

"Let's see, I've heard something about that before: poisonous snakes have a spade-shaped head, haven't they?"

"That's what they call it, sir. It is really a great swelling at the back of the jaws on either side of the neck. This swelling is made by the poison bags which communicate with their hollow fangs. You'll see if you shoot the big gentleman I saw crawling back into his hole this morning. I dare say he's out again now, to be in the hot sun. Why, what's the matter, Master Nic?"

"Matter?"

"Yes, sir; you keep going off in a dreamy way, and not listening."

Nic frowned and was silent.

"I beg your pardon, sir; it is like my impertinence to ask you. I forget sometimes, when you are ready to treat me like a human being, that I am only a convict."

"Don't take it like that," said Nic hurriedly. "It was only because I was thinking, Leather."

"Yes, sir, I see: some little trouble at home."

"Oh, no!" cried Nic, ready to blurt out everything now. "You see I like you, Leather."

The man's eyes flashed and then softened for a moment, while his lips quivered; but his hard, cynical, bitter aspect and tones came back—the manner born of years of misery and degradation, and he cried mockingly:

"Why? Because I behaved like a brute to you, and made believe to throw you down into that gully?"

"Don't bring that up," cried Nic angrily; "and don't talk in that way, Leather. It isn't you. It's only put on."

"Indeed," said the man bitterly. "Well, I didn't put it on, sir. It was fate."

"There, I didn't like to speak to you," continued Nic; "but I must now. I've long wanted to, for of course I can't help seeing how different you are from Brookes and old Sam. You are always showing me that you are a man of good education, and what a deal you know. It makes me ashamed sometimes."

"Why?" said Leather sternly.

"To ask you to do all kinds of rough work when I feel that you are better educated than I am—that you must have been quite a gentleman."

"Ah, don't, boy!" cried Leather passionately, and with his face convulsed. "For Heaven's sake hold your tongue."

"I can't now," cried Nic, as excitedly. "I feel as if I must know. I do like you, Leather—I do really; and it worries me. I think of it at night when I go to bed, and it makes me wild to hear Brookes talk to you as he does."

"Brookes is an honest man, sir; I'm a convict," said Leather bitterly.

"There you are, going back to your old way!" cried Nic; "and it isn't fair, after I've told you I liked you."

The convict caught the boy's hand, and his eyes softened again; but he dropped the hand and drew back, sending a pang through Nic, who felt that he must have been guilty of some terrible crime, and they stood looking in each other's eyes for some little time. Then the boy spoke in a husky whisper—for he said to himself, "Poor chap, he must be very sorry for it now,"—"What was it you did, Leather?"

"Nothing."

"Then why were you sent out here?"

Nic started, and repented having spoken, for the convict drew himself up, with his eyes flashing and his face convulsed by rage, scorn, and indignation.

"Why was I sent out here, boy?" he raged: "because a jury of my fellow-countrymen said I was guilty, and the judge told me that I deserved the greater punishment because I—a man of education, holding so high and responsible a position, and who ought to have known better—was worse than a common ignorant thief; and that he must make an example of me, that the world might see how government servants found no favour when they sinned. He said I had had a fair trial, that my countrymen condemned me, and that he quite agreed with their verdict; and he sentenced me to twenty-one years' transportation,—he might as well have said for life."

Nic stood looking at him in pain and misery, and the convict began pacing up and down in the agony evoked by this dragging up of the past.

"I'm sorry I spoke," faltered Nic.

"No, no: I'm glad. It is like stabbing me, but if I bleed, boy, it is a relief. Transportation for twenty-one years, and to what a life of horror, misery, and despair! Companion to the greatest scoundrels and wretches that ever breathed; loathed and hated by them, because I was not what they, called their sort. Then, when sent out for good behaviour as an assigned servant, hated and scorned and trampled upon by every honest man. You have seen—you know. The convict from the chain gang, a branded felon. Nic, boy!—I beg your pardon, sir," he cried bitterly—"Master, your slave wonders sometimes that he is alive. I tell you I've prayed night after night for death, but it would not come: no spear, no blinding stroke from the sun, no goring by the half-wild bullocks which have chased me; no fall when I have desperately climbed down the side of that gorge. No! spite of all risk I have grown stronger, healthier, as you see—healthier in body, but more and more diseased in mind."

He stopped and threw himself down upon his breast, to bury his face in his hands; and just then there came a low, chuckling sound, as of laughter, from one of the great grey kingfishers in the tree above them, followed by a wild, dissonant, shrieking chorus from a flock of parrots, as if in defiance at the cruel laugh.

"I don't mind your speaking to me as you did, Leather," said Nic at last, as he turned his head aside to hide his emotion, and he sat down to watch his beautiful horse quietly cropping the grass, thinking how much happier the dumb beast was. "I only mind when you talk in your bitter way.—I'm sorry for you."

"God bless you, my lad!" said the convict, in smothered tones: "I know it. You've shown it to me a score of times. My life has not been the same since you came here."

"And I can't help seeing that you are sorry too. How could you have done so bad a thing?"

"I? Did that!" cried Leather, springing up on one arm. "I tell you I am innocent as a child. Dominic Braydon, mine was a high position, and large sums of money passed through my hands. There came a day when a heavy amount was missing. It was gone, I could not explain how. Everything seemed against me. My explanations were ridiculed, and until I had been out here a couple of years I could not see the light. It came one day, though, like a flash—when it was too late."

Nic looked at him inquiringly.

"My subordinate was the guilty man: the meek, amiable wretch who broke down in the witness-box and wept at being forced to tell all he knew. Even I believed and liked him at the time—poor weak fool that I was! If it imposed on me, who listened to every word he spoke, seeking for some way of escape, how could I wonder that judge, jury, and counsel were deceived? But it was too late when I read the truth, and that to save himself he sacrificed me—me who had helped him in every way."

"Then you really did not take this money?" cried Nic.

"Not one penny. I? But, there, why did you drag this all from me, boy? You made me speak. I do not say it to excite your sympathy. It is my fate, and I have tried to bear it like a man. I have borne it like a man, boy, though it has made me hard, callous, and brutal. Dead to all who knew and loved me, I have still lived, thinking that perhaps some day the truth may rise like the sun and throw its light around. Then I know it will be time to join the only one who believed me what I am."

"And who was that?" said Nic hoarsely.

"She who was to have been my wife. It was her death."

There was the hot stillness of the Australian midday around them, and for some time neither spoke.

Then all at once Leather sprang to his feet.

"There, sir," he said, "you are the first who has heard my tale. The law has branded me a convict, and I can only say 'Please let all this be as if it had never been said.' And yet I don't know," he continued, with his eyes softening; "it has done me good. Still I don't ask you to believe me, sir. There is plenty of deceit out here, and I have met some clever actors of innocent parts in the different gangs."

"But I do believe you," cried Nic earnestly — "every word. Oh, I felt that you could not have been so bad."

"Thank you, my lad," said the convict, smiling; and Nic thought what a fine, handsome, manly fellow he was when his face lit up. "No: I cannot shake hands. Some day, perhaps. I should like to help you, not drag you down. It is master and servant, you know. Yes," he added, after a pause, as he gazed earnestly in Nic's eyes, "you do believe me. There, I shall work more easily now, for life is brighter than it was."

He sprang to his feet now, and moved to go, but came back.

"We were forgetting the execution of the poisonous snake, sir," he said, with a little laugh. "This way."

"No," said Nic quietly; "let it live another day."

He walked to his horse, lifted the rein and threw it over the animal's neck, then sprang upon its back.

"Master Nic!"

"Yes."

"This is our secret, sir, and you must keep your place."

"Secret? Why shouldn't I tell my mother and father that you were condemned for that which you did not do?"

"I'll tell you, sir," cried Leather. "Because they cannot listen with your ears, nor see me with your eyes."

"My father is everything that is just," said Nic proudly, "and my mother all that is gentle and true."

"God bless her! yes, my boy," said the convict softly; "but if you speak, Mrs Braydon, knowing me for what I am, will say, 'This man has wormed himself into my son's confidence—he has obtained an influence over him that is not healthy—he had better go,' and I should be exchanged, Master Nic, as they would exchange a horse or bullock. Don't speak, sir, and have me sent away!"

Nic looked in the pleading eyes, and saw that the man's lips were quivering from the strong emotion which animated him.

"Our secret, then," he said; and at a touch of the heel the horse bounded away, with its rider feeling that every word the convict had spoken must be the truth.

Chapter Twenty Five
Nic Takes the Helm

"Bad news," said the doctor, about a couple of months' shepherding and track riding later, as he held a letter out to his wife before coming to where a couple of men were carefully rubbing down the heated horses they had hitched up to the fence kept for the purpose.

"Come in, my lads," he said. "I'll have your horses seen to. They must have a couple of hours' rest. There'll be a meal ready for you directly."

"What is it, mother?" said Janet and Hilda; and Nic looked at her eagerly.

"It is bad news indeed," said Mrs Braydon. "The letter is from Lady O'Hara, who is in the deepest distress about Sir John. She says he is dying, and that there is only one man in the colony she believes able to cure him."

"Father!" cried Hilda, flushing.

"Yes, my dear; and she begs that he will come to her in her great distress. Here he is."

For the doctor, after showing the men round to the stable, where they preferred to attend to their horses themselves, re-entered the room.

"Well, my dear, what do you think? Lady O'Hara forgets that I have not practised for so long."

"Lady O'Hara knows that she has spoken the truth," said Mrs Braydon proudly.

"Then you wish me to go?"

"No," said Mrs Braydon sadly; "but it is a duty you must fulfil."

"It means going and leaving you all in a couple of hours' time," said the doctor.

"Yes, you must go at once," sighed Mrs Braydon.

"Yes, I must go," said the doctor. "Perhaps I can save him." Then cheerfully, "Now, Nic, my boy, you must step into my shoes and play the man. I leave the Bluff and all that is dear in your charge. You manage old

Samson and Brookes better than I do, and as for Leatherhead he has become twice the man he was since you have been here."

Nic flushed a little, for the secret pricked him.

"And I am glad to see, my lad, that you keep him in his place with a tight rein. I was afraid at first, and Brookes dropped a few unpleasant hints about the way he said that you were making friends with him. I am glad to see, however, that all this is at an end."

"But, father—" began Nic, whose conscience was uneasy.

"No, no: I don't want to hear any explanation. You will do your best, I know. Now help me to pack my saddle-bags, all of you. See to the gun and ammunition, Nic; hobbles for the horse, and what is necessary. Hilda, my dear, haul the meal bags in, and see that we have plenty of flour, tea, and sugar for our ride, What's the matter, mamma dear?"

"I—I was thinking about the blacks," said Mrs Braydon nervously; and then, in an apologetic tone; "You made me speak, dear."

"Yes, and I'm glad you have. The blacks for miles and miles are friendly to us, for we have done them no harm. There is not the smallest likelihood of any evil-disposed tribe coming near. If one did, you have a brave son and trusty men to defend you till one of our own fellows went over to Mr Dillon's for help. Now are you satisfied?"

"Yes, my dear, quite."

"And Janet and Hilda, both of them to fight for their mother, if there is need."

"Of course," said Hilda merrily.

"Janet had better use the poker," said the doctor, taking his cue from his younger daughter, and laughing too, so as to hide the pang he felt at the near-at-hand parting.

"You know I can fire a gun, father," said Janet.

"To be sure: yes," said the doctor. "But, Hilda, my dear," he continued, "if you have to shoot at a blackfellow, be sure and remember that it is the wooden stock you hold to your shoulder, not the muzzle of the gun."

"Oh, father, what a shame!" cried Hilda. "Did I point the stock at that big hawk I shot for coming and stealing my beautiful little chickens?"

"No: I remember now. But bustle! those men want a good tea meal."

Two hours had not elapsed when, with the two government messengers well refreshed, and their horses dry and ready for a long afternoon's work, saddle-bags and blankets strapped on, guns and ammunition ready, the doctor sprang upon his horse, and Nic moved toward Sorrel, whose rein was thrown over a post, the boy meaning to ride a few miles of the way.

But the doctor took his hand.

"No," he said; "your place is here. Keep about the station, except when you take your daily rides round to see to the stock. I leave you in charge, my boy, so take care. I'll be back at the earliest moment I can."

The next minute he had embraced Mrs Braydon, touched his horse's sides, and cantered off after the men, turning twice to wave his hat to the watchers by the door.

Chapter Twenty Six
"When the Cat's Away"

The girls, seeing how pale and depressed Mrs Braydon looked at breakfast next morning, began by way of a diversion to banter their brother by solemnly asking him for orders—whether he was going to be very strict and severe in his rules; whether he intended to put the station in a state of defence, and drill them or train them in the use of their weapons.

Nic took it all in good part, as he made an excellent breakfast, his appetite being sharpened by two hours' busy work with the men and inspecting some of the stock, ending by finding for the three Englishmen tasks that required performing close about the house, and others for the three blacks, who had promised to be very industrious while the master was away, were also found close at hand.

"They'll all be here if wanted," Nic confided to his sister Janet; "for I must go a very long round to drive in some of the cattle on the far run. Father meant to have gone with me to-day."

"It is hardly necessary to be so particular, dear," said Janet; "but it will make mother more comfortable. I don't think I would say that you are going far."

"No, I did not mean to," replied Nic. "I shall go round and see that the men are at work all right, and then mount and be off just as if I were only going a little way."

"When will you be back?"

"About three or four o'clock at the latest."

Directly after breakfast he went and saw that the men were at work, said a word or two of praise to the blacks, whose faces shone with satisfaction; then going to the stable he saddled his horse, led it to the fence while he fetched his gun, mounted and rode off, unconscious of the fact that Brookes, who was busy in the wood-shed, was watching him.

Samson also rested upon his spade in the garden, and gazed with a smile at the lithe, active lad as he cantered easily away, looking as if he and the beautiful little highly bred horse were one.

Then Leather caught sight of the lad, and his face darkened, as he felt low-spirited and had an intense longing to go with him somewhere far away from the work about the station.

Just at the same moment Bungarolo, who had been busy weeding, raised his keen eyes, noted the direction Nic had taken, gave his trousers a hitch, grinned, dropped upon his chest, and began to creep rapidly like a slug toward the gate in the fence, through which he passed, and continued his way to where the other two blacks were busy cleaning out the cow-shed.

What followed did not take long. There was a whispered jabbering, a happy grin upon each face, and then, as if by one consent, the three blacks stripped off their shirts, unbuttoned and kicked off their trousers, and stood up in their native costume of a waistcloth.

The clothes were bundled together into a corner, three spears and as many nulla-nullas and boomerangs drawn from where they were tucked in the rafters, and the trio astonished a cow tied up in a corner with her tender calf by going through a kind of war dance, and all in silence.

Then the cow felt better in all probability, for there was no sign of the calf being stunned with a club to be cooked for a holiday, the performers of the dance stepping lightly to the door, out of which Bungarolo peered cautiously before dropping down upon his breast and crawling rapidly off to the garden fence, without disturbing the two collies, though Nibbler, who lay as if asleep, opened one eye, lifted his tail, and brought it down with a rap and closed the eye again.

He opened it, though, twice more as the other two blacks passed him in the same way, gave two more sharp raps with his tail, and then sniffed at the last black as if wondering how he would taste. But as he had had a pretty good piece of a drowned sheep, he subsided and closed the eye, not even turning his head to gaze after the three blacks as they glided on right under the fence on the side farthest from the house, and close by where old Sam was contentedly digging, in perfect unconsciousness that the three great children were off to the bush for a jovial day, hunting for fat grubs, honey, snakes, and other picnic delicacies in the glorious open wilds.

Half an hour had passed, during which Brookes went to the door of the wood-shed three times to scowl at Leather; but the convict was hard at work at the end of the wood-yard, chopping away at rails which he was splitting, tapering at the ends and piling on a heap, ready for some fencing that was to be done as soon as there was a little time.

Brookes felt ill-used. He would have liked to find the assigned servant yawning and doing nothing, or taking advantage of the master's absence to have a nap, and give him cause, as he was in his own estimation head man now, to let loose his tongue at the man he hated intensely.

But there was no excuse, and Brookes went back into the shed.

"I shall catch him yet," he muttered. "Only let him give me a chance."

But Brookes could not rest. He pitched the soft bundled-up fleeces about irritably, for they annoyed him. He wanted something hard, and growing more restless from a desire to show his authority, he went to where the two blacks should have been cleaning out the cow-shed.

Brookes had come out of the blinding sunshine, and the shed was dark and cool. He did not see the blacks, but he was not surprised, for their faces would naturally assimilate with the gloom.

"Here, you two," he growled, "nearly done?" an unnecessary question, for he knew that their task to be done thoroughly would take them some hours at their rate of working.

"Do you hear, you charcoal-faced beggars?" he shouted; but of course all was still, and satisfying himself, by picking up a manure fork, that they were not asleep in a heap of straw by jobbing the handle in savagely, after making an offer with the tines, he uttered a low growl, and, fork in hand, went out to look sharply round about the yards; but not a soul was in sight.

"Ah!" muttered Brookes, "that's it, is it? Cuss 'em, I might have known." Then, urged by a sudden thought, he went back into the long cow-shed, and looked round till he caught sight of the old trousers and shirts lying in a heap.

"Hah!" he ejaculated, shaking the fork handle, "just wait till they come back. I'll make them see stars."

Then, striding out, he made for the garden, where, with his sleeves rolled up and the neck and breast of his shirt open, old Samson was digging away, turning over the moist earth, and stooping every now and then to pick out some weed that was sure not to rot.

"Hi, Sam!" cried Brookes.

"Hullo!" said the little old fellow, going on with his digging, whistling softly the while.

"Where's Bungarolo?"

"Down yonder weeding."

"Nay," he cried.

"Yes, he is. I saw him ten minutes ago."

"He's started off with the other two."

"Nay!"

"He has, I tell you!" cried Brookes. "They've left their rags in the cow-shed, and all gone."

Samson showed his yellow teeth and chuckled.

"Just like 'em," he said; "just like 'em."

"I don't see anything to grin at," growled Brookes.

"Nay, you wouldn't, my lad; but I do. 'When the cat's away the mice will play.' I wonder they've stopped steady at work so long."

"What?"

"They're on'y big savage children, lad," said the old man, "and you can't alter 'em. ''Tis their natur' to.'"

"Natur' or no natur', they shan't play those games while I'm master here."

"Eh? Didn't know you was, Brooky."

"Then you know it now. P'r'aps you're going to give yourself a holiday."

"Having one," said the old man, breaking a refractory clod.

"And going to take yourself off to the bush to have a corroborree with the blackfellows."

"And if I was I shouldn't ask your leave, Snaggy," said the old man, showing more of his teeth. "There, let 'em go. They'll come back and work all the better after."

"Heugh!" cried Brookes, giving vent to a final grunt; and he turned away and stalked out of the garden, striking the fork-handle down at every step.

"Lookye here," said old Samson, taking up a spadeful of earth, and addressing it as if part of the dust of the earth of which he was made, and therefore worthy of his confidence: "sooner than I'd have old Brooky's nasty temper I'd be a kangaroo or a cat. I'm sorry they sloped off, though. Hang the black rascals! Master Nic'll be so wild, an' nat'rally, when he comes back."

Brookes turned and glared once at old Samson, who occupied the position about the place that he felt ought to be his; and, going straight back past the various sheds, he looked round toward the wood-yard, and then his eyes glistened with satisfaction. Short as the time had been, Leather had left his work.

He paused for a moment or two, to make sure that there was no regular *chop-chop* at the end of the rails, and with a grin of satisfaction he walked quickly to the spot where he had seen the convict at work.

He looked about the stacks of wood, stepping softly and peering round into shady corners, expecting and hoping to see his fellow-servant asleep; but he was disappointed, and five minutes elapsed before the convict came back, axe in hand.

"Seen either of the blacks about, Mr Brookes?" he said.

"Why?" snarled Brookes.

The convict looked surprised, but he said gently: "I want one of them to come and turn the grindstone handle. This axe is getting very dull."

"You lie, you lazy hound!" roared Brookes. "I've had my eye upon you. Your master's out, and so you think you're going to skulk, do you? If there's any more of it, over you go to Dillon's for a taste of the cat."

The blood flushed through the convict's bronzed skin and his eyes glistened, but only for a moment, and he said quite gently, for he saw Nic in his mind's eye: "It was the simple truth. I was wasting time."

"Yes, I know you were wasting time!" roared Brookes. "You're always wasting time, and I won't have it. Your master's out, and I won't have it. Get on. I'll have that pile o' rails done before you leave off to-night; so no more shirking, do you hear?"

A feeling of fierce resentment made the convict's nerves quiver; but he thought of Nic, and, controlling his anger, he took a step or two to the block on which he cut the rails, picked up one, and gave it a couple of chops.

"Quicker there, lout!" roared Brookes; "and none of your sulky looks with me."

The convict took up another rail, while Brookes stood over him with the fork-shaft playing up and down in his hand; while, emboldened by the other's meekness, he went on with a brutal tirade of abuse, calling up every insulting expression he could think of, and garnishing them with bad language, till the convict winced as if under blows.

"Trying to humbug me with your lying gammon about the axe. It's as sharp as sharp."

"It is not, sir," cried the convict, angrily now. "Take it and judge for yourself."

He held it out so quickly that Brookes started back, and brought down the fork-handle with all his might, striking the axe from the man's hand.

"What!" he roared. "Would you, you murderous dog? Take that—and that—and that!"

As he spoke he struck again savagely with the stout ash handle, the second blow falling heavily upon the convict's shoulder, the third coming sharply upon his head and making the blood spurt forth from a long deep cut.

Then the fork was raised for another blow; but, quick as lightning, the convict flung himself forward, and his fist, with all the weight of his body behind it, caught his assailant full in the face, sending him down to strike the back of his head against the edge of the wood block, and lie there yelling for help.

"Murder! help! Sam!" he roared, as he lay there, a ghastly object, with the convict's foot planted upon his chest, he too bleeding freely from the wound in his head.

At one and the same time Mrs Braydon, her daughters, and old Samson came running up in alarm.

"Here! what's the matter?" said the latter, while Mrs Braydon turned sick at the horrible sight, and caught at her elder daughter's hand.

"Can't you see what's the matter?" cried Brookes. "Get a gun, Sam, quick! He tried to murder me."

"No, no!" cried the convict, startled by the charge, and shrinking from the horrified and indignant-looking Mrs Braydon and the two girls.

"He did, missus," cried Brookes, struggling to his feet. "I had to speak to him for idling, and he struck at me with the axe. There it lies, and if I hadn't had this fork he'd ha' killed me. You see, he's most mad: why don't you get a gun, Sam?"

"I don't want no gun," said old Sam snappishly. "He didn't cut your head like that with the chopper, did he?"

"Yes, yes: look! I'm bleeding 'most to dead."

"Looks more as if you'd gone down on the block. There, missus: hadn't you and the young ladies best go indoors?"

"No; not yet," cried Mrs Braydon indignantly. "In my husband's absence too! Man, man, have you not been well treated here?"

"Yes, madam," said the convict hoarsely.

"Such an outrage—such a cruel outrage on Dr Braydon's trusted servant!"

"What he said, madam, is not true," cried the convict, recovering himself now from the giddiness produced by the stunning blow. "I did not, I could not raise the axe to him."

As he spoke he turned his eyes from Mrs Braydon to her daughters, and he shivered as he saw Janet's indignant look.

"I tell you he did," cried Brookes, holding the fork now threateningly, as soldiers would bayonets. "He tried to murder me. Sam, are you going to fetch a gun?"

"Yah! I'm going to fetch a bucket o' water if you won't do it yourself. Missus—young ladies, why don't you go? This ain't the place for you."

"No," said Mrs Braydon, taking Hilda's hand. "Come in, Janet."

But for a moment Janet did not stir, held as she was by the convict's imploring look as he said, addressing Mrs Braydon, though as if for her:

"Indeed, madam, it is not true. This man struck me brutally: I forgot myself—I did strike him in return."

"Yes," said Mrs Braydon coldly; and; uttering a sob, Janet gave the convict a reproachful look and followed her mother into the house.

Chapter Twenty Seven
Brookes Strikes Back

"That's better!" said old Sam. "The masters both out, and we're having a nice day here."

Leather stood as if turned to stone.

"Let's look at you," continued the old man, as he roughly spun Brookes round. "Where's yer 'ankycher?"

Brookes made a movement to seize the axe, but old Sam kicked it away.

"Let it alone, stoopid! What did you want to tell that lie for? He didn't hit you wi' that."

"I swear he did," cried Brookes fiercely.

"Then you'd swear anything," said Sam, binding up the rough cut. "But do you think I'm a fool? Any one can see that wasn't made with the edge of a chopper. Did he give you that lovely crack in the mouth with the chopper too?"

"I'll let him see—I'll let him see!"

"I wouldn't till I'd washed my face. Sarves you right: you're allus letting out at somebody. If I warn't a nat'ral angel in temper I should ha' let you have it years ago."

"I'll let him see—I'll let him see," muttered Brookes savagely.

"Better shake hands like a man," said old Sam.

"Convict or no convict, he's only give you what you asked for."

"I'll let him see," snarled Brookes; and he went off toward the stable.

"Gone there to one of the buckets," growled old Sam. "I was going to take you there. Here, let's have a look at your head."

"Oh, it's nothing—nothing," said Leather hastily.

"Nothing! when you're bleeding like a pig. Come along to the bothy, and let's bathe and tie it up. Why, Leather, this looks as if he'd used the axe! Reg'lar clean cut."

"No, it was with the fork handle. There, it will do me good. Let out some of the hot, mad blood."

"Ay," said old Sam, guiding him, for he staggered, to the men's bothy, and bathing and tying up the wound. "It's a pity, my lad. I wish you hadn't hit back, for you see if he should turn nasty and complain—"

Leather looked at him wildly.

"And him like that, there's no knowing what might come."

The convict uttered a groan, and caught the old man's arm.

"I'll say all I know, my lad; but you see—"

"Yes, yes," said Leather hoarsely, "I know"; and he sat there on a block of wood which served as a stool, while the old gardener finished the dressing.

"There, that's a spontanous bit o' grafting," he said, "and— 'Ullo! what's that mean?"

He turned to the doorway, through which they could see Brookes mounted upon one of the horses and cantering straight away.

"Leather, my lad," said the old man sharply, "he's our fellow-servant, but he's a cur. What'll you do, my lad? He's gone to Dillon's, for a silver pound; he'll make up his tale, and it means the cat."

Leather sank back against the wall, and gazed wildly toward the house.

"If it was me I'd take to the bush, and—"

"What! not face it out!" cried the convict fiercely. "Own that I was in the wrong! Not if they flog me and send me back to the gang."

The sudden excitement passed away, and the convict sank sidewise to the floor, perfectly insensible, for he had fainted dead away.

"And I thought I was going to have a good quiet day's gardening!" said old Sam. "There's hundreds o' things wants doing badly, and I'm 'bliged to give up my time to cultivate convicts. I wish to goodness the master was at home; then all this mess wouldn't ha' took place."

But as the old man muttered he kept on acting. Taking some fresh water, he bathed the convict's temples and tried hard to revive him.

"Give you a clean face if it don't give you a clean character, my lad. I don't like you because you're a convict, that's all. You're a good, manly sort o' chap, and if you'd ha' been a honest man I should ha' said you were as good a fellow to work as ever was. Nothing never comes amiss to you, and you and me never had a word in our lives. But you see you are one of the gang and a blackguard and a thief; not as you was ever a blackguard here, nor stole so much as one o' my taters, which I will say has been big enough and fine enough to tempt any man as was digging 'em, as you was. I know they tempted me, Leather, for I took a dozen nubbly ones and roasted 'em three at a time in a bit o' fire as Bungarolo made for me; but then I did grow them taters and had a sort o' right in 'em."

Old Sam left off talking to the insensible man, and looked at him anxiously as he kept on bathing his face.

"I don't want to be hard on you, my lad, even if you are a convict. 'Temptation sore long time you bore,' p'r'aps before you took it, and your head maybe wasn't as strong as your hands. But I say, are you a-coming to? None o' that nonsense! Here! Hi! Leather! Don't die! Don't be so stoopid as that just for a whack on the head as'll heal up in a fortnit."

He gave the insensible man a shake in his excitement, but it made no impression.

"What am I to do? If I goes and tells 'em at the house it'll frighten the women, and they can't do no good. They'd want to burn feathers under his nose. Here, Leather, rouse up, man; don't be a fool! D'yer hear? Wait till you get back to town, where you can be buried properly; don't die here!"

Sam began to mop and splash the water almost frantically, as the motionless features before him seemed to grow hard and stern.

"Well, I thought you had more good stuff in you, Leather—that I did," said the old man piteously. "I don't wish no harm to nobody, but I wish to goodness you were old Brookes lying here instead o' yourself, for he's the wiciousest warmint as ever lived. I never see things go so orkard: it's worse than locusts or blight. Master going off like that, too, just when he's wanted. Poor lad! and I can't do nothing for you, or I would. There, I don't care what you done, Leather," he said, "convict or no convict, I forgive you, whatever you did, and here's my fist."

He took the strong labour-hardened hand in his, and then dropped it hastily, for just as he pressed it there was a deep sigh and the convict opened his eyes to stare blankly in the old man's face. Then, as recollection came back, he struggled up into a sitting position, rose to his feet, and stood with one hand resting against the boarded side of the bothy.

"Come, that's better," said old Sam. "You're a-coming round now. I tell you what you do: just you lie down in your bunk and get a good sleep; you'll be all right then. I began to think as you'd had a lob just a bit too hard. Here, what are you going to do?"

"Go on with my work," said the convict.

"Yah! That's foolishness; you can't do it, Leather."

"I must," said the man gravely. "Thank you for what you've done, Samson. It was not true. I did not raise the axe against Brookes."

"I know that, my lad. He'd say anything when he's nasty. But I'm sorry you hit back—very sorry."

"Yes, I know," said the convict; and he walked slowly out of the low wooden building, and five minutes later the regular *chop, chop* of the axe was heard, and the rattle of rails as they were laid back in a heap.

"Well," said old Sam, "that's better than him being as I thought I suppose I may go on with my work now, and get that garden in a bit of order. Well, all I've got to say is this: if Brooky's gone to lay a complaint before the magistrate he's no man."

Man or no man, midday had not long passed before old Sam, as he raised himself up from his digging to give his back a bit of a rest, caught sight of a flash of something bright, and there was another flash—the sun glinting from the barrel of a gun; and turning his eyes, there about a mile away, spurring across country, he made out a party of five mounted men advancing at a trot.

The old man drove his spade savagely into the ground and trotted out of the garden and round to the wood-yard, where Leather was going on slowly and laboriously with his rail trimming.

"Leather, my lad," he said, in a quick whisper, "they're a-coming over the hill: hadn't you better go off for a month or two?"

"To be hunted down by the dogs and blacks?" said the convict bitterly. "No, old man; I shall get Justice Day, here or—in the next world."

"But, my lad," pleaded the old fellow, "they're close here."

"I am ready," said the convict quietly; and there was a pause.

Then he spoke again.

"Perhaps I shall be sent somewhere else, old man. I shall be marked as dangerous now, and not fit to be at a station where there are ladies. But you'll tell young Mr Nic the whole truth?—you know what I've had to bear."

"Ay, my lad, I do know."

"Thank you, Samson. You've always been a good fellow to me. Good-bye."

He passed the axe into his left hand and held out his right, but quickly placed the axe back and stood up firmly, as a heavily built, florid-looking man, mounted upon a fiery horse covered with foam, cantered up, followed by four more men, three of whom, like their leader, bore guns, while the fourth was Brookes with his head tied up, his face swollen, distorted, and still smeared with dried blood—altogether a horrible-looking object—but he sat his horse firmly enough.

As the leader rode up he lowered the gun he carried and spurred his hesitating horse close up to the convict, as if fully prepared to drive in the spurs and ride him down.

"Surrender!" he shouted. "Down with that axe, quickly, or I'll send a charge of buckshot through you."

Leather looked him straight in the eyes and threw down the axe.

"Here, Belton: handcuffs."

One of his men dismounted, handed his gun and rein to a companion, took a pair of heavy handcuffs from the strap which held his blanket to the saddle, and advanced to where the convict stood with folded arms.

These were dragged roughly apart, and *click!*—one iron was about a wrist. Then the other arm was seized, dragged downward, and *click!* the convict's wrists were secured behind his back, just as Mrs Braydon and her two daughters came hurrying out; and seeing what had taken place, Janet uttered a low cry, and would have fallen but for her sister's arm.

The convict saw it, and his lips quivered for a few moments. Then he stood up with his head erect, gazing straight before him.

"Mr Dillon!" cried Mrs Braydon.

"Your servant, my dear madam," said the new arrival, raising his hat as he rode forward. "Young ladies, yours. Don't be alarmed, Miss Braydon: there is no danger now. I am very sorry that this outrage has taken place in the doctor's absence. Your poor man rode over, and I came instantly.—Too glad to have been of service."

Mrs Braydon's lips moved, but no word was heard.

"Where is the young squire?" continued the visitor.

"My brother has gone out on a round, I suppose, Mr Dillon," said Hilda quickly. "But—but what are you going to do?"

"What a neighbour should, my dear young lady. What your father would do for me or any of our friends. See that wives and daughters are protected in every way."

Then, turning quickly, he rode back a few yards.

"Go on, my lads," he said to his followers. "I'll overtake you directly."

The man who had handcuffed Leather loosened one end of a hide rope from his saddle-bow, and secured it to the irons on the convict's wrists.

"Say, Mr Dillon, sir," said old Sam, who had been dividing his time between scowling at Brookes and watching what was going on. "That there poor chap can't walk ten mile over to your place. He's only just come out of a swound."

"Indeed!" said the visitor, with a laugh. "We shall see. Now forward!"

The little procession moved off; Belton first, with his prisoner, and the two others with their guns across their saddle-bows following.

Then Mr Dillon rode back to the ladies.

"I am very sorry, Mrs Braydon. I wish you had kept away from this painful scene."

"Yes, it is very terrible," said the trembling woman. "But—it was in a fit of passion, I suppose, Mr Dillon. You will not be very severe?"

"I have a duty as a magistrate to perform, ladies, and I must be just. Your man has been barbarously attacked; and living as we do with these convict servants about, more in number in places than we are ourselves, any hesitation would be stamped by them as weakness, and our very existence would be at stake."

"But he has always been a good, hard-working man, Mr Dillon," pleaded Janet.

"And so long as he behaved, my dear Miss Braydon, the government said, 'You can have almost your freedom.' He and other assigned servants know the bargain with the government. Good behaviour—liberty; bad behaviour—punishment."

"But till my husband returns," faltered Mrs Braydon, "you will wait?"

"These things cannot wait, madam. The law here must be administered firmly and sharply."

"But you will investigate the case?"

"It has been investigated, Mrs Braydon," said Mr Dillon stiffly. "Your man came to me, with witnesses who cannot lie, branded upon his face. Ladies, I respect your gentle, merciful feelings; but if you had the governance here, in a short time the Crown Colony would be a pandemonium, ruled over by a president too vile to live."

"Hear him!" growled Brookes.

"D'yer want me to kick yer?" whispered old Samson savagely.

"But you will wait? Keep him a prisoner for a time, Mr Dillon," pleaded Mrs Braydon, as she saw her elder daughter's agonised look.

"My dear madam, I must study your husband and the commonweal of this colony," said the magistrate firmly. "Good morning."

"But—you wish refreshments?" faltered Mrs Braydon.

"Some other time, madam. My visit now must be very painful to you all."

He raised his hat, spurred his horse, and galloped off after his men; while, as Mrs Braydon stood gazing after him, Janet uttered a low wail, flung her arms about her sister's neck, and whispered, "Take me in, dear. I cannot bear it, take me in."

"Janet, my child!" cried Mrs Braydon; and in an agony of suffering she helped to lead the agitated girl into the house, while old Sam trotted off into the stable, and came back with a halter in his hand to where Brookes stood, shading his swollen-up eyes with one hand, holding the rein of his horse with the other.

"Thank ye, mate," he said, as he saw the halter, "but I dunno as I want it. Take the horse in for me; I want a wash. Don't s'pose Mr Leatherhead'll hit at me again."

"Yes," said old Sam in a husky voice, "I'll take the poor horse. Here, ketch hold. How are you a-going to face Master Nic when, he comes back?"

"Face him!" cried Brookes savagely: "I'll face him and show him what his fav'rite has done. He shall see my face, and then he may go and look at his convict's back and see how he likes that."

"Here, ketch hold," cried old Sam, shaking the rope.

"Tell you I don't want it," cried Brookes savagely.

"And I tell you you do," said the old man fiercely. "Take it and go right off to the first big green bough in the bush."

"What for?" cried Brookes, with his swollen eyelids opening wide.

"To use it—on yourself; for such a man as you ain't fit to live."

Chapter Twenty Eight
And all in Vain

"Cooey—cooey!" shouted Nic, as he came cantering up over the soft, fine grass a couple of hours later toward the house; but no one was in sight, and he turned off toward the stables just as Brookes came out of the wool-shed.

"Why, hullo! What's the matter? Had a fall?"

"Had a fall!" cried the man savagely. "Look here." But old Sam had been watching for his young master's return, and he hurried up.

"Won't you listen to me, Master Nic?" he cried. "Let me tell the tale."

"Nic! Nic! come here quick!" cried Hilda, running from the house.

The boy looked wildly from one to the other, threw the rein to old Sam, and ran to his sister.

"Hil dear, what is the matter?—mother?" For answer she threw her arms about her brother's neck, and sobbing out told him all.

"And Janet—fits of hysterics?"

"Yes; I don't understand her, Nic. Mother can't leave her. What shall you do?"

"Go in to them!" said Nic firmly; and giving his sister a push toward the house, he ran back to where the two men stood growling at each other and the horse impatiently stamping as it stood between them and tugged to get away.

"Here you, Brookes," cried Nic imperiously, "tell me how it happened."

"He was as nasty as nasty, because the blacks—" began old Sam.

"Silence!" roared Nic. "I did not speak to you." Old Sam started in amazement, for it seemed to be a strong man speaking, not a boy.

"Now you, Brookes."

Brookes told the same tale he had told Mr Dillon when he rode over to Wattles Station, embellishing it with cuts—that is to say, showing his wounds.

"No chopper would make a place like that!" cried Nic fiercely. "I don't believe a word of it, you brute. It's a lie."

"So it is, Master Nic," cried Sam, showing his teeth. "He give it to the poor fellow brutal."

"Tell me, then—all you know. Quick, man, quick!"

"Oh, if father had been at home!" as soon as he had heard the old man's tale. Then snatching the rein, he threw it over Sorrel's head, touched the beautiful little creature's sides and went off at a gallop.

"Who's that?" cried Janet, starting up wildly as the hoofs were heard beating on the turf.

"Nic!" cried her sister, running to the window to look out. "He has gone off at a gallop."

"Gone!" cried Mrs Braydon—"and at a time like this!"

"He has galloped off. I know: he has gone over to save that poor fellow."

Janet uttered a low sigh, and as Mrs Braydon turned to her wonderingly the poor girl fainted away.

Meanwhile, urged now as he had never been urged before, by voice and heel, Sorrel forgot his long morning's ride, and stretching out like a greyhound skimmed over the soft turf like a swallow in its flight.

Nic rode on with his heart a prey to varying emotions. He knew perfectly well that the convict's fate would be that of all unruly assigned servants. He had heard it from old Sam again and again,—how that if Jack did not behave well, he was sent by his master to another station, where he would have so many dozen lashes of the cat-o'-nine-tails and be sent back; while another time Joe, who had behaved ill at that next station, was sent across to the first. So the masters avoided the administration of punishment to their own men, but punished those of their neighbours. It was the rough-and-ready custom in the early days of the colony, and common enough for small offences. Where a convict servant's offence became a crime, he was returned to the prisons—marked.

To Nic, then, it was horrible that the man for whom he had gradually grown to feel a warm sense of friendship should suffer this horrible indignity. It would be, he felt, an outrage; for he was as fully convinced as if he had been present that Leather had been maddened by Brookes's ill usage until he struck him down.

The boy felt old as he galloped on in the direction of the Wattles Station. He had never been there, but he knew it lay some ten or a dozen miles away to the north, and he hoped to find it by riding on and on till he came upon flocks of sheep, and then going up some one or other of the eminences, and looking about till he caught sight of white buildings, which would be the place. This would come the easier from the fact that stations were built close to water, but high enough up to be beyond the reach of floods.

When he had gone three or four miles he began to repent not bringing Nibbler, who would, in all probability, have been there in his time, and consequently might take it for granted, when going in that direction, that his young master was aiming at this place. But in his excitement he had thought of nothing but getting over there; and faint, hungry and hot, he began now to find that he had done a foolish thing.

A chill ran through him at the idea of missing the place, and he was about to change his direction and ride up a hill to his left; when it suddenly struck him that after once starting he had done nothing in the way of guiding his horse, which kept right on in one direction, merely deviating to avoid great trees or patches of scrub.

Then he uttered a joyful cry, for gazing down he could see hoof marks faintly on the thick grass, and it dawned upon him that these were quite fresh, and the horse was following them as steadily as if going along a main road.

Elated by this he slackened the rein just sufficiently to feel the horse's mouth, and left it to itself. And then it galloped in its easy, swinging pace, with its rider leaning forward, heart-sick where the footprints were invisible, and exultant as he caught sight of them again and again, after feeling that all was over and the trail entirely lost.

"If I only were clever as one of the blacks," he thought. "Bungarolo, Rigar, or Damper would follow the faintest trail."

But their services were needless here. The sorrel nag had been to the Wattles more than once before its young master's time, and, besides, its natural instinct led it to gallop along where its fellows had been before.

Two great ostrich-like birds started up from right and left, and though he had not come across them before Nic knew that they must be emus; but he only glanced at them as they raced away, with the rapid motion of their legs making them almost as invisible as the spokes of a running wheel. Twice over, too, he saw a drove of kangaroos, which went flying over the bushes in their tremendous leaps; but they excited no interest now. He must get to the Wattles soon, or he would be too late.

It was a long ten miles—more probably twelve—and Nic's heart was low, for he seemed to have been riding three hours, and he began to fear that the horse would go on following tracks until rein was drawn, so he stopped; when all at once, as they turned a clump of magnificent gum trees standing alone upon a beautiful down, there below him, and not a mile away, was the place he sought—a group of buildings, with the sheep and cattle dotting the country as far as his eye could range.

And now he checked his horse's speed to a gentle canter, and thought of what he should do.

He knew that he would be most welcome as a stranger, much more so as Dr Braydon's son; so he rode straight up to the fence, leaped down, and hitched his rein over a post close to where several saddles rode upon a rail, and was going up to the door of the house, when Mr Dillon himself appeared, and came to meet him with a friendly nod.

"Dr Braydon's son, for a wager!" he cried.

"Yes," said Nic; and before he could say another word the big, bluff-looking squatter shouted:

"Hi, Belton! Come and rub down and feed Mr Braydon's nag. Now, my lad, come in. We're just going to have a meal, and you must be hungry after your ride."

Nic was hungry after his ride, which was a far longer one than Mr Dillon guessed, for the boy had had nothing since the morning, and the mention of food struck a responsive chord in his breast. But he had not come to visit, and, flushing slightly, he spoke out at once, plunging boldly into the object of his coming, though he felt that the magistrate knew.

"Thank you, no, Mr Dillon," he said. "I have come over about our man."

"So I supposed," said Mr Dillon, smiling; "but we can talk as we eat."

"I can't at a time like this, sir," said Nic. "I've come for him, please, to take him back with me."

"Indeed!" said Mr Dillon, smiling. "Do you know all that happened?—while you were out, I presume?"

"Yes, everything, sir, and how you were misinformed."

"Misinformed, was I?" said Mr Dillon pleasantly. "I think not."

"But you were, sir, indeed. I know both the men so well."

"I suppose so, my lad. Let me see, you have been in the colony quite a short time?"

"Yes; but I've seen a great deal of them," cried Nic, whose face burned with annoyance at the magistrate's look of amusement.

"And you are, of course, a good judge of convict servants?"

"I know nothing about any but our own men, sir. But I have heard everything, sir, and I am sure that our man Leather does not deserve to be punished. It would be unjust."

"You think so?"

"Yes, sir: I'm sure of it."

"And you want to take him back with you?"

"If you please, sir—now. I know the man so well, and I am certain that I can answer for there being no more trouble."

"That's speaking broadly, my boy," said Mr Dillon, slapping Nic on the shoulder; "but comes tea—dinner's ready, and we can continue our argument as we have it."

Nic shook his head.

"I couldn't eat, sir, with that poor fellow in such trouble," he said.

"Well, that's very kind and nice of you, my boy," said Mr Dillon, "and I like you for it; but come now, let's be reasonable. You see, I am the magistrate of this district, but I want to talk to you, not like a man of law, only as your father's friend and neighbour."

"Yes, I felt that you would, sir," said Nic, who was encouraged.

"Your father has, I suppose, left you in charge of his station?"

"Yes, sir."

"Well, boys out here have to act like men, and I like your manly way about this business. You came back, found out the trouble, and rode over directly to set it right?"

"Yes, sir—exactly."

"That's all very right and just; only as a man of long experience, young Braydon, you see, I know better how to manage these troubles than you possibly can—a lad fresh over from school."

"Yes, sir, I suppose so," said Nic, "in most cases; but I do know our man better than you."

"You think so, my lad; but you are wrong. He was my servant first."

"Still, you will let our man come back with me, sir?"

"In your father's absence, my boy, I have too much respect for him, too much interest in the safety of your mother and sisters, to send back unpunished a desperate man."

"Don't say that, sir. You don't know Leather indeed."

"'Nothing like Leather,'" said Mr Dillon, smiling. "Yes, I should think he was a great favourite of yours. But, come now, my boy; you have done your part well. Here, come in and have a good meal. Your man has done what many more of these fellows do—broken out in a bit of savagery. He is shut up safely in yonder, too much done up for me to say anything to him to-night; but tomorrow morning he will be tamed down a bit, and kept for three or four days to return to his senses, and then he will come back and go on with his work like a lamb."

"Mr Dillon, you don't know him, sir!" cried Nic earnestly. "Such a cruel act would drive the poor fellow mad."

"I know him, and I know you, my boy. There, you are young and enthusiastic; but I see, plainly enough, you have been too much with this fellow. There, frankly, you have been with him a good deal?"

"Yes, sir," said Nic.

"Precisely. And he has not corrupted you, but he has made you believe that he is an injured, innocent man. Frankly, now, is it not so?"

"Yes, and I do believe," said Nic quietly.

"Exactly. Well, my dear boy, you see I do not; and if you will take my advice you will have nothing to do with him in the future."

"Mr Dillon, you are mistaken," cried Nic. "Pray—pray do not punish him!"

"My dear young friend, pray—pray don't you interfere with a magistrate's duties."

"Then you will not let him come, sir?"

"Certainly not, for at least a week."

"But, Mr Dillon, promise me that—that you—you will not flog him," said Nic, in a husky whisper.

"I promise you, my good lad, that tomorrow morning I shall have him out in front of my men and my four assigned servants—convicts, and have him given a good sound application of the cat. Now that business is settled in a way that ten years hence you will agree is quite just; so come in like a sensible young neighbour, have a good feed, and I'll ride part of the way back with you after."

"Do you mean this, sir?" said Nic hoarsely.

"I always say what I mean, boy, and act up to it. Once more, come in."

Nic walked straight to where the man was rubbing down his horse, stopped him, picked up and girthed his saddle, saw to the bridle, and then mounted, while Mr Dillon stood watching him, half amused, half angry.

Then a thought struck Nic, and he bent down as if to reach the cheek-piece of the bit, and slipped a shilling into the man's hand.

"Where's our man shut up?" he whispered.

"In the big shed behind the house," said the man, staring.

Then at a touch Sour Sorrel started off.

"Going now?" shouted Mr Dillon.

Nic raised his hand to his hat as he galloped off, but he did not turn his head.

"The conceited young puppy!" cried Mr Dillon angrily, as he watched the boy's receding form; "and he wouldn't eat bread and salt. He deserves to be flogged himself for his obstinacy. I don't know, though: I wish I'd had a boy like that."

He re-entered the house, and Nic rode on homeward, the slowest, saddest ride he had had since he entered the colony, for as soon as he was out of sight of the house he drew rein and let Sorrel walk.

Chapter Twenty Nine
A Night's Work

"What shall I do?" said Nic to himself.

Being faint, and feeling half stunned, no answer came; and he looked round at the beautiful country, which appeared newer and more beautiful than ever in the orange-gold of approaching evening, while all within was black with misery and despair.

He never knew before how much he liked the stern, manly fellow who that next morning was to be tied up and flogged; and the more Nic thought of the horrible punishment the deeper grew his misery, as he felt what a helpless boy he was in the matter; and a number of wild plans began to enter his head.

He had no gun with him now, but he could ride back, fetch it, and wait till morning. Then he would ride up to the Wattles just when they were going to tie up Leather, take his place beside him, and, with presented gun, dare any one to touch his father's servant.

Then the weak tears came into the boy's eyes, and he laughed a piteous, contemptuous laugh at himself for harbouring such a silly, romantic notion.

And all the while Sorrel went on at his steady walk, growing cool and comfortable, refreshed too by the light feed he had had and the rub down.

They went slowly on till sunset, when Nic drew rein, and sat gazing at the large orange ball sinking away beyond the mountains.

"So beautiful!" he said, forced into admiration of the glories of the coming evening; "and poor Leather lying there handcuffed and waiting to be flogged."

He leaped from his horse and threw the rein over its head.

"There!" he cried, patting the soft arched neck, "eat away, old chap. You needn't be miserable if I am. I can't go and leave poor Leather like this."

He threw himself down on the grass to think—to try and make out some plan, while the birds winged their way overhead back to their roosting places, and here and there the kangaroos and their many little relatives began to steal out of the woodland shelters they had affected through the heat of the day, to lope about like huge hares, look around for danger, and then begin to browse.

At first the only idea that would come to the boy was that he would wait there till daybreak, and then ride the three or four miles he had come in his homeward direction back to the Wattles, getting there in good time; and when the preparations were being made for punishment he would ride boldly up and make a final appeal to Mr Dillon to either let Leather off or to defer everything till the doctor returned.

"Poor Leather!" he said to himself: "he'll see that I have not deserted him."

Crop, crop, crop; the horse went on browsing away upon the rich grass, but keeping close at hand, as if liking its master's company, and raising its head now and then to whinny softly.

The sun had gone down, and the glorious tints were dying out on and beyond the mountains. Then a great planet began to twinkle in the soft grey of the west, which rapidly grew of a dark purple, lit up again with a warm glow and grew purple once more, with the planet now blazing like a dazzling spot of silver hung high in the heavens.

Soon after, it would have been dark but for the glorious display of golden stars which now encircled the vast arch overhead, far more beautifully in that clear air than Nic ever remembered to have seen at home.

And all this splendour of the heavens made him the more miserable, for it seemed to him as if at such a time everything ought to be dark and stormy.

The night birds were out, and strange cries, wails, and chuckling noises reached his ears, mingled with the whirr and whizz of crickets and the soft pipe and croak of frogs in and about a water-hole not far away.

Once or twice, half startled, Nic thought he saw dusky, shadowy figures stealing along, and his heart beat fast; but he soon told himself that it was all fancy, for if any one had approached the horse would have been alarmed, whereas it was close at hand cropping the grass contentedly, its loud puff of breath with which it blew away insects upon the grass sounding regular in its intervals.

It was restful lying there, but Nic's faintness increased, and he was glad to pick a few leaves and blades of grass to chew and keep down the famished feeling which troubled him. But that calm night-time was glorious for thought, and before long he had determined that, come what might, he would wait for another hour or two and ride back to the Wattles and set Leather free.

For he knew whereabouts the convict was imprisoned. The man who attended to Sorrel had said it was behind the house. Then what could be easier than to ride round, and, close up, find which was the big shed, and give Leather a signal; and then, with one working outside, the other in, it would be easy enough. Why, if he could not get the wooden bar away with which these big sheds were mostly fastened, he could guide Sorrel alongside, stand on the saddle, and remove some of the bark or shingle roofing.

Nic forgot hunger, misery, and despair in the glow of exultation which came over him, and he felt contempt for his readiness to give up and think that all was over.

"More ways of killing a cat than hanging it," he said, with a little laugh, and lying upon his back in a thoroughly restful position he set himself to watch the stars, till all at once they turned blank, and he leaped to his feet in alarm and went to pat his horse.

"That won't do," he muttered. "Done up, I suppose, and it was the lying on my back and leaving off thinking. But I couldn't have slept for many minutes."

For the matter of that the time might have been two or three hours, for aught he could have told; but as it was he had not been asleep a minute when he sprang back into wakefulness, and, determined now not to run any more risks, he stopped with his horse, resting against its flank and thinking of what a great solitary place he was in, and how strange it seemed for that vast country to have so few inhabitants.

His aim was to wait until everybody would be asleep at the Wattles, and then ride softly up, when he felt that there would be light enough for his purpose, which ought not to take long.

The time glided away slowly, but at last he felt that he might start, and after seeing that the bridle was all right he proceeded to tighten the girths. But Sorrel had been pretty busy over that rich grass, and Nic found that if he did anything to those girths he ought to let them a little loose.

"You greedy pig!" he said, patting the horse affectionately, "eating away like that and enjoying yourself when your master starves."

The horse whinnied.

"Ah! don't do that," said Nic in alarm. "You would spoil everything."

He mounted and cantered back for a good two miles, finding no difficulty, for the horse went over the same ground again. Then Nic drew rein and walked on and on till he thought he must have missed the place in the dark; but all at once below him he saw a faint light move for a few moments, and disappear.

Evidently a lantern which some one had carried into the house.

Nic checked his horse for quite a quarter of an hour, and then walked it slowly down the slope, till there, dimly showing up before him, he could make out building after building, looming all dim and ghostly-looking, but plain enough to one whose eyes had grown accustomed to the dark.

But there were fences to avoid, and there was an enclosed garden; so the boy felt that the wisest plan would be to take a pretty good circuit round and then go up to the back.

Starting to do this, he was very nearly thrown, for Sorrel suddenly made a tremendous bound and cleared a large tree trunk, which had been felled and lay denuded of all its branches right across his way.

This was a shock; and it had other effects, for at the heavy beat of hoofs a deep-mouthed dog suddenly set up a tremendous bark, which was taken up by half a dozen more in chorus, accompanied by the rattling of chains in and out of kennels.

Nic paused, with his heart beating, but the barking went on, and a voice was heard to shout faintly:

"Lie down!"

But the dogs still barked, and a window was opened and a loud voice, which Nic recognised, shouted:

"Hullo! What is it, my lads?"

The barking turned to a burst of whimpering and whining, and after a few sharp commands to lie down Nic heard the window closed; and the rattling of the dogs' chains began again, a whimper or two, and then all was silent once more.

Meanwhile Nic had peered carefully round, and became aware of the fact that there were several pieces of timber lying about, as if a group of trees had been felled where he stood, and cautiously dismounting and leading his horse, he began to guide it out of the dangerous place.

But he had hardly achieved this when the barking broke out again, making Nic mount and ride slowly off, while the window was once more thrown open, and the voice the boy had recognised as the magistrate's cried sharply:

"What is it there, boys?" the dogs barking wildly in reply.

Just then a shrill whistle rang out, and directly after a man shouted.

"All right, sir, here!"

"What's the matter with the dogs, Belton?"

"Dunno, sir. Dingo, perhaps."

"Or something else. Here: go and see if that scoundrel's all right."

"He's all right, sir. I've been twice. Just come from there now."

"Humph! That's right, my lad. But they seem very uneasy."

"Well, yes, sir, they do," said the man; "but they often have a fit like this. Lie down, will yer!"

There was a general rattling of chains at this, while every word had come distinctly to Nic's ears in the soft silence.

"Good night."

"Good night, sir."

There was shutting of the window, and then the man said slowly:

"I'll bring a whip round to some on yer directly. Hold yer row!"

One dog barked as if protesting.

"Quiet, will yer!" cried the man. "Think nobody wants to sleep?"

Then silence, an uneasy rattle of a chain, the banging of a door, and Nic wiped the perspiration from his brow.

The case seemed hopeless, but he would not give up. Twice over he tried to get round to the back of the house, but the dogs were on the alert; and the last time, just as he drew rein closer than he had been before, the window was opened, two flashes of light cut the darkness, and there came the double report of a gun, making Sorrel bound and nearly unseat his rider.

"See any one, sir?" cried the man, hurrying out.

"No; but I'm sure there's some one about. Get your gun. I'll be down directly, and we'll keep watch."

The window closed, and Nic heard the man growl at the dogs:

"You've done it now. Keep watch, eh? But I'll pay some on yer to-morrow."

The dogs burst out barking again, for Nic was guiding his horse away in despair, feeling that he could not accomplish his task; then he waited till he was a few hundred yards distant, and cantered on, feeling that in all probability some of the dogs would be loosened and come after him.

As he rode he listened, and there was the yelping as of a pack, making him urge Sorrel into a gallop; but the sounds died out, and at the end of a mile he drew rein, for there was no suggestion of pursuit.

Nic walked his horse beneath one of the great trees, and sat there like a statue, thinking, and trying hard to come to some determination. To get at the building where Leather was imprisoned was not the easy task he had thought. In fact, he felt now, that with all those dogs about, that he had not noticed the previous afternoon, when they were probably away with the shepherds, it was impossible.

"What shall I do?" he said to himself again; and he cudgelled his brain in the hope of some idea coming, but all in vain.

And so a good hour passed, when, sick and in despair, he determined to make one more essay, for he argued, with a bitter smile, "The dogs may be asleep." At any rate he would try, and if he failed he would ride up in the morning, and they should not flog the poor fellow while he was there.

"Yes," he said, "the dogs may be asleep; but suppose Mr Dillon or his men are keeping watch."

He had put his horse in motion, and was riding out of the black shadow, but drew rein sharply, and Sorrel stopped short, for away in the distance came the loud yelping and baying of dogs in pursuit of something, just as he had heard them in the Kentish woods at home when laid on the scent of a fox, but not with the weird, strange sound heard now on the night air.

"What does it mean?" thought Nic, as his heart seemed to stand still and then began to beat with heavy throbs; for the idea came that Leather had broken out—was escaping—was coming in his direction; and at that moment there was a pause—a silence which jarred the boy's nerves.

Had they got him?

No; for the dogs were in full pursuit once more, probably on the fugitive's scent, and faintly heard there were shouts as of some one urging the pack on.

How long what followed took Nic never knew, for he was listening, intensely excited, and agitated as to whether he should go or stay, when the thought came that perhaps the dogs were on his scent; but he cast that idea away as foolish, for he had been mounted nearly all the time.

Then all at once, as the hounds were evidently coming nearer and the shouts plainer, Nic felt that he must sit out the affair and hear what had happened; when Sorrel drew a deep breath, there was a heavy breathing, and a man came on at a steady trot straight for the shadow in which Nic sat, so that the next moment he was upon him.

"Back, for your life!" came hoarsely, as the man raised his arm.

"Leather!"

"You here!" panted the convict. "But quick—they're after us. Canter right away."

As he spoke he took a firm grip of the nag's mane, and as it sprang off ran easily by its side, the docile beast making straight for home.

For some minutes they went on like this, with the sounds growing fainter; and then the convict broke the silence.

"Master Nic," he whispered, "I am innocent, my lad. I did not use the axe. That ruffian struck me with the fork handle till my manhood revolted against it, and I knocked him down with my fist, boy—my fist."

"Yes, I know: Sam told me," said Nic hoarsely. "I came to try and get you away."

"God bless you, my lad! I couldn't bear to stay there and be disgraced more than I have. It was too hard."

"How did you escape?"

"Broke the handcuffs apart, climbed to the rafters, pulled open the bark thatching and let myself down; but the dogs gave the alarm."

"Well, they shan't have you now," cried Nic, pulling up. "Jump on and ride home. I'll run beside you. They can't take you away again."

The convict laughed bitterly.

"You foolish boy," he said gently, "the law is on their side. No. Good-bye, lad. Don't forget me. You know the truth, but you must not be mixed up with my escape. You have done nothing yet. Off with you—home!"

"But you, Leather, what are you going to do?" said Nic huskily.

"Escape if I can, and I think I shall."

"But where—what to do? Wait till father comes home?"

"No. What can he do? Dillon will send me to the chain gang as a dangerous man; and I am now, boy—I am, for it shall only be my dead body they shall take."

"Leather!"

"No, Nic. Frank Mayne, an honest man. Home with you, boy!"

"But you?"

"I? There's room enough yonder. To begin a new life of freedom—a savage among the blacks."

There was a smart blow of the open hand delivered on the horse's neck, and the startled beast sprang forward into a wild gallop, which the boy could not for the moment check. When he did, and looked round, there was the darkness of the night, the cry of some wild bird; the baying of the dogs had ceased, and he was quite alone.

"He can't be far," thought the boy, and he whistled softly again and again, but there was no reply. He tried to pierce the darkness, but it was very black now, and he noticed that the stars had been blotted out, and directly after there came *pat; pat, pat*—the sound of great drops of rain, the advance-guard of a storm.

It would have been useless to try and follow the convict, and at last Nic let his impatient horse move on at a walk, then it cantered, and then galloped straight for the Bluff, as if trying to escape from the pelting rain, while it quivered at every flash and bounded on as the lightning was followed by a deafening roar.

"There'll be no trail to follow," cried Nic exultantly; "it will all be washed away, and he'll shelter himself under some tree. But hurrah! I shall see him again. Let old Dillon flog the whipping-post, or, if he's disappointed, let him have old Brookes."

For a peculiar feeling of exultation had come upon the boy, and the storm, instead of being startling, seemed grand, till he rode into the enclosure, seeing that lights were in three of the windows, and a trio of voices cried:

"Nic, is that you?"

"Yes, all right," he shouted. "So hungry. In as soon as I've seen to my horse."

Five minutes after he ran in dripping wet, and had hard work to keep Mrs Braydon from embracing him.

"Not till I've changed, mother," he cried.

"But where have you been?"

"Over to Dillon's, to get him not to punish Leather, and let him come away."

"Yes, Nic?" cried Janet excitedly.

"He wouldn't let him come."

Janet heaved a piteous sigh and sank back in her chair, while Nic hurried to his room to get rid of his soaking garments.

When he came out to go to the room where the meal had been kept waiting all those many hours for his return, he met Janet.

"You coward!" she whispered: "you have not tried."

"I did my best," whispered Nic. "But, I say, Jan, can you keep a secret?"

"Yes: what?" she cried excitedly.

"Old Dillon must be as mad as mad. Leather has escaped, and has made for the myall scrub."

Janet uttered a peculiar sound: it was caused by her pressing her hands to her lips to suppress a cry, as she ran to her own room.

"Poor chap!" said Nic to himself. "I'm glad she likes him too."

Chapter Thirty
The Quest

As Nic had supposed would be the case, hoof-marks were either obliterated or looked faint and old from the heavy soaking they had received in the storm, while those made by a man were invisible, unless to the ultra-keen eyes of some natives.

He noted this when he went out that same morning in pretty good time, for he felt convinced that Mr Dillon would give him the credit of helping Leather to escape.

It was a glorious morning, the dust being washed away by the storm, and everything looking beautifully fresh and green in the sunshine.

When he went out he was soon aware of something else being wrong, for Brookes was rating the three blacks, who had thoroughly enjoyed their truant holiday, and would have stayed away for days in the myall scrub, but the bush in wet weather is to a blackfellow not pleasant, from the showers of drops falling upon his unclothed skin. Consequently the storm had sent them back, and they were all found clothed and curled up fast asleep in the wool-shed by old Sam, who had roused them up.

His words had brought Brookes on the scene, armed with a stout stick, with which he was thrashing them, while the rascals were hopping about in a peculiar shuffling dance, whose steps consisted in every one wanting to be at the back and pushing his fellow to the front.

Bungarolo was the least adept player, and Damper and Rigar managed to keep him before them as a kind of breastwork or shield, behind which they could escape the threatening stick.

"Baal mumkull! baal mumkull! (don't kill)," he kept crying piteously.

"But that's all you're fit for, you lazy rascals. Where did you go?"

"Plenty go find yarraman. Budgery yarraman (good horses). Plenty go find. Run away."

"I don't believe it. What horses ran away?"

"Kimmeroi, bulla, metancoly (one, two, ever so many)," cried Rigar, from the back.

"It's all a lie. Come: out with you!"

"No, leave him alone, Brookes," said Nic sternly. "I'll have no more quarrelling to-day."

The man faced round sharply.

"Look here, young master, are you going to manage this here station, or am I?" he cried.

"I am, as far as I know; and I won't have the black-fellows knocked about."

The three culprits understood enough English to grasp his meaning, and burst out together in tones of reproach:

"Baal plenty stick. No Nic coolla (angry). Black-fellow nangery (stay), do lot work."

"Work! Yes," cried Nic. "Go away with you, and begin."

The three blacks set up a shout like school-children who had escaped punishment, and danced and capered off to the work that they had left the day before.

"Look here, sir—" began Brookes again.

"Why don't you hold your tongue, Brooky?" cried old Sam. "You ain't looked in the glass this morning, or you'd see enough mischief was done yesterday."

"Who spoke to you?" cried Brookes fiercely.

"Not you, or you'd get on better. Young master's quite right. You can't deal with the blacks that way."

"Breakfast!" cried a clear voice; and Nic turned to find his sister Janet coming to meet him, looking very pale, but quite contented.

"I shall keep it a secret, Nic," she whispered. "I'm so glad, for all that seemed so dreadful to me."

At that moment Mrs Braydon appeared at the door, she too looking pale, but eager to welcome her son; and no allusion was made during breakfast to the previous day's trouble.

But hardly had they finished when Nibbler burst into a deep-toned volley of barking, which immediately started the two collies, and they rushed round to the front.

"Some one coming," cried Hilda. "Oh,—they're bringing back poor Leather!"

Nic sprang to the window, to see Mr Dillon, followed by five of his men, three blacks, and seven or eight dogs, among which were three gaunt, grey, rough-haired, Scottish deer-hounds.

The boy had expected that Mr Dillon would come, but his sister's words staggered him and gave him a sharp pang.

The next moment, though, he saw that she was wrong; and turning from the window, he exchanged glances with Janet, as he said quite coolly, "What does he want so soon?" and made for the door, thinking that he knew well enough that they were on a man-hunting expedition, but congratulated himself on the convict's long start.

"Good morning, Mr Dominic," said the magistrate, riding up, while the two collies ran on to investigate the strange dogs, and Nibbler tore furiously at his chain.

"Good morning, sir," said Nic. "Here, Rumble—rumble! Come here, both of you! Hi, Samson! Shut these two dogs up in one of the sheds."

"Yes," said the visitor, "or there'll be a fight." Then, as Sam came running up and relieved Nic of his task of holding the pair by their black frills, "Will you be good enough to walk a little way from the house, young man? I want a word or two with you."

"He can't know I was there," thought Nic; and he walked beside the visitor's horse till it was checked, and the rider looked down sharply at the boy.

"Now, young gentleman," he said, "I don't want to quarrel with your father's son, but I am a man who never allows himself to be played with. You played me a pretty trick last night."

"I, sir? How?"

"Do you want telling?"

"Of course, sir."

Nic felt the magistrate's eyes piercing almost into his very thoughts; but, at the same time, he saw those armed men and that pack of dogs ready to hunt down the convict, and if he could avoid it he was determined not to say all he knew.

"You came over to my place last night and broke a way out for that fellow to escape."

"I did not," said Nic firmly.

"Do you mean to tell me that you did not bring over a handcuff key which your father has, and climb in at the roof and unlock the bracelets?"

"I do tell you so!" said Nic. "I did not know we had such a thing."

"On your word as a gentleman?"

"On my word as a gentleman," said Nic. Then to himself: "If he asks me if I came over, I must say Yes."

"Then I beg your pardon," said Mr Dillon. "But you have him here?"

"No," said Nic, "he is not here."

"I must ask your men. Will you summon them?"

"The blacks too?" said Nic.

"Yes, all of them, please."

"Hi, Sam!" cried Nic, as the old man banged to and fastened the door where he had shut up the dogs. "Call Brookes and the blacks; then come here."

"Right, sir," said the old man; and Mr Dillon went on:

"He got away somehow, and the dogs were after him till the storm spoiled the scent."

"Then you can't flog him," said Nic in triumph.

"Not this morning, of course," said Mr Dillon good humouredly. "All right, my young friend, you'll come round to my way of thinking."

"Never," said Nic firmly.

"That's a long time, squire. But don't you look so satisfied. You really do not imagine that our friend can get away?"

"There's plenty of room," said Nic.

"To starve, my led. But, mark my words, if we don't run him down this morning, he'll come back before long to ask for his punishment, if the myall blacks have not speared him and knocked him on the head."

Just then the men came forward, and the magistrate's attention was taken up, so that he did not see Nic's shudder.

"Oh, Brookes," said Mr Dillon, "that fellow broke out and ran for the bush last night?"

"What?" cried the man, changing colour.

"Has he made you deaf?" said Mr Dillon. "Your Leather got away last night. Have you seen him?"

"No, no," said Brookes, who looked unnerved. "But you'll run him down, sir?"

"Of course. And you, Samson?"

"No, sir, he hasn't been back here. Here, you—Bung, Rig, Damper: have you seen Leather 'smorning?"

"Plenty mine see Leather chop rail."

"Yes, yes, that was yesterday. 'Smorning?"

The three blacks made a peculiar sound, and threw up their chins.

"No good, Belton," said Mr Dillon. "Back to the bunya clump. I have an idea that he struck off there, so as to keep up by the river. Don't care to mount and come and see a convict hunt, squire, I suppose?" said the magistrate inquiringly.

Nic gave him a furious look, and Mr Dillon nodded good humouredly and rode after his men, the dogs beginning to bark as they started back, to be answered by Nibbler and the collies, who thrust their noses under the bottom of the door.

"Won't take them big stag-hounds long to hunt him down," said Brookes, trying to hide his nervousness with a grin.

"Think they'll catch him, Sam?" said Nic.

"Well, sir, it's just about like a pair o' well-balanced wool scales," said the old man rather sadly. "Dogs has wonderful noses of their own. But there, I 'spose we shall hear."

Nic went off to the stables, for he had not the heart to go indoors. And as he stood by his horse the desire came upon him strongly to mount and ride after Mr Dillon's party, so as to know everything that happened, but he felt that it might appear to the poor fellow that he was with the party trying to hunt him down, and he stayed and hung about the station all day.

"Bung," he said toward evening, "you like Leather?"

"Plenty mine like damper."

"No, no; I mean did Leather ever knock you about?"

"Baal, no. Budgery (good)."

"Go over to the Wattles, Mr Dillon's, and find—did catch Leather. You pidney? (understand)."

The man gave him a sly look, laughed, and ran into the cow-shed, to come out directly after in his dress clothes, and armed. Then with a shout he ran off at a long, quick trot toward the track.

It was getting toward midnight when he returned, to cooey under the boy's window.

"Well, did you find out?"

"No catch. White fellow plenty run along myall bush."

"Here, catch," cried Nic, and he pitched the man a big piece of damper and the blade-bone of a shoulder of mutton; and then, as he closed the window, he fancied he heard whispering outside his door, and another door closed.

Chapter Thirty One
Black Sympathy

Nic found the next day that in their tiny world of the Bluff there were others sufficiently interested in the convict's fate to have been making inquiries about the proceedings instituted by Mr Dillon; for on going round the place in the fresh early morning to see how the live stock was getting on, the first person he met was old Sam, who saluted him with one of his ugly smiles, and a chuckle like that of a laughing jackass—of course the bird.

"They didn't ketch him, Master Nic," he cried.

"Why, you ought to be vexed, Sam," replied the boy.

"Yes, I know that, sir; but I ain't. I don't like Leather 'cause he's a convict, and it ain't nice for honest men to have them sort for fellow-servants. But I don't want him ketched and flogged. Not me."

"But will they catch him, do you think, Sam?"

"Ah, that's what nobody can say. Most likely yes, because if the dogs get on his scent they'll run him down."

"But the rain?"

"Ay, that's in his favour, sir. But, then, there's another thing: the blacks will be set to work again."

"But they can't scent him out."

"Nay; but they can smell him out with their eyes and run him down. Bound to say, if I set our three to work, they'd find the poor lad."

"They are very keen and observant."

"Keen, Master Nic? Ay! It's a many years now since I shaved; but if I took to it again I shouldn't use rayshors, sir, but blackfellows' sight. Steel's nowhere to it."

"But how do you know they didn't catch him?"

"I sent Damper and Rigar to see the fun, and they came back to me grinning, and told me."

"But did Mr Dillon set his blacks to work tracking?"

"Ay, that he did; but it strikes me they didn't want to find the poor chap. It's like this, you see, Master Nic. Yes'day morning, as soon as our three found out, from Brooky's face looking like a bit o' unbaked damper, and his tied-up head, that he'd been having it, they asked me how it was, and I told 'em. Next minute I goes into the cow-shed to see what the noise was, and them three chaps—for they're just like little children—there they were, with jyned hands, having a crobbery sort o' dance."

"Why?"

"Why, sir? Just because they were precious glad that Brooky had found his master. They didn't say so, but I knew. You don't suppose, because a chap's face is black, he likes to be hit with sticks, and kicked, and sneered at. They're little children in big black bodies, master; but they like the man who shares his damper and mutton with 'em and never gives 'em a dirty word a deal better than him as treats 'em as if they was kangaroos."

"Of course, Sam."

"They get their likes same as little children do. The lazy black rascals!" continued the old man, grinning; "they always want to be at play, and I give it 'em well sometimes, but they know they deserve it; and, after all, they'd do anything for me, Master Nic, and so they would for you."

"Oh, I've done nothing to please them, Sam."

"Oh yes you have, Master Nic, often; and just you look here—they didn't show their white teeth for nothing."

"What do you mean?"

"I'll tell you, sir. They was along with Dillon's blackfellows yes'day most o' the arternoon, and Dillon's blackfellows didn't find old Leather."

"No; you said so before."

"Ay, I did, sir; but don't you see why they didn't hit out Leather's track?"

"Because the rain had washed it away."

"Nay!" cried Sam, with a long-drawn, peculiar utterance; "because our fellows wouldn't let 'em. They belongs to the same tribe."

"Ah!" cried Nic.

"That's it, sir. Our boys give 'em a hint, or else they'd ha' found him fast enough."

"Then he'll escape!" cried Nic eagerly.

"Nay! There's no saying. Government's very purticlar about running a pris'ner down. 'Bliged to be. Soon as it's reported as Leather's jumped for the bush, some o' they mounted police'll be over, and they'll bring blackfellows with 'em as don't know him and don't belong to our boys' tribe, and they'll find him. 'Sides, there's black tribes in the bush as'd take a delight in throwing spears at him. And then again, how's a white man going to live? He ain't a black, as'll get fat on grubs, and worms, and snakes, and lizzars, and beadles, when he can't get wallabies and birds. But there, we shall see. I'm sorry he jumped for the bush; but don't you go and think I want to see him caught and flogged."

"I don't, Sam."

"Then you're right, Master Nic; on'y raally you mustn't keep me a-talking here. I say, though," he whispered confidentially, and chuckling with delight all the time, "Brooky won't enjy his wittles till Leather is ketched."

"What do you mean?"

"He's going about, sir, in the most dreadfullest stoo. He walked over in the night to the Wattles, and come back all of a tremble, and he's got a loaded gun behind the wool-shed door, and another behind the stable."

"Yes; I saw that, and wondered how it came there."

"He put it there, sir," chuckled the old man. "Just you watch him next time you see him. He's just like a cocksparrer feeding, what keeps on turning his head to right and then to left and all round, to see if Leather's coming to pounce on him and leather him. The pore chap don't know it, but he's sarving out Mister Brooky fine. There, now I must go, sir, raally. One word, though: Brooky's doing nothing but grumble, and look out for squalls, and the master away—not as that matters so much, for the way in which you're a-steppin' into his shoes, sir, is raally fine. But I want things to look to-rights when he comes back."

Chapter Thirty Two
A False Scent

Two days, three days glided by, and the convict was not found. Then a week passed, and another, and he was still at large; but a letter was brought up from the post, a couple of the mounted police being the bearers. This letter, from the doctor, told that Sir John O'Hara was dangerously ill, and that his life was despaired of; it was impossible to leave him till a change took place; and the letter ended affectionately, with hopes that Nic was managing the station well, and that all was going on peacefully.

The mounted police were going on to Mr Dillon's, and on their return in three days they were to take back Mrs Braydon's answer.

The men had just ridden off after a rest and a hearty meal, when, as Nic turned to re-enter the house and hear the letter read over again, he saw old Sam's head over the garden fence, and the handle of his spade held up as a signal.

"Want me, Sam?"

"Ay, sir; come in here. I don't want Brooky to see me talking to you as if I was telling tales. We has to live together, and we're bad enough friends without that."

Nic went round by the gate, and the old man sunk his voice.

"He's been at 'em, sir."

"Who has been at what?"

"I don't mean what you mean, sir. Brooky got at them two police. Know what that means?"

"About Leather?" cried Nic.

"That's it, sir. There'll be another hunt 'safternoon and to-morrer; and if they don't ketch him then, when they go back they'll take a 'spatch from Mr Dillon, and we shall have a lot of 'em down here."

Nic's face contracted from his mental pain.

"Don't you look like that, my lad. They ain't got him yet. Do you know, I shouldn't wonder if he's gone right away with Bung's tribe, and they won't get him. But I say, Master Nic, you won't go over to the Wattles, will you?"

"No, certainly not."

"But you'd like to hear?"

"Yes, of course."

"Then I tell you what, sir: just you tell our three that, as they've been very good boys, they may have a holiday and go and get a good lot o' bunya nuts."

"Get a lot of what?" said Nic, in a tone of disgust.

"Bunya nuts, sir: grows on them trees something like firs. They ain't half bad, I can tell you."

"But I don't want to send them out nutting," said Nic. "They're better at work."

"You don't understand, sir. I saw them staring over the fences at the perlice. You give them leave, and off they'll go and watch everything, just as if they were on'y playing about. Then we shall know everything."

In the result, there was very little to know; for when the three blackfellows came back that night, they could only tell that there had been a long hunt for the convict. They got to know, too, that there was to be another next day.

Then the police returned, received their letters for the doctor, and as they rode off for their long journey to the port they told Nic in confidence not to make himself uncomfortable, for they would be back soon with a little troop and some trackers, and that then they would soon catch the escaped man.

"I don't suppose he'll venture near the station, sir; but if he does, and don't surrender, you're justified in shooting him down."

Nic drew his breath hard as he went back to the house very thoughtfully, but he said nothing indoors.

That afternoon he mounted, and sent the two collies nearly frantic by whistling to them to come after him; and as they dashed on Nic rode after at an easy canter, to take a long round amongst the grazing, off-lying cattle, and carry out another project he had in mind.

It was very pleasant riding there through the far-stretching, park-like place, and that afternoon the number of birds he passed was enormous, but Nic did not shoot at them. A large iguana, a hideous, dragon-like creature, ran to a big tree, making Sorrel start as it crossed his path, and then the great lizard crept up among the branches, puffing itself out, waving its tail, and looking threatening and dangerous. But Nic paid no heed to it, instead of shooting it for the blacks' supper. And twice over large snakes were left unmolested, in spite of the furious barkings of the dogs, and their reproachful looks, which seemed to say, "Why didn't you shoot?"

For Nic had been thinking that if he extended his round day by day, he would, sooner or later, come upon Leather, who must be in hiding somewhere near, for he would never dare to go right off into the wilds and seek starvation.

There were the dogs too; and in all probability they would scent him out, and he could warn him of the coming of the police.

But though Nic extended his rounds more and more, the days glided by, and neither in open glade, deep ravine, ferny gorge, hollow forest monarch, nor dense patch of bush did he come upon the slightest token of the convict ever having been there.

Then in despair he tried a new plan. He quietly got the three blacks together and explained to them what he wanted, and rode behind them in high glee as they trotted on, spear in hand.

"What a stupid I was not to think of this before!" he said to himself; full of confidence. But that night he rode back low-spirited and dull. The blacks had shown him holes in trees, out of which they chopped opossums; the lairs of kangaroos; the pool where a couple of egg-laying, duck-billed platypi dwelled; and trees bearing a kind of plum, and others with nuts: but no signs of Leather.

He tried the next day, and at another time would have been fascinated by the unusual-looking objects the blacks pointed out; but now he wanted to find the convict, and everything else was as nothing; for he felt certain that if the party came over from Port Jackson, the result would be that Leather would be hunted out, refuse to surrender, and be shot down.

But the trips with the blacks all proved to be dismal failures.

Oh yes, they understood.

"Plenty come along find Leather. Corbon budgery. My word, come along."

But they found him not; and when bullied, they smiled, looked stupid, or shook their heads.

"It's because they won't find him, Master Nic. They know all the time," said old Sam.

Acting upon this idea, Nic attacked the three blacks separately, telling them he was sure they knew where Leather was in hiding, and insisting upon being told; but the only result he obtained in each case was a stare of surprise and puzzlement. The man's face puckered up, and at last he mumbled out:

"No pidney (understand). Mine no take Leather fellow in myall. Mine no been see it mandowie (tracks)."

"Be off!" said Nic; and the others talked in a similar way, and went "off;" looking the quintessence of stupidity.

"You're all wrong, Sam," said Nic, the next time he ran against the old man.

"What about, sir—them calves?"

"No, no—about the blacks. I questioned each of them, and they were all as stupid as could be."

"No, I ain't wrong, sir. You get 'em all three together, and promise 'em plenty of damper, some sugar, and a pot each of your ma's jam; then you'll see."

"I'll soon do that," said Nic. "They're in the wool-shed."

"But Brooky's there, sir."

"No, I saw him go off toward the fern gully an hour ago, with a gun upon his shoulder."

"Look here, sir. You'd better lock up all the guns, and keep 'em till they're wanted, or maybe we shall be having mischief done."

"What do you mean?"

"Mean, sir? As Brooky's always going about with a gun, and on the watch. He don't want a gun to go and look round o' they cows. He feels as Leather's close handy somewhere, and afraid he'll take him unawares. If you was to ask him, he'd tell you he was sure the blacks knew where Leather's hiding. There, I'm sorry for him after all."

"So am I, poor fellow."

"Nay, I don't mean Leather: I mean Brooky. He can't even sleep of a night for fear Leather should come and pay him out. It sarves him right, I know, for he always was a brute to Leather; but there, he's being paid back pretty severe. You go and talk to them there black boys. You'll get it out of them with that jam."

Nic strode across toward the wool-shed, and found the blacks jabbering away hard, and evidently quite excited; but they heard his steps, and three rough black heads came softly into sight, one round each doorpost, and the other above a couple of broad boards which ran in grooves, used to keep pigs or other animals from entering to make a warm bed in the wool. But the moment they caught sight of their young master they disappeared, the middle man going off cart-wheel fashion, like a black firework, with arms and legs flying, so as to get behind a stack of wool.

"Here, you fellows," cried Nic, looking over the board, "come here!"

"Baal go floggee blackfellow," protested Bungarolo.

"No mine no flog," cried Nic.

"Mas Nic corbon budgery (very good). All come along."

This brought out the other two grinning.

"Mine come fish?" cried Damper.

"No; I want to find Leather fellow. You boys pidney where he is."

The faces ceased grinning, and looked as if carved out of some burned wooden stump, all hard, solid, and immovable.

"There, I know: so no nonsense. You all take me and show me Leather fellow's mandowie, and I'll give you plenty damper, plenty mutton, plenty sugar and jam."

"Mine no find mandowie (tracks)," said Rigar. "You pidney (know), Damper?"

"Mine no pidney," said Damper. "Mandowie myall. Bungarolo pidney?"

"Bung no pidney," said that gentleman.

"Yes, you all pidney—more sugar, more jam, more damper," cried Nic.

But the men only stared blankly; and growing impatient at last with the three ebony blacks, Nic left them to go back to Sam, but turned sharply, to see that they were all three watching him with their faces in a broad grin.

This exasperated him so that he made a rush back to look into the long dark shed, where he could see wool everywhere, but no traces of the blacks, who seemed to have disappeared.

"I'll bring a whip," he shouted, and then went away, laughing at the way the men were scared.

"Sam's right," he said: "they are like big black children. Here! Hi! Samson," he shouted, and the old man came to meet him. "They don't know."

"Don't know, sir? What makes you say that?"

Nic related his experience, and Sam grinned.

"And they laughed at you," he said, showing his teeth. "Why was that? On'y because they enjoyed being as they thought too clever for you, Master Nic. They know, sir; but it's no use—they won't tell. They like you and me; but if they'd speak out to us as they do to one another, they'd say, 'No mine tell Leather fellow, Mas Nic, plenty mine jam, damper. Leather fellow mumkull.'"

"Mumkull? Afraid Leather would kill them for telling?"

"That's it, sir, safe."

There was something to stir the pulses of Nic soon after, and he somehow felt glad that he did not know the convict's hiding-place, for a dozen of the colonial mounted police rode up, followed by half a dozen black trackers and a couple of chained and muzzled, fierce-looking dogs, whose aspect sent a shiver through Nic, excited the indignation of the collies, and drove Nibbler into a fit of fury, making him bound to the end of his chain so savagely that he dragged his tub kennel out of its place and drew it behind him, making him look like some peculiar snaily quadruped trying to shed its shell.

"Better shut up your dogs, sir," said the policeman who had been once before. "Letter for Mrs Braydon."

The dogs were quieted and shut away, so that they could not commit suicide by dashing at the powerful brutes held in leash; and once more, while the police were being refreshed, Mrs Braydon read her letter over to her children, who learned that the governor was no better, that the doctor was bound to stay, and that while he regretted this, and the bad news about the assigned servant, every assistance ought to be given to the police who had come to fetch him back to the chain gang.

Nic said nothing, but after a time he saddled Sorrel, and rode with the police leader as they started for their first search.

"Now, Mr Braydon," said the man, "your father said that we must take this fellow; so as in all probability you know where he is, perhaps you'll tell us which way to go and capture him."

"I don't know," said Nic quickly.

The man smiled.

"You needn't disbelieve me," said Nic warmly. "I tell you I haven't the least idea."

"And if you had, you wouldn't tell us, eh?"

"I'm not going to answer questions," said Nic. "But mind this: if you find him, I won't have him shot down."

"Then he mustn't shoot at us, sir," said the man, smiling, "so you'd better send him word if you know where he is. Forward!" he cried, and the party trotted toward the Wattles, but turned off a little over half-way there, and to Nic's horror he felt that they had hit upon the place where he and the convict parted that night just as the storm came on. And here, after a few words from the head of the little force, two of the blacks came forward and began to quarter the ground like dogs, their bodies and heads bent forward, and their eyes searching the grass with the keenest eagerness.

But it was a long time before either of them showed that he had found signs.

Then one stopped short, dropped upon his knees, uttered a cry, and his fellows ran softly up behind him, keeping close to each other, and being careful not to go near the track or whatever it was that he had found.

Then began a low excited jabbering, during which the mounted men sat fast, one of them holding the leash which restrained the dogs.

At last the quick discussion ended, and the first black rose from his knees and made a sign to the police leader to come forward, Nic without hesitation following and peering over the blacks, who gave way a little, while the first pointed down to something which Nic expected to find was a footstep, but which proved to be a big common knife, rusted by exposure to rain and air.

This was picked up now and handed to the leader, while Nic's eyes dilated a little, for he felt sure that he had seen the knife before; and in the convict's hands, when he was eating his cold meat and damper beneath a tree.

"Yes," he said to himself with a little shiver, "that is his knife. He must have dropped it here. It had a buckhorn handle, and on the other side three crosses had been filed pretty deeply." He remembered that fact well.

Just then the police leader turned round sharply, saw his interested look, and said, in a decisive, imperative tone of voice:

"You know that knife, sir?"

To gain time the boy held out his hand, drawing his breath hard, and striving to control his voice and make it firm.

Then, as he took the knife, he examined it as if in doubt, hesitating about turning it over, and then handing it back, saying firmly, "No."

"That's a lie," thought the man, as he retook the knife, "and my lord here is trying to keep the lair hidden. He knows."

But the knife had no crosses filed in the handle, and Nic was breathing freely, when he noticed that the black was pointing to something else—a faintly marked footprint, evidently made by a coarsely made sandal or shoe. Beyond this was another, and again beyond another.

"That's right—go on!" rang in his ears, and the next moment the party was again in motion, with the blacks bending low, and from walking beginning to trot, while the policeman pressed his horse closer to Nic's.

"Easy trail to follow, sir," he said. "Now, then, don't you think you'd better save us further trouble by taking us straight across country to your man's form?"

"I told you I did not know where he was hiding," said Nic shortly.

"You did, sir, but I thought I'd save trouble. These birds are a bit desperate when run down, and I'm sure you wouldn't like to see him shot when he refuses to surrender. Now, would you?"

"No," said Nic, rather faintly.

"Out with it then, and we'll take him by surprise—surround him after dusk. Then it will mean a flogging or two, and another year in the gang, and perhaps a fresh chance. Better than being buried, sir, in the bush."

Nic remained silent, but with his brow contracted.

"Very well, sir, but you see. Why, I can trace that track as I ride. We could find him now without the blacks."

Still Nic held his peace, and rode on beside the man, as mile after mile was traced, leading, to the boy's surprise, toward the Bluff, but curving off a mile from home, as if to go round it to reach the other side.

And so it proved, the blacks trotting on till they did pass the house half a mile away; and Nic jumped to the conclusion that the poor fellow had made for the fern gully, up which, somewhere probably on the riverside, was his lair.

They went right on, without once being at fault, the footprints, with the left sole badly cracked across, showing clearly at times in the soft soil, till the place where the black-fish were caught was passed, and the valley slope mounted for the open ground, where the sheep was kicked into the rift that ran down toward the water.

From here the footsteps went right across toward the station, and the leading black ran them easily and triumphantly right up to the men's bothy, at whose door Brookes stood hollow-cheeked and anxious.

"Got him?" he cried hoarsely, when, to his surprise, the blacks dashed at him and had him down, while the leader secured and held up one of his boots with the sole toward the head of the police.

"Mine find," he cried, pointing to a crack across the sole; and Nic forced the nag away, and trotted off to the stable to hide his laughter, and then stood patting his horse, feeling quite heartsick from the tension now relieved.

For he had made sure that so as to be in a place not likely to be searched Leather had come by night to the station, and that he would be found hidden in one of the piles of wool, whereas it was evident that Brookes had been over to the Wattles, and had come that way back, searching along the fern gully, to make sure of Leather not being in hiding there.

For two days more the police hunted in every direction, but neither the keen eyes of the blacks nor the senses of the dogs were of any avail, and at last the search was given up.

"We shall find him back here some day," said the head policeman, "if he's still alive. But,"—the man looked significantly at Nic—"they don't always have life left in 'em when we do find 'em. Good day, sir. We may look you up again."

They rode off, and the station was free of them, for they had made a sort of barrack of the wool-shed, where the fleeces made most satisfactory beds; and as they grew less and less, Nic turned away, to see the light all at once blaze, as it were, into his darkened mind.

"How stupid!" he said, half aloud. "Why, I know where he is hiding, after all."

He looked up, and there was Brookes watching him with curious eye.

Chapter Thirty Three
In a Trap

Sleep did not come very readily to Nic's eyes that night, and he looked very heavy and thoughtful at breakfast time next morning.

"How thankful I shall be when your father comes home, my dear!" said Mrs Braydon.

"A bag of flour would be the best thing," said Nic to himself.

"I know, of course, my dear, that you are doing wonders," continued Mrs Braydon, looking uneasily at her son, and misinterpreting his heavy look into showing annoyance at her remark. "Both the girls and I are astonished at the rapidity with which you have taken up this wild farm life, and gone on with it as if you had been working for years; but we cannot help longing to see your father back to take the management and give us that feeling of protection which we miss."

"I ought to have guessed it at once," muttered Nic.

"Is anything the matter, Nic?" said Hilda.

"Matter? No. Why?"

"You seem so dull, and you are not eating your breakfast."

"Oh yes, I am," cried the boy, with forced merriment; and he rapidly attacked the meal and made mother and sisters more uneasy by eating tremendously and talking rapidly at the same time about how glad he would be to have the doctor back.

Soon after breakfast Nic went to the storehouse and filled a bag with meal, carrying it afterwards to the stable.

"I suppose one of the horses is ill," said Hilda. "Nic has been to fetch some flour to make it a mash."

"Then that's what made him so anxious and thoughtful at breakfast time," cried Mrs Braydon. "Poor boy! it worried him. He wants to get it well again before your father's return."

Janet said nothing, but attributed it to the right reason—that her brother was troubled about the convict—and she trembled in her longing to ask him, but did not dare.

Meanwhile Hilda had her thoughts; and the consequence was that Nic grew angry, as he busied himself about the place, going here and there looking after the men, inspecting the cattle, and carefully watching that no tasks were being left undone.

"I never saw anything like it," he said to himself: "go where I will it's just as if some one was watching me. They surely cannot suspect anything."

Then, too, four or five times, when he had made up his mind to start, old Sam or Brookes or his mother wanted him about some matter. But still it was yet good time in the morning, when, taking his gun, the mounted Sorrel, slung the big bag of meal across the saddle-bow and rode out.

"You will not be late, my dear?" cried Mrs Braydon. "Oh no, mother; back in good time." Then to himself, "Don't—pray don't ask me which way I'm going."

"It must be for some bullock at a distance," said Mrs Braydon, as she thoughtfully noted the bag across the saddle-bow, the fine sacking having now assumed an hour glass shape, at which Janet gazed curiously, feeling puzzled, though she could not have told why.

"At last!" muttered Nic, as he pressed his horse's sides and rode off, feeling very guilty, and yet bright and exhilarated, quite confident too of having solved a problem, though he was doubtful still as to whether he would be able that night to write down mentally QEF.

He cast an eye to left and right to see if he were being watched, but every one seemed to be busy over his or her affairs, and he began to think that his start was exciting no interest whatever, when he saw Brookes crossing the big field beyond the garden.

But the man did not turn his head in Nic's direction; and the next minute, after forcing himself not to look round, the boy had placed the trees between them, and cantered away quite out of sight of the house, keeping down in a hollow leading toward the fern gully, as if going to visit some cattle on the other side of the hills lying to the south-east. As soon as he was beyond those hills he bore away to the north, as if making for the Wattles; and when a mile or so in that direction he bore to the left again for some distance, and then made for the west—just the very opposite direction to that which he had taken in starting.

The morning was delightful as he rode on, now in the full sunshine, now in shade; and the feeling of exhilaration which came over him seemed to be shared by his horse, which began to dance about and strain to get away for a swift gallop.

A word or two always checked it, and the beautiful creature, whose satin skin glistened in the sunshine, playfully tossed its head and ambled on.

"Nobody can have imagined which way I was coming," thought Nic; and then, "Bother the old flour!" he said, half aloud; "how it works through the bag! Why, Sorrel, your back will be as white as my knees. Woa!"

The nag stopped short, and Nic stood at the edge of a glade dotted with clumps of acacia in full bloom, everything seeming to be covered with tiny golden balls.

"Why, you two wretches, how dare you come hunting?"

Nic sat like a statue among the trees watching, as he saw the two collies suddenly come into sight about five hundred yards away and then run among the low growth for which they were making.

"Well, it won't matter," he said. "They can't tell tales. But they may come again and show some one the way. I'll send them back."

He pressed his horse's sides, and walked it toward where the dogs had disappeared, putting up a flock of the tiny zebra paroquets, which flew a little distance to another tree.

"Poor fellows! I should like to give them a good run," he said to himself, "but it's best not. I suppose I'm doing something very unlawful, but the law did wrong to that poor fellow, and I feel as if I must help him. Oh, what a thick-headed noodle I am not to have thought of it before! Why, I remember quite well now all he said about it. Hullo! what are those? They must be the great hawk parrots old Sam talked about. Bother the birds! I've got something else to think of to-day. Why, there goes another of those great iguana things! Where did the dogs go?"

He had ridden on slowly, startling bird and lizard, and completely lost trace of the collies, when all at once he heard a smothered growl in a dense patch close at hand.

"They've found a snake," he said to himself, cocking his piece. "I mustn't have them bitten."

He pressed forward, peering in amongst the bushes, passing some young clean-stemmed trees; and as he rode unconsciously by one, a nude black figure, neatly ornamented with two or three stripes of white pipeclay on its breast, pressed close up to the tree holding a spear erect, and, as the horse passed, moved so exactly round that the tree was kept between it and Nic.

That tree did not appear to be thick enough to hide the black, but so cleverly did the man move that Nic saw nothing, though he was not ten yards away; and the black would have been unnoticed if it had not been for the action of the dogs, which suddenly charged out playfully, one going one side, the other the other, and then stopping barking at a respectful distance from the tree.

"You vagabonds!" cried Nic; "how dare you come! Here, what have you found? Fetch it out!"

Rumble dashed forward barking; and Nic noted that the dogs did not look excited or angry, but playful, and as Rumble charged on one side Tumble made a bound forward on the other.

"It must be a 'possum," thought Nic; but he altered his mind the next moment, for he saw a spear come forward with a poke on one side of the tree, and then drive at the second dog on the other.

Nic lowered the gun and moved round toward the other side cautiously; but the black edged himself along, as he did so cleverly keeping the tree still between them, and would have continued to keep himself in hiding if it had not been for the dogs, which, encouraged now by their young master's presence, made a playful dash together at the black's legs, and made him bound from the tree to keep them at bay with his spear.

"Why, Bung! You?" cried Nic, who felt considerably relieved, while the dogs now scampered around, barking and leaping as if at the end of a game of hide-and-seek. "What are you doing here, sir?"

The black grinned, and, supporting himself on one leg by help of his spear, made playful clutches at the delighted dogs with his right foot, whose toes worked about as he used it as if it were a great awkwardly shaped hand.

"R–r–r–ur!" growled the dogs together, as they now justified their names, and blundered over one another in a make-believe attempt to bite and worry the foot; Nic looking on amused as they threw themselves down, rolling over and grovelling along on their sides and backs to get close up and feel the black's toes tickle them, and catch hold of their shaggy hair.

"Why don't you speak, sir? Why are you not at work?" cried Nic.

"Little White Mary say, 'Bung, go along see master.'"

"What! did my sister send you?"

The black nodded and laughed.

"Then just you go back, sir, directly, and take those dogs with you."

"Little White Mary say come along," persisted the black.

"I don't care what any one said," cried Nic. "Be off back."

"Little White Mary say, 'Gun no shoot—mumkull.'"

"Put down that spear," cried Nic, who now pointed the gun at Bungarolo, who replied by striking an attitude, holding his spear in a graceful position as if about to hurl it at the boy's head.

"No mumkull Bung?" cried the black.

"Not if you run off back," cried Nic. "If you don't I'll pepper you."

"No pepper Bung, no mumkull. Baal shoot gun. Little White Mary fellow say Bung come."

"You go back home," cried the boy, following him up.

"Little White Mary say—"

"Go home."

"Little—"

"Will you go, sir? Here, Rum—Turn! Run him home."

The dogs made a rush, and the black darted off, but a hundred yards away ran behind a tree, where the dogs hunted him out.

"Home!" roared Nic, and the black darted on again, Nic riding after him again and again, till, satisfied that the black was really making for the station, followed by the dogs, he made a circuit in among the trees, and rode hard for a time, altering his course at last, and not pausing till he was close up to the precipitous edge of the huge gorge.

Here the boy dismounted in a patch of rich grass surrounded by mighty trees, hobbled his horse, removed the bit, which he hung to the saddle, and then paused to think.

"He's here somewhere," the boy said to himself, "but the thing is where."

He was not long coming to the conclusion that the convict had devoted himself during his shepherding tours to hunting out some place where he could descend the terrible precipice into that glorious valley far below, where there were sheep and cattle, plenty of water, and no doubt wild fruits to enable him to subsist.

"And if he found his way down, why shouldn't I?" said Nic, with a little laugh. Then, shouldering his gun, he dived in among the trees and wattle scrub which lay between him and the edge of the precipice, with the intention of keeping cautiously along it, first in one direction and then in the other, till he found traces of some one having climbed down.

Two hours' work convinced him that he had undertaken a task that might have made Hercules sit down and scratch his ear, for it promised to be hard enough to equal any of the celebrated labours of that mythic personage. Nic had toiled on in one direction only, forcing his way through thorns, tangles, and over and between rocks, pausing from time to time, whenever he came to an opening, to gaze across the tremendous gap at the glories of the rock wall opposite, or to look shuddering down into the beautiful paradise thousands of feet below, where the tints of green were of the loveliest hues, and he could see the cattle calmly grazing, mere dots in the natural meads which bordered the flashing waters seen here and there like lakes, but joined possibly, for the trees shut out broad stretches of the river in the vale.

For a time he would lie there, resting and listening to the whistling calls of birds whose names he did not know, to the shrieks of parrots, and now and then catch sight of what seemed to be tiny fragments of paper falling fluttering down, till he saw them turn, and knew that he was gazing at cockatoos.

Then, after yielding to the fascination of peering down into the awful depth, he would turn suddenly away, for a cold chill would run through him as he experienced the sensation as of something drawing him downward, and he would creep yards distant and sit there wiping the perspiration from his face.

He soon recovered, though, and once more continued his search for a way down.

"It is as if it would take years," he said to himself; "but I don't care, I shall come again and again and keep on trying. I will find it," he said half aloud, as he set his teeth in dogged determination, and for another hour he struggled on, till, feeling utterly exhausted, he seated himself at the edge of the precipice at a point where he could divide the bushes and look down. Here, only a few yards away, he saw that there was a broad shelf some fifty feet below, and along it a mere thread of water trickled to a lower edge and disappeared, leaving among the stones amidst which it had meandered patch after patch of richest green, showing its fertilising power.

That water was tempting in the extreme, for his mouth was dry; he was faint, and he knew by the position of the sun that he had been struggling through the dense growth for hours without refreshing himself, though all the time he had a cake of damper in his pocket, keeping the powder-flask company.

If he could get down there, he thought, he might have half an hour's rest, and then tramp back to where he had left Sorrel, and ride gently home in the cool of the evening.

"And come again." For come again he would till he had found poor Leather, "unless," he said to himself with a shudder, "he has fallen down this terrible place."

And yet it was not terrible, he thought the next moment. It was grand, glorious, lovely, and the shelf below him, with its water, more tempting than anything he had ever seen before.

"I must get down," he said; and going farther along he sought for a means, but had not far to go, for he soon grasped the fact that this shelf was only some eighty or a hundred feet off the top, which had slipped a little and then stopped. It had broken away, gone down some fifty feet, and then been checked.

While as he gazed down at the old edge of the precipice, and over it into the gorge below, he could hear the soft, whistling, humming trickle of the water, and it increased his eagerness. He must get down, he thought—but how? There were no overhanging boughs, no roots which had forced their way between cracks in the rock and gone on down and down searching for the moisture of that tiny rill which went over the edge to its present depth; and there were no stout bushes growing in the side beneath him. All there was clean, broken-away stone, which could only be descended by stepping from projection to projection, while if any one slipped—

"Well, what if he did?" said the boy contemptuously, as he gazed down: "he would, at the most, only get a few scratches and bruises. Here's the best spot, and I'm going down."

Without further hesitation he laid down his gun, turned upon his breast and lowered his legs, found footing easy to get upon a ledge, and lowered himself more and more till he was at the full stretch of his limbs, when a horrible thought occurred to him: suppose, when he jumped down upon that broad shelf formed by a sliding of the rock till it was checked by some inequality, his weight should be sufficient to start it going again, and he should be carried with it backward into the gulf.

"What nonsense!" he thought; "why, my weight upon it will be no more than that of a fly;" and he lowered himself a little more, found it harder, moved to the right, and got on to a firm ledge, and from that to another, and was soon half-way down.

There he came to a stop, for he could find neither foot nor hand hold; and there he was at last, spread-eagled against the perpendicular rock, unable to go down, and, upon determining to go up instead, utterly unable to retrace his steps.

"Oh, this is absurd," he thought, and looking sidewise, he saw a little projection which seemed as if it would do then, feeling that if he stopped longer in his cramped position he would be less able to act, he measured the distance with his eyes, gathered himself together, made a clumsy spring, got a foot on the projection, but missed the crevice into which he meant to thrust his right hand, and went scrambling and sliding down the other five-and-twenty feet, to come into a sitting position on the broken stones, scratched, bruised, and uttering a loud groan of pain.

"Oh my bones!" he cried, with a laugh and a wince of pain, as he began to rub himself; and then, as he looked up, a sudden chill struck him, for, he said to himself:

"Why, it's like a trap. I can never get up there again. I ought to have looked farther before I leaped."

He limped a little as he stood up, and his arms both required a rub, especially about the elbows; but while he performed these little comforting offices he was not idle, for he carefully inspected the shelf. Escape on the one side did not seem possible, for it was over into the gorge; the other side, a curve, was one nearly perpendicular wall of rock, along which he walked from where he stood to the ends at the edge of the precipice and back.

"It is a regular pitfall," thought Nic; and then, determined to make the best of things, he lay down upon his chest over the clear murmuring water, lowered his lips, and took a long, deep, delicious draught of the sparkling fluid.

"That's refreshing," said the boy to himself, and he came to a sitting position on the warm stone, took out his piece of bread cake, and looked up at the wall facing him, as he broke off a morsel of damper.

"Doesn't look so high as it did before I had that drink," he said, with a laugh. "Not half so high; and by the time I've eaten my bread it will only look half as high once more. Pooh! I can climb up. Cake's good."

He sat munching away contentedly enough now, stopping from time to time for a fresh draught of water; and as he ate and drank he forgot the awkwardness of his position in wonder and admiration of the mountain precipice before him, and at last crept to the edge of that upon which he had been seated, to obtain another look down into the mighty gorge.

"Ah, it's very grand," he sighed; "but it's time I climbed out of this."

He started, for he heard a sharp double click, like the cocking of a gun, and looked up behind at the edge from which he had descended.

"Cricket or grasshopper," he thought; and then he felt, to use a familiar old saying, as if his blood ran cold; for a slight movement at the top had caught his attention, and he found himself gazing at the muzzle of his gun, so foreshortened that there seemed to be no barrel—nothing but a round hole, and behind it a glittering eye.

Chapter Thirty Four
Trust for Trust

"Some one found my gun and taking aim at me," thought Nic, feeling thoroughly how bad a plan it was for any one to bring out a gun for self-defence and then leave it for an enemy to seize.

That watch kept upon the gun muzzle did not last many moments, for a rough, mocking voice said loudly:

"Well: come to take me? Here I am."

"Leather!—I mean, I mean Frank Mayne," cried Nic joyously, as he sprang to his feet; "found you at last!"

"Yes," said the convict bitterly, "you have found me at last. Where are your men?"

"What men?" said Nic, staring.

"The bloodhounds you've brought to hunt me," said the convict.

"Don't talk nonsense!" cried Nic sharply. "You don't think I should bring any one to hunt you?"

"Why not?"

"Because you know I wouldn't be such a brute. But, I say, I was right then. I've been trying ever since you went away to think out where you could be gone."

"And sending the police after me," said the convict bitterly.

"You know better than that," cried Nic; "but, I say, I was right then. I felt sure you would be here."

"Why should you be?" said the man suspiciously.

"Because, don't you remember once, months ago, talking about the gorge?"

"True, I did; I had forgotten. But where are the police now?"

"Gone back to the port. How did you know they had been?"

"From the blacks."

"There, I knew it!" cried Nic. "The cunning rascals, and they pretended they had no idea of where you were."

"Poor fellows," said the convict, smiling bitterly; "they are faithful enough."

"But they might have told me," said Nic. "Even you don't seem to trust me now."

"How can a man, who is hunted like a wild beast with dogs and black trackers, trust any one, boy?" cried the convict fiercely. "You know what it would have been if they had found me, and I had run instead of surrendering. They would have shot me down like a savage beast."

Nic nodded as he gazed up at the fierce countenance, whose eyes seemed to glare down at him.

"There," continued the convict, "you have found me. Of course you know there is a heavy reward. You can earn it for pocket money."

"Yes," cried Nic, speaking fiercely now, "and go over to the village tuck shop, and spend it with my school-fellows."

"Of course," said the man banteringly. "Only there's one drawback, boy. You are caught in a trap there, and when you are found there will only be your bones."

"Oh, I say, Leather, what a savage you have turned! I say, have a bit of damper? I have some left."

The man made no reply for a few moments. Then, in an altered tone:

"Have you found any way out?"

"No. It is a regular trap; but I was thirsty, and I came down to drink. Fell half the way," said Nic, holding up a bleeding hand.

"I went down the same way," said the convict quietly.

"Then there is a way out?" said Nic sharply.

"Yes, over the brink yonder."

"Oh yes, I found that out," said Nic, with a laugh; "but I don't want to break my neck. How did you get out?"

"Over there," said the convict quietly. "It requires a steady head, but you can creep along a narrow ledge, and get back to the top here, three or four hundred yards farther on. I did not find it out till I was nearly starved to death."

"Poor old chap," said Nic quietly. "I say, this sounds more like you."

"Does it? Did any one see you coming?"

"Bungarolo. But I sent him home before I was halfway here."

"He would not tell tales, poor fellow. They have had my life in their hands ever since."

"But, I say, Leather, it's awkward talking like this. I'll come up to you;" and he moved toward the edge.

"No, no, don't stir," cried the man fiercely. And Nic stamped angrily upon the rock.

"Why don't you shoot me?" he cried. "You've got the gun. There, be off; I don't want to see which way you go. Look here, Sorrel's over yonder somewhere. Go and find him, and ride off up the country as far as you like. Only send him back some day by one of the blacks, I'll pay him with blankets and things. I can't give him to you, because, as you know, he was father's gift. There's a pack of meal on his back; I brought it in case I could find you; but you'd better take this lump of damper too."

The convict made no reply for some minutes, but lay there at the edge of the rocks gazing sadly down at Nic, who had thrown himself upon his chest, and was looking into the gorge.

"Nic," he said at last.

"Well," was the reply; but the boy did not turn his head.

"Don't misunderstand me, lad; I said don't try to come up, because the risk of going along there made me shudder. I'm coming down to help you — where's your hand?"

"Oh, I say, I beg your pardon," cried Nic, springing up. "I didn't mean — I thought — I — I say, Leather, mind how you come."

"Yes, I'll mind," said the man. "But the gun. It is not safe to pitch it down to you."

"No; leave it up there."

"For another enemy to get hold of it. No, my lad, that won't do. There, if I hold it crosswise like this, and drop it down, you can catch it."

"Yes, I think so."

"Then try."

As he spoke the man went down upon his face, held the gun at arm's length as far down over the edge as he could, and then after a warning let it fall.

"Right," cried Nic, catching it cleverly. "Now, how are you going to manage? I came down just there."

"And I'll try twenty feet to my left here," said the convict; and, selecting a place, he lowered himself down until he hung by his hands, and then began to descend with wonderful activity, reaching the bottom without a slip, solely from the rapidity of his movements.

"Why, Leather," cried Nic, grasping his hand, "you are as active as a squirrel."

"A man needs to be to lead my life, boy," said the convict quietly. "Hah! that seems to put humanity into one again. The blacks are friendly enough; but it is for the touch of a white hand one yearns."

"Have some damper?" said Nic suddenly, so as to hide a peculiar feeling which troubled him.

The convict took the bread cake, broke it, and began to eat, seeking refuge in the act for the same reason.

"Hah!" he said, smiling, "it tastes good. Nic, boy, you forgive me all I have said?"

"Of course I do. But, I say, how have you managed to live?"

"The same as a black would. This is the first bread I have eaten since I broke away and became a savage."

"Do you think they will manage to catch you?" said Nic, after a pause.

"Not alive, my lad. Well, let's have just a few words together, and then you must go."

"You will stop about here, I suppose?"

The convict shook his head.

"Hunted beasts stay where they are safe. Hunt them, and they go farther away."

"You have been hunted, but you have not gone farther away."

"No, boy, because this is my sanctuary. There, you see I trust you, and I know that I am safe in your hands. Let's sit down."

Nic willingly did so, and the convict went on eating the bread cake, talking quietly the while.

"There is no place I could find where I should be so safe, Nic," he said; "and this is near human nature, which one likes, even if it is unkind. I had often thought of breaking away and making for the bush, feeling convinced that if I reached the place I could manage to live where so many poor wretches who have escaped found their end. But I was servant to a just man; your mother and sisters treated me when they saw me as if they were sorry for me, and I could not go. Then you dame, boy, and tied me tighter to the place, making all the petty troubles caused by that overbearing brute seem like nothing."

"I tied you tighter to the place?" cried Nic.

"Yes. Why, the hours I spent with you when you found me out in the run were the only happy ones I had had for years."

"Oh, I didn't do much," said Nic hurriedly. "I'm afraid it was because I liked to talk to you about birds and things. But, I say, do you mean to keep to this life?"

"Do you think I can give up and submit to that worst punishment of—to be flogged?"

"No," cried Nic firmly; "you can't do that. You must wait. And look here, I tell you what: try and find a way down into the gorge, and keep it a secret. Why, you can build yourself a gunyah (bark hut) somewhere below, and live there, and make your garden and keep fowls, and there are sheep and cattle. I'll bring you a live chicken now and then, and seeds and cuttings, and tea and sugar and flour when I come, and then we can go fishing and hunting and collecting together. Why, it will be capital."

The convict smiled.

"I don't see anything to laugh at," said Nic.

"I suppose not, you young enthusiast."

"That I'm not," cried the boy. "It's you who take too miserable a view of things."

"With cause, boy."

"Well, yes, there is plenty of cause," said Nic: "but you really could live down there safely for years without being found out—if you could get down."

"I can get down, and I have been down there since I broke away. I have made myself a bark gunyah, and for the present that is my home, Nic."

"Capital," cried the boy eagerly. "Take me and show me."

The convict shook his head.

"No," he said; "you and I must never meet."

"Why?" said Nic, in rather an ill-used tone.

"Because you would be disgracing yourself by associating with a man of my character, and you would be breaking laws made for the protection of the settlers who employ convict servants."

"You are not a man of bad character," said Nic quietly; "and as to law—well, I suppose it would be breaking that; but then the law doesn't know any better. It does not know you like I do."

"There, boy, we will not argue the question. I'm black enough as it is, but I want to do you good, Nic, not harm. Come," he continued, rising, "time is going on, and you are some distance from home. Where is your horse?"

"Miles away."

"Then you must be moving."

"There's no hurry," said Nic.

"Yes, there is. You have a dangerous ledge to go along."

"I can get along better when I am more rested," said the boy.

The convict smiled.

"Then let me put it in a more selfish way," he said. "It is close on sundown, and I have a long way to go to my home. A more dangerous way than yours, and I could not attempt it after it begins to grow dusk."

"I'm ready," said Nip, springing up; "but tell me this: when will you meet me again?"

"Perhaps never," said the convict.

"Then I shall come hunting for you every day till I find the way down into the gorge."

"And bring the government people on my track?"

"No, I won't do that," said Nic; "but I will find you out, and I can now that I know where you are."

"I doubt it, boy. The gorge is enormous, and I am the only man who knows the way down."

"Pooh! The blacks would know. Bungarolo would show me now he knows I have seen you."

"The blacks do not know, Nic. I should not know if I had not discovered it two years ago by accident when trying to save the life of a sheep which had fallen. There, be content. You have seen me. Some day we may meet again. Now then, we must lose no more time."

"Very well," said Nic; "only mind this: I will not do anything to risk having you discovered; but I will come to you."

"I know you will not do anything to harm me, my lad; but you are deceiving yourself, my boy. You will not come to me. Now, are you ready?"

"Yes. Where's this dangerous shelf?"

"I will take you along it. Where is your handkerchief?"

"It was too hot to have it round my neck," said Nic, smiling, as he took it from where it was tied about his waist.

"I am going to bind it round your eyes," said the convict.

"What! For fear that I should find the way down into the gorge?"

"No; because your head may turn giddy when you see the depth below you. I want you to trust me, Nic, to lead you safely along the shelf. Can you do this?"

Nic was silent for a few moments.

"I feel as if I want to trust you," he said at last; "but I don't feel as if I can—no, no, I don't mean that. I mean that I want to trust you, but I can't trust myself. No, that isn't it exactly. I suppose I'm afraid. Why can't I walk close behind you?"

"Because I doubt your doing it without practice. I expect that you would go along half-way and then lose your nerve, and I don't think I could lift and carry you then. Won't you trust me, Nic?"

The boy looked sharply into his eyes for a moment, and then leaned forward for his eyes to be bound, thinking the while of the log bridge over the fern gully and his feelings there.

"There," said the convict, as he secured the knot firmly. "Now listen: I shall take hold of your hand to hold it tightly, and I want you to try and make yourself part of me for the next ten minutes, obeying every touch, and taking step for step with me. Don't pause, don't hesitate; only keep on feeling that I am guiding you safely through the darkness. There is no risk if you do this."

"I'm ready," said Nic; "only begin quickly, please, and let's get it done."

"Then come along."

Nic felt his hand seized in a strong, firm grip, and followed as he was led, hesitating once, and showing a disposition to hang back, but it was only for a moment. The next he was walking slowly and steadily behind the convict, who led him between two or three bushes, and then along a narrow shelf which passed round the end of the rock slip; and as soon as it was cleared the buttress at that end grew still more narrow, so that the boy felt his right arm brushing against the perpendicular rock wall, while his left hung free.

He could not see, but he knew that his left fingers must be pointing down into the tremendous gulf; and in imagination he saw with wonderful accuracy through the golden transparent air the various plants which grew from the interstices of the titanic wall, the bushes and shrubs, the pendent vines and clinging creepers, the shelves and faults in the strata here and there deeper down, and then lower and lower still the gaps and hollows whence stalwart trees had risen from seeds dropped or hidden by some bird—trees which had grown out almost horizontally, and then curved up into their proper vertical position, to rise up and up as the years rolled on, though now they looked mere shrubs a handbreadth high.

And as the boy walked on he saw lower and lower the forest monarchs dwarfed to shrubs, and lower still patches of timber that were indistinct and looking hardly more than grass, while here and there the light of the setting sun gleamed ruddily from the water of the chain of lakes.

It was but the picture raised by memory from where it was printed upon Nic's mind, but it was very accurate, and almost exactly what he would have seen had his eyes been free during that long, long walk, as it seemed—a walk of a few brief minutes though, and then his hand was dropped.

"Don't do that till you've unbound my eyes," said Nic sharply.

"Why not, boy? we are in safety now."

Nic's breath was exhaled in a hoarse sigh as he felt the kerchief drawn from his face, and he looked round to see that they were among trees.

"Was it very dangerous?" he said.

"Very; or I would not have asked you to be bound. Now, my lad, good-bye."

"No, no; I have quite a load of meal for you on the horse."

"There is no time to fetch it. Leave it for me on the chance of my finding it."

"But where? You never will."

The convict thought for a moment.

"I'll tell you," he said. "Lay it in the crack close to the edge of the precipice where I held you half over that day. Cover it with grass. It will be on your way home, and I shall be able to find it if the coast is clear. Once more: straight away for where your horse is grazing. Can you find it, do you think?"

"Oh yes. I can follow my way back," said Nic. "I shall see my tracks here and there."

"Then once more: good-bye."

He turned sharply and disappeared, while, tired and disappointed, Nic had a hard task to retrace his steps to the horse, whistling for it as he drew near where he felt that it ought to be, and gladdened at last, just as darkness was falling, by a responsive neigh.

The long bag of meal was hung up in a tree that Nic felt he could find again, and then he rode home.

"Poor Leather will think I have deceived him and be suspicious, but it's impossible to find that place by the precipice to-night."

Chapter Thirty Five
Nic has Suspicions

The next day Nic walked over to the spot where he had hung up the bag of meal, took plenty of precautions to make sure that he was not observed, and carried it from place to place, halting, resting, and taking a look round as if he were stalking birds, and finally reaching the proposed spot, where he dropped the bag into a narrow crevice, covered it with green, and all the time carried his gun ready as if to aim at a bird.

The precautions, however, appeared to be perfectly unnecessary, and he was satisfied that he had performed his mission unseen, but it remained to be proved whether the convict had been earlier and gone away disappointed.

Making this an opportunity for looking over some sheep, Nic walked about a mile out of his way going back, and had just finished his casual inspection when he came upon Brookes, gun on shoulder, who immediately stood his piece against a bush and began to examine some of the flock, throwing so much energy into the task that Nic felt suspicious, and a chill ran through him as he thought it possible that the man was on the watch.

But Nic felt that the only course open to him was to assume a careless air; and walking over to where the man had caught a sheep, thrown it, and was examining its fleece, he exclaimed:

"Anything the matter with it, Brookes?"

"My word, Mr Nic, how you made me jump! Why, where did you come from?"

"Over yonder. I was here ten minutes ago, and didn't notice anything wrong then."

"Oh, you've been a-shepherding, sir, have you? That's right: sheep's things you can't be too 'tickler about. No, there's nothing very wrong. I'll come round here with a bucket o' dressing, though, to-morrow."

"Shall I go or stay?" thought Nic, as the man turned over layer after layer of the thick wool which opened down the animal's sides as if divided by a series of partings like that leading to the crown of a human being's head. "If I stay I shall make him suspicious. If I go it may disarm him."

"Oh," he said aloud, "that doesn't look bad. I shall go on and get Sorrel. I'm going to ride round the bullocks. Not coming yet, I suppose?"

"No, sir; I'll just run my eye round that hundred over yonder with Black Damper. Haven't counted 'em 'smorning, I s'pose?"

"I haven't been there," said Nic.

"Ah, they'd better be counted. One'd think the blacks could count a flock of sheep, but not they. It's *bulla* and *kimmeroi* and *metancoly*, and saying that over and over again. They can eat as many as you like, but counting beats 'em."

"Yes, they are stupid that way, Brookes," said Nic; and he went straight off for home, looking perfectly unconcerned, but feeling particularly uncomfortable as he turned over in his own mind the possibility of the man finding the convict's hiding-place.

For now it seemed such a very simple thing, and he wondered that the men from the Wattles and the government police had not gone straight for and made some efforts to get down to the bottom of the great gorge.

By degrees, though, he grew better satisfied, as he recalled that this place bore the reputation of being impossible of access, and even the blacks declared that no man had ever been down.

Then came a horrible thought.

"Suppose Brookes should encounter the convict and use the gun he always carried now! Leather was unarmed, but—"

Nic shuddered as he thought of what a strong, active man would do if driven to bay. The gun would only go off once, but a desperate man would find weapons in sticks and stones.

The boy made an effort to cast off the unpleasant sensation, and hurried home, where the calm aspect of everything and the look of content he saw in his mother's and sisters' eyes altered the current of his thoughts; and he hurried himself, saddling Sorrel, and rode off, after promising that he would be back in good time to take tea.

He had a long round, found the cattle wanted driving in a bit, and after performing this duty by the help of his two dogs, he cantered towards home, coming round by where Rigar was playing shepherd with another flock. But all was right here, save that the collies helped to bring them half a mile nearer the station to new pastures; after which Nic turned his horse's head homeward, arriving in good time and finding Brookes busily helping old Sam and looking more like himself.

A couple of days elapsed, and on the following morning Nic announced that he was going to take a long round, the consequence being that his satchel was well filled with bread, meal, and cake; and he rode off after seeing that all was going on right about the place, and in a matter-of-fact sort of way as if he had been used to it for years.

He cantered gently till he was out of sight, and then gave Sorrel his head and skimmed over the ground till he was compelled to draw rein and walk the horse in and out among the trees, besides being careful to avoid the blocks of stone which here and there thrust their grey heads out of the slope.

For he was nearing the spot where he had hidden the meal, and he had determined to fetch it and carry it over his saddle-bow as nearly as he could to where he had parted from the convict.

To his delight, on reaching the hiding-place he found that the bag was gone, and for the moment he was convinced that Leather had fetched it; but Nic's next thought was startling:

"Suppose Brookes had been suspicious—had seen it and taken it away."

The thought was horrible, but he dismissed it, telling himself that he was too ready to imagine things; and, determined to try and find the convict again, he mounted and rode along parallel with the edge of the gorge till he was as nearly as he could guess to where the patch of rock had slipped down.

Here, in a shut-in tract of grassy land, he dismounted, cast his hobbled horse loose to graze, and shouldering his gun, went in among the trees and tried to find the stone trap in which he had been caught.

He looked around him, and then started off in the direction Leather had taken that evening, keeping about fifty yards from the edge so that this distance would serve for his guidance back, and kept looking to right and left for some signs of the convict having passed that way, but finding none.

Every step he took for quite an hour led him through fresh beauties. He had no desire to use his gun; so, as if in consequence, birds of brilliant plumage flitted from tree to tree, or rose in flocks to fly shrieking to the coverts. Twice over he saw snakes; lizards seemed to be wonderfully plentiful wherever the stones lay scorching in the sunshine. Every now and then he saw the Blue Mountains, rising up tier after tier, across the gorge, and as he peered through the various openings he could not help noticing how thoroughly they deserved their names.

But he only saw one natural object in his mental view, and that was the great deep crack, which he felt sure he would encounter before long, running at right angles across his path, and this he felt equally sure would be the way down into the gorge and to Leather's home.

"And if he can go down it," said Nic to himself, "I can, and what's more, I will."

But at the end of another hour there was no sign of any rift such as he had pictured, and beginning to grow hot and weary, he turned to find a sheltered spot where he could rest and refresh himself with some of the provisions that he had intended to share with the convict, when, to his astonishment, he found himself face to face with him, for Leather stood with his back against a stone.

Chapter Thirty Six
In Sanctuary

"You here?" cried Nic excitedly.

"I have been following you for the last hour," was the quiet reply.

"And I've been tramping along here for nothing. Why didn't you speak?"

"Because I wanted you to tramp along there for nothing," replied the convict. "You were not looking for me—I could see that. You were trying to find a way down there below."

"Well, yes, I was," said Nic, who felt startled by his companion's keenness; "but I *wanted* to see you too."

"Well, have you found anything?"

"You know I've not," cried Nic. "I say, you might trust me. How do you get there?"

"Why should I show you the way to the only place of safety I have got?"

"Because you like me," said Nic, with a smile, as he held out his hand, which the other grasped and held.

"Yes," he said; "you made me like you, Nic, and brought me back a little to a better belief in human kind just when I was growing day by day more and more into a brute—a savage. Well, I will show you; but you are tired now."

"Not too tired for that," said Nic eagerly, for there was a suggestion of adventure which attracted him. "I'm ready. Are you going to bind my eyes again? You can if you like, and then you can lead me down and I shall not know the way."

"Why should I do that when I said that I would trust you? Besides," said the convict rather grimly, "you will want your eyes."

"Is it dangerous?" cried Nic.

"In places; but you will not shrink."

"Is it far?"

"A mile from here. This way, then. But wait a few minutes."

Nic stared, for the convict suddenly darted to one side and disappeared, leaving the boy wondering at his singular behaviour. Then there was utter silence, and it seemed as if he had gone for good.

All at once he reappeared from quite a different part, and came quickly up to Nic.

"I am obliged to be watchful," he said. "I did not know but that you might have some one following you; but all seems to be clear. Now then, come along."

He struck off in among the trees, and Nic followed closely, till, wondering at the course his companion was taking, he said suddenly:

"Are you making some short cut? Does the gorge bend round anywhere here?"

"Oh no: I am going quite right."

"But you are leaving the edge of the precipice right behind."

"Yes; that is right. No one would look for the way down where I am leading."

Nic gazed at him wonderingly, for the man's manner seemed moment by moment to grow more strange; but they trudged on for quite a quarter of an hour, through a wonderful chaos of rocks and stunted trees, which formed a dense thicket through which it was hard to pass, and which was at last barred by the rocks closing in.

Here the convict turned sharply to his left, went in, and out for a couple of score yards, and then came to a halt at a rock face, from beneath which a little stream of water gurgled down a long gully for a short distance, and then disappeared.

"Is the water good?" said Nic eagerly.

"Delicious. Drink."

"Then you have been coming to find that?" cried Nic, after taking a long, deep draught. "It is good. But I thought you were going to show me the way down into the gorge."

"Yes: there it is."

"What? Why, where?" cried Nic, staring.

"Down there, where the water goes. Follow that, and you will reach the great valley."

"But," cried Nic, gazing in wonder at what seemed to be a mere split in the rock, down which the light penetrated but a short distance, "that goes underground."

"Yes, nearly all the way."

"A cavern."

"A series of caverns. You do not care to go now?"

"Well, it looks—It is so—One can't hardly—Yes, one can," cried the boy, ceasing his stammering and drawing himself up. "I am quite ready. Will you go first?"

The convict smiled, bent down a little, and passed out of the boy's sight.

"You can jump down boldly here," came in deep, echoing tones: "there is good foothold. A little slippery, but I'll catch you if your foot glides away."

It requires a little effort of mind to leap down off *terra firma* into a black-looking hole whose bottom is invisible, and Nic hesitated for a moment or two. Then:

"Trust for trust," he said to himself, and leaped, to feel for a brief instant or two that strange sensation experienced when rushing downward in a swing. Then *splash*! and his feet sent the water flying as he landed upon soft sand, while a hand grasped his shoulder, and he could dimly see the convict's swarthy face.

"All right?"

"Yes. Did I hit you with the gun?"

"Pretty hard, boy; but, never mind—it didn't go off."

Nic looked round, and by the light which gleamed from above through a lovely lacework of overhanging ferns he could see rugged rocks, which looked of a glistening: metallic green, but in places of a soft rippled cream, as if the rich produce of hundreds of cows had trickled down the walls and turned to stone. Water was flowing about his feet, but only an inch or two deep, and beyond where the convict stood there was black darkness.

"I say, is this really the way down to the bottom of that great gorge, Leather—I mean Frank Mayne?" said Nic breathlessly, for his heart, in spite of his having gone through no exertion, still laboured heavily.

"Yes, and a gloriously easy way, as you will soon see."

"See?" cried Nic.

"Yes; come along."

"One moment," said Nic, pausing to look upward at the arching ferns eight or ten feet overhead. "No one would think of coming down there to look for a way. But how about footmarks in this soft sand? One of the blacks would trace us directly."

"The water trickles over them and washes them full of sand directly, Nic. I am safe in that."

"But did you venture into this black darkness without knowing where you were going? One might slip down into some horrible pit."

"I slipped down into a horrible pit years ago, boy," said the convict bitterly, "and I felt that I could only lose my life in an adventurous search. But I did not go far in the dark. Come on a few yards, and I will show you. There is nothing to mind."

"Does the water get deeper?" whispered Nic, in an awe-stricken voice.

"Never more than an inch or two, except in rainy time, and then of course it becomes a rushing torrent and impassable. Come along: it is always a soft sandy or rippled path formed of petrifactions like that you saw just now."

Nic braced up his nerves and followed the *wash, wash* of the convict's footsteps till his companion cried, "Halt!"

"Now," he said—"hold this."

"This" proved to be a great piece of soft, crumbling touchwood, which felt as if it had been torn from some dry, rotting gum tree; and directly after *nick—nick—nick* came the sound of a flint against a steel: tiny bright scintillations glistened in the black darkness, and soon there was a faint glow as the convict began to blow one spark which had fallen upon the wood Nic held. Then the spark grew brighter and brighter, and at last shed a faint luminous glow sufficient to make darkness visible; and this was increased by the convict taking the piece of wood and waving it softly to and fro.

"A poor light," he said, "but it takes off the worst part of the gloom, and it is comforting. I have not begun making myself candles yet, Nic."

"What's that?" whispered the boy, as there was a peculiar fluttering noise and something swept his cheek softly.

"Only bats. There are plenty here. Don't you smell them?"

"Yes, there is a black-beetly smell; but I thought it was the wood. Are there any—any dangerous beasts down here?"

"There are no dangerous beasts in this country," said the convict, "except poisonous snakes and the crocodiles in the rivers, and I have never seen one of them. No, Nic, there is nothing to fear here but flood after a storm. Now, come along; step out boldly. It is nervous work the first time. I felt a bit scared when I explored it. I could walk through now in the darkness with my hands in my pockets. One only has to let one's feet follow the water."

"But if you did not follow the water?"

"Then you might wander away into one of the side passages, or go down some wide rift and lose your way."

"Is it so big, then?"

"Farther on. There it opens out into huge caverns, and rises up into great cracks and chambers caused by the petrifying stony water. There are sheets and columns and hummocks of stone all made by the drip from above. This place has all been formed by the water eating away the limestone rock, dissolving it here and piling it up there."

As the convict walked on, and Nic followed close behind, the splashing of their feet echoed softly from the walls, and the man's voice sounded shut in and smothered. The air felt hot too, and oppressive, while the smouldering wood glowed and made the convict's figure stand out like a solid carved block moving dimly outlined before Nic as he went on.

Then, all at once, the echoes of the disturbed water grew louder, and went whispering away; and as Leather went on talking his voice seemed to grow free, and the air was cool and damp.

"Now listen," he said; and he paused, waved his smouldering torch, and uttered a loud *cooey*.

Nic caught at his arm, for there was a crash, and a bellowing roar as the cry went echoing away and then gradually died out in whispers.

"Startling, isn't it? But only sound. The cavern is enormous here."

"It's dreadful!" panted Nic.

"No: wonderful and grand, boy. Ah! who knows what may be deeper down in the interior of this mighty world on which we crawl! Come along; you'll have other chances of exploring here—that is, if you come to see me, Nic. Would you venture alone?"

"No," said Nic frankly. "I don't think I should dare."

"Familiarity breeds contempt—even for darkness, Nic," said the convict with a laugh, which sounded horrible. "Don't be in a hurry to say that. I believe that with a lantern you would come. Forward, boy!"

"Is it much farther?"

"Oh yes—a long, long, long way. I was months before I got right through."

"What!" cried Nic in a startled voice; and he wished he had not spoken, for his exclamation sounded as if it would bring down the rocks upon their heads.

"No, no; not as you take it," said the convict laughingly, as he waved the torch and made it glow. "I mean that after I discovered it one day, as I told you, through a sheep falling down into that well-like opening, I made myself a rough lamp from an old pannikin, some melted mutton fat, and a bit of rag, and when I had chances I came down and followed the stream a little farther and a little farther, led on and on by the interest of the place, always expecting to find that it would end with an underground lake."

"And it did not?"

"No, this little stream joins the river in the great valley, as you will see. But we are losing time. Come on."

Nic followed in silence, but with the creepy, shivering sensation passing off; and a feeling of intense curiosity and wonder taking its place.

"Is it much farther?" he said at last.

"Like to go back now, boy?"

"No," cried Nic firmly—"of course not."

"Well, as to being farther to go, I could turn off in several places, and we could wander on for longer than I could say. You can bring friends and explore it some day, perhaps; but down to the valley is not a great way now."

"Down! Are we going down?"

"Of course: flowing water is always going downward. There, you can hear that the rocks are farther away to right and left. Farther on they close in again till it is like a crack, and they run up to a point far above our heads. We must have a good light some day, Nic, if I am not taken. You would like to explore the place?"

"If you are taken!" cried Nic. "Why, you could defend yourself against a hundred people here, and set them at defiance."

"Yes, but I might be surprised. I can't live without sleep, Nic. They'll take me some day. Friend Brookes will find out that you come to see me, and track you to the opening."

"He would not dare to come along here."

"No, but he would send those who did. But never mind that now. Let's enjoy life while we can, even if it is such a poor life as mine."

"I say, Frank Mayne," said Nic, after a thoughtful pause, during which he had listened to the *whish, whish* of their feet through the water, and the whispering echoes, now close at hand, now far away.

"Say on, boy."

"I'm going to the port as soon as my father comes back."

"Going, boy? I'm sorry. But you will come back?"

"I hope so; with news. I shall go and see Sir John and Lady O'Hara, tell them your story, and get you pardoned."

"No. The governor did what he could: I was allowed to go out as an assigned servant; I have disgraced myself, and I should have to go back to the gang."

"Not if he knew that you were innocent."

"My character with which I came out spoils that, boy. Don't talk about it. Mine is a hopeless case."

"But Lady O'Hara is my friend."

"Hush! It is too late."

They went on and on through the obscurity in comparative silence now, Nic feeling as if he were being led always by that black shadow of a gigantic man, beyond which there was a faint glow.

Always the same tramp, tramp through the splashing water, and along its soft bed, which was never more than four or five feet wide at that time, and the flowing stream kept them easily in the right way. Once or twice Nic felt startled at the want of light from the smouldering torch, but a few waves in the air brightened its faint glow again, and they went on and on as if their journey were to be right through the grim bowels of the world.

"Is it much farther?" said Nic at last, to break the painful silence.

"Not much."

"But we seem to have come miles."

"I dare say it is two," said the convict, "but imagination makes it longer. My first journeyings made me think that it must be at least twenty. Come closer here."

Nic stepped up and touched the arm which bore the light.

"Now look straight on."

"I can see nothing."

"You are not looking the right way. Try again."

"Yes, I see now. What is it? A spark?"

"Of daylight. We are nearly through."

Nic's heart throbbed. He felt as if a huge load had been taken off his brain; a thrill ran through him, and he stepped on briskly, with the faint light ahead rapidly growing brighter. Five minutes later they could see the golden glow of sunshine, and in another minute they were wading in deeper water at the bottom of a vast rift overhung by the ferns which grew on the ledges higher and higher. The next minute they stepped out into broad daylight on the sides of the deep cleft, and in a short time, after some sharp climbing, they were at the bottom of the mighty gorge, with Nic shading his aching eyes.

"My little kingdom, Nic," said the convict. "Welcome to my savage home!"

Chapter Thirty Seven
Castles in the Air

"Don't try to find any more adjectives, boy," said the convict about an hour later. "Be content with beautiful. That's what it is."

They were sitting in front of a loosely made bark gunyah, bare-footed, and with their shoes and well-worn stockings placed upon a scorching sheet of rock to dry. The wallet was empty, for they had made a hearty meal; after which Nic had been piling up all the words he could think of to express his admiration for the valley shut in by those tremendous walls, or his delight with the beauty and novelty of the place.

The troubles of his life seemed to have dropped from the convict, who laughed and talked as if he were a dozen years younger, and free from care. The hard, bitter look had gone from his eyes, and he entered with boyish zest into the proposals his young companion made.

"Oh yes," he cried, "we must have plenty of shooting and fishing. How many birds have you collected and skinned?"

"Two," said Nic, making a grimace. "I've been so busy."

"Never mind; you can come here and shoot. I'll skin for you, and you can get a fine collection."

"Birds ought to be plentiful here."

"They swarm," said the convict. "You can get the beautiful lyre bird, with its wonderful curved tail. I can show you the bower birds' nests, with their decorations. Then there is that beautiful purply black kind of crow—the rifle bird they call it. As to the parrots and cockatoos, they are in flocks."

"The kangaroos are plentiful enough, too, seemingly."

"Herds of them, from the little wallaby rats right up to the red old men."

"And snakes?"

"Too many of them; I'm obliged to be careful. We can have some grand hunts, Nic, and I can feast you afterwards on roast cockatoo and mutton."

"And I shall bring you—I say, I'd forgotten: did you bring the flour down here?"

"No," said the convict, smiling; "you forgot to hide it where you said."

"It was too dark that night to find the place, but I put it there next day. Didn't you get it?"

"No; some one must have seen you hide it, and taken it away. One of the blacks, I suppose."

"Or Brookes."

"Was he anywhere near, Nic?"

The boy nodded.

"That's bad, my boy," said the convict, with the bright look fading out of his face, to leave it cold and hard. "There, the sun is getting low; we have the tunnel to go through, and then you have a long walk back to your horse. We have been going too fast, Nic. I'm afraid you must wait some time before you come again."

Nic looked pained, and sat gazing at his companion sadly.

"Must I go now?" he said.

"Yes."

Nic thrust his stockings into his pocket, tied his shoes together to sling over his arm, and picked up his gun. Then reluctantly he followed his silent companion to the mouth of the tunnel-like cavern, where a bigger piece of touchwood was lit, and they commenced the return journey.

It was up hill, but it did not seem half so far; and at last they stopped close to the well-like opening, down whose side the water trickled musically.

"Frank," said Nic, "I'm going to leave you my gun."

"What for?"

"To protect yourself."

"Don't leave temptation in my way, boy," was the stern reply. "No; I will not have it. Brookes and I might meet. There are plenty of trees to cut myself a stout stick for a weapon, or I can defend myself with my hands. Look, there are three notches in the stone where you can place your feet. Up with you! You can find your way. Good-bye."

Nic could not say "good-bye," but he grasped the convict's hand before climbing up the narrow shaft-like place and raising his head cautiously above the level.

A kangaroo loped gently by—evident proof that there was no danger—and, drawing himself right out, Nic dived in among the trees and rocks, and began to return by the way he came.

He had so much to think of that the way back did not seem to be so very long; and at last he reached the spot where he had left his nag, mounted, and rode home, wondering whether Brookes had found that flour and suspected anything.

Chapter Thirty Eight
Nature at Home

If Brookes suspected, he made no show, but went about his work watchful and quiet as could be, Nic noting that he never went to perform the simplest duty about the station without a gun, and always seeming to be on the look-out for danger lurking behind bush, tree, or fence.

"He must feel that Leather is somewhere near at hand," thought Nic, "and he'll betray him if he can."

The convict protested; but, after taking candles and going through the cavern alone, Nic took him flour, tea, and sugar, and various other things to make his solitary life more bearable.

"There, I'm very weak," the poor fellow said one day; "but these are the only happy moments I have had for years, Nic. You have made me like a boy again, and I feel as if I had begun to live a new life. But it is too good to last, Nic. There is too much sunshine, and the storm and flood will come. When does your father return?"

"Don't talk of him as if he were a storm," cried Nic.

"But you will have less liberty then."

"Oh, I don't know; I shall go on taking long rides round after the sheep and cattle. I say, I never told you: we've lost two sheep during the past fortnight."

"The blacks."

"That's what we all thought; but Bungarolo and the others are sure that there have been no blackfellows in the neighbourhood. They went out for two days afterwards, and came back and declared they had seen none. If they had, of course I shouldn't be here. I think it's the dingoes, though we found no skin or bones. Old Sam and I are going to take the dogs and have a hunt. Let Rumble and Tumble run them to bay, and then let loose Nibbler at them."

"Try it," said Leather laconically.

That day, in accordance with a promise, the convict took Nic for a long walk through the open gorge, where the gum trees grew of gigantic size, and on down the river for some miles, to where it spread out into a wide lagoon, completely shut in by the forest, and with the borders fringed by reeds and tall grasses, offering plenty of cover for them to approach. The ducks were in abundance, and Leather laughingly spoke of it as his larder where he fished for them, hiding among the reeds, and sending a small fish sailing among them at the end of a line, with the result that he often hooked one and drew it ashore for a meal.

But it was not to catch a shoal of ducks that they were come, the convict cautiously leading the way to a broad extent of marshy ground, from which the water had retired in consequence of the drought, and here, upon their crawling up to the screen of reeds, Leather drew aside for the boy to peer through to see pretty close at hand a flock of over a hundred grey stork-like birds marching about gravely, and darting their bills down sharply here and there at some fish or frog in a pool. Others were standing on one leg, with the other and the long neck regularly folded up, and the bill tucked neatly away among the feathers.

All seemed grave, calm, and deliberate, every motion being made in the most solemn fashion, one of them the root of whose beak itched scratching it with a claw in a gracefully zigzag mode.

They were fine tall birds, fully four feet in height, and of a beautiful grey; but after kneeling in a damp place for about a quarter of an hour Nic grew weary, and turned to look at the convict, who smiled, nodded, and held up a finger, as much as to say, "Be patient."

"Things never do what you want at the right time," thought Nic; but hardly had he mentally spoken when one of the storks farther off uttered a peculiar cry like the low note of a cracked clarionet, and in an instant the long-legged birds from all quarters came trooping up, some of them helping their movements by extending their wings a little, till all were collected in a rough kind of circle, one remaining almost motionless in the middle of the ring.

A few more of the quaint trumpeted-out notes were heard, and these were uttered by one of the cranes nearest to Nic, who could see the scissors-like beak open, the bright eye, and the gay scarlet ear-lobes of the solemn-looking bird, which drew itself up, took a look round in a stately way, and then seemed to Nic to have gone mad; for it suddenly began to dance and caper about, bowing and shaking its head to its companions again and again before leaping in the air and coming down upon its feet, to go through a series of the wildest gambols imaginable. It waltzed, advanced, retreated, set to partners, skipped here and there with wonderful activity, and began again.

Its actions were contagious, for the next minute fully a hundred of the long-legged bipeds were capering about the marsh in a frantic dance, snapping their bills, and evidently enjoying this ebullition of fantastic gambols.

Nic would have roared with laughter had he not been afraid to send the birds away and so end their game; and this went on for some minutes, ending in a regular wild country dance peculiar to bird-land, after which all was still. Some of the cranes rested on one leg, with a heel projecting from beneath their tails, others stood still with their heads cowered down between their shoulders, and the rest stalked solemnly about, peering here and there in search of frogs or small fish, and it was hard to imagine that these grave and reverent-looking grey signors could ever have been guilty of such antics.

On some days Nic arrived late, and when the moon rose went opossum shooting, the skins being prepared by the convict for a bed. One evening he stayed late to be taken to see the lyre bird come dancing down a green lane between dense casuarinas, to a favourable spot for these beautiful creatures. And once he saw the peculiar bird, large as a pheasant, spread its curious tail, dance, rattle its wings, and indulge in a series of cries and calls—now it would be whistling, at another time making a sound like the cracking of a whip, and at another time justifying its native name of bullan-bullan.

Mayne had always some new natural history object to introduce to Nic, throwing himself heart and soul into his pursuits, and announcing at last that he had seen emus about in one particular spot, and saying he was sure that there must be a nest.

Nic had longed to get specimens of the great dark green eggs, and he heard the announcement with delight.

"Just what I wanted," he cried; "but I meant for us to explore the cavern next time I came."

"If we soon find the nest, we shall have time to do some exploring as well," replied Mayne; "so bring your candles, and I'll get some of the bunya wood and dry it in the sun. It burns well, and it will help to light up some of the dark parts. When will you come over?"

"Day after to-morrow."

"If your father has not returned," said the convict sadly.

"Well, if he does, on the next day. I say, don't look so downhearted. You see that was all fancy about Brookes suspecting anything."

"I don't know," said the convict thoughtfully.

"I think I do," said Nic, laughing. "He has been as nervous as can be for fear of your coming back to punish him for laying information about you with Mr Dillon. If he felt that you were anywhere near, he would soon go over to the Wattles again. Sam says you've gone right away a hundred miles up in the myall scrub to join the Gunalong tribe, and married and settled."

"Indeed!"

"Yes, he said we should never see you again. Good-bye."

The convict grasped his hand, and they parted at the mouth of the cavern.

"Nic, my dear," said Mrs Braydon that night. "You will be obliged to have some more shoes; those last have quite rotted away at the stitching. You seem to be always wading and getting your feet wet. Do be careful, my dear; it is so difficult to get anything new. Is all well about the station?"

"Everything, mother, excepting the loss of those sheep. We must have a dingo hunt. It won't do to lose any more before father comes home."

Mrs Braydon sighed.

"It seems so long since we have heard, my dear," she said. "If it were not that I don't like to spare you, I would get you to ride over and see how Sir John is getting on."

Nic thought he would like to go; but he, too, felt that it would not be possible to leave home, and for more reasons than one.

Chapter Thirty Nine
A Double Surprise

"'Nother sheep gone, Master Nic," said Brookes next morning.

"Then we'll have the dogs out and have a hunt round. Whose flock was it among?"

"Bung's."

"All right, then; we'll have a turn at once."

Old Sam was told of what was to take place, Damper and Rigar were fetched from their charges, and gladly joined in, while the dogs nearly went mad—all three seeming to fully understand what was going to take place, and displaying their mad delight by charging and rolling one another over, and a sham worry all round, that suggested horrors for any unfortunate dingo with which they were not at play.

As Nic rode on between his two men, with the dogs and blacks in front, he began to feel a little suspicious of the latter, from the way in which they talked and laughed one to the other, as if they enjoyed the loss of a sheep as a very good joke; and the boy could not help asking himself whether they were taking advantage of his inexperience to help themselves to the wherewithal for an occasional feast.

This impressed him so much at last that he mentioned his suspicions to old Sam.

But the man shook his head.

"No, sir; I think not," he replied. "We look too sharp after 'em, and they're too well fed. I won't say what a hungry blackfellow mightn't do, but our boys ain't hungry, and that makes all the difference. What do you say, Brooky?"

"I say it ain't the blacks; but I know."

As the man spoke he examined the pan of his gun, and then took out his knife and began to chip the flint, so that it might be certain to strike out sparks.

"What do you know?" said Nic, looking at the man wonderingly.

"What do I know?" said Brookes, giving him a defiant look: "why, I know it's that there Leather as is skulking about like a rat, and snatching a sheep whenever he likes."

"Absurd!" cried Nic indignantly.

"Oh, all right, sir, it's 'surd, then; you know best, o' course. You're master, and I'm on'y a servant; but I say as that there Leather killed all them sheep, and if the doctor was at home he'd soon stop that."

"Go on, dogs!" shouted Nic, riding forward to hide his annoyance and fidgety looks, for Brookes had looked at him in a way which troubled him.

The blacks led on among the trees and over the pastures, now nearly brown for want of rain; and to Nic's annoyance the men made for the stretch of country which ran along by the side of the gorge. Then suddenly one of the collies uttered a sharp bark, which was taken up by the other, Nibbler gave forth his deep growl, and as they started off on the scent of something, he followed, and the blacks trotted close behind.

Nic felt a peculiar, sense of hesitation; but his two men started in a run, and he felt that he must go too, though this part of the country seemed to him the least likely for dingoes, and he began to wonder whether the dogs had taken up the scent of a man who had passed that way, and if so, would it be the convict?

Ten minutes later he felt ready to stop the hunt, for the dogs were right on the line he would have himself taken to reach the spring which ran down to the tunnel-like cavern. Certainly it was miles away, but, going at a pretty good speed, Nic felt that the dogs would quickly reduce the distance, and his horror increased.

"They'll soon have him, Master Nic," panted old Sam, who ran, in spite of his years, better than his companion, the blacks being now out of sight.

"Have whom?" cried Nic; but he repented directly, for Brookes turned and gave him another curious look.

"Why, that there dingo, sir," said Sam.

"*Cooey—cooey!*" came from a distance, as the faint barking of the dogs ceased; and Nic pressed forward, to arrive, in a quarter of a mile or so, at a dense thicket, within which he could see the blacks and hear the dogs whining and snuffling about.

"Got him?" cried Nic, with an intense feeling of relief.

"Mine help dog follow find him," cried Bungarolo with a broad grin; and the boy urged his horse in through the bushes, to find a skin tossed down, and plenty of evidence of a sheep having been lately killed there.

He was staring down at the remains, while the dogs stood whining and snuffling round, eager to make a feast of the offal, but kept back by the blacks, who each held a nulla-nulla with its melon-shaped knob in front of their noses.

"He! he!" laughed Brookes. "That's a clever sort o' dingo, Sam. I never see one skin his sheep before and dress him."

Old Sam rubbed one side of his nose and looked at Nic, who turned sharply to the blacks.

"Here, you!" he cried angrily—"you killed this sheep!"

"Baal! Baal!" they cried in angry chorus. "No kill—no mumkull sheep fellow. Plenty mutton—plenty. White Mary gib plenty mutton. You pidney (know)."

"No, I want to pidney," cried Nic. "Here, Bung, who killed the sheep, then?"

"No pidney. Soon find."

The man, imitated by his fellows, began to search about, and soon took up a barefoot trail and pointed to a drop of blood now and then where it lay dried upon a leaf.

"Could Leather have killed a sheep and taken it away?" thought Nic. "No—impossible!" and he was following the blacks in a hesitating spirit, when Brookes stopped short.

"What is it?" cried old Sam, imitating his action.

"I ain't going to walk into no hambudges," growled Brookes.

This roused Nic into action.

"Here!—Hi! Bung, all of you stop!" he cried, and the blacks paused and waited till they came up, looking at their young master inquiringly.

"Find tracks?" asked Nic.

"Plenty mine find mandowie."

"Black fellow's?" cried Nic.

"Baal! Baal! white fellow!" cried all three—"white fellow."

Brookes gave a ghastly grin and cocked his gun.

"I ain't going no farther," he growled. "It's walking into a hambudge. Black fellows don't kill sheep like that."

"No plenty mumkull sheep," cried Damper. "White fellow."

"P'r'aps we'd better not go on, sir," whispered old Sam uneasily.

Nic said nothing, but rode slowly back to where the remains of the sheep had been discovered, followed by the rest, the blacks chattering together in a great state of excitement, and the dogs whining and uneasy.

"Pick up the skin, Sam," said Nic; and the old man made one of the blacks carry it shouldered over his spear.

Nothing more was said, Nic riding along feeling sadly puzzled, and trying to follow out a peculiar line of thought without success. It had something to do with an idea about, spite, and whether it was possible that Brookes had killed these sheep on purpose to make it seem that Leather was lurking about destroying his late employer's property, so that, when once this idea took deep root, another expedition might be planned for the purpose of hunting the convict down, and relieving him of an object which caused him constant dread.

But Nic gave Brookes the benefit of a doubt, and rode silently on till he was in sight of the house, when he suddenly pressed his horse's sides and galloped forward.

For he had caught sight of a light waggon drawn up in front; there were horses and men about, and he felt that something important had taken place in his absence.

Ten minutes later he was grasping his father's hands, and then those of the governor, who looked very pale and thin. Lastly those of Lady O'Hara, who held his tightly.

"Oh! just look at him," she cried; "why, he's brown as chestnuts and getting as big as a man. Sure, and what do ye water him with, Mrs Braydon, to make him grow like that?"

"Yes, he has grown," said Nic's mother, smiling with pride.

"Grown! why, he's shot up like a palm tree. Nic, boy, we've come up with your father for me husband to get quite cured: will you have us for a bit?"

Nic's eyes silently gave their answer as he clung to lady O'Hara's hand, just as he did that day when she came to the Friary to fetch him from school, not so very long back; but so many events had happened since, that it seemed an age to the boy, who felt how different he was since then.

"You don't deserve for us to come, Mrs Braydon," said Lady O'Hara as they sat over their homely meal that evening, "for you never come to stay with me, nor the girls neither."

"You see what a simple farmhouse life we lead," said Mrs Braydon, smiling. "We are not fit for Government House."

"Now just hark at her, John!" cried the lady. "Do we want her to come and see Government House? It's to see us."

"Mrs Braydon knows that," said Sir John gravely, "and how deeply we are in her debt. Here we are, after robbing her of her natural protector all this time, come to trouble her more."

"Then let's go back, John," said Lady O'Hara dilly; "sure we're not welcome. We're too foine for her."

"Lady O'Hara!" cried Mrs Braydon indignantly.

"That's brought her to her senses," said the visitor, rising and going to Mrs Braydon to kiss her affectionately. "Don't you know that you're all the dearest and best friends we've got in the world? Hasn't the doctor been sitting up with John night after night, and saved his life?"

"Oh, nonsense! nonsense!" said the doctor quickly.

"It's quite true, Mrs Braydon," said the governor warmly; "and God bless him for it!"

"There!" cried Lady O'Hara, "now let's all be comfortable. Why, it's like being at home, at the old place from which John fetched me when he was only Lieutenant O'Hara, and hadn't a grand handle to his name. Gyurls, I'm going to enjoy myself with you while the governor gets strong and well. Sure I can make butter as well as either of you. Didn't we have two Kerry cows at home? As for bread, there I'll bate—beat I mean—either of you. Nic, boy, you'll take me round with you when you go to see to the stock; only I must have a quiet ould mare—none of your great tatthering savage craytures that want to go like the wind. I've brought my strong riding habit. And you gyurls, you'll ride too?"

"Of course," cried Janet eagerly.

"Then we're going to have quite a happy time; and John'll get quite strong, won't he, doctor?"

"Yes, he'll be a new man in a month."

"What!" cried the lady, with an assumed look of alarm: "John, darlin', order the waggon and horses out. Ring for the men. We'll go back home directly, and try the new doctor that's just come out."

"Why?" said Sir John, smiling.

"Sure, didn't he say he'd make a new man of you? Don't I want you the same as you always were? A new man, indeed!"

A merry evening was passed, but before they parted for the night the doctor said:

"I've asked no questions, Nic, boy; but all seems to be right."

"Nearly, father—not quite."

"Not quite? Well, that doesn't sound very serious. But I want to know fully what this upset has been about the assigned servant."

Nic briefly told of the trouble.

"Ah, well, we'll have that over in the morning, Nic. I'm sorry, though, for I thought the man was trustworthy."

Nic gave his father a pained look, as the doctor went on: "I shall ride over and see Dillon. Well, what next?"

"Three sheep have gone, father, one after the other."

"I am not surprised," said the doctor drily.

"But, father—" began Nic.

"Not to-night, my boy. I know what you are going to say. This man was rather a favourite of yours. Now, what other troubles?"

"None, father."

"That's good. Then you've done well, boy. But I was very anxious to get back, for there has been a serious rising among the convicts, and two parties have escaped to the bush. I was afraid you might be having a visitation."

"They're taken by this time, Braydon, depend upon it," said Sir John. "My people will not rest till they are. There, I'm tired out. You'll excuse me to-night?"

"I beg your pardon, O'Hara," said the doctor. "Yes, bed for us too. Good night, Nic. To-morrow you will have to render me an account of your stewardship."

Nic sought his bed that night with mingled feelings of pleasure and pain.

It was delightful to feel the warm grip of his father's hand again, and to see Lady O'Hara's merry, cheery face; but, on the other hand, after being captain of the station so long, there was a slight suspicion of regret at having to give up his independent position; and then there was the trouble about the convict. His father said he would go and see Mr Dillon, and there was what the magistrate would say about him. Then his conscience smote him for that which was a lapse of duty. He had made so great an intimate of Leather, and he felt as if he had been helping him to defy the law. Sir John O'Hara was sleeping under their roof now, and he was governor, judge—a regular viceroy in the colony. What would he say?

Above all, what would the doctor do?

It was a long time before Nic could settle off to sleep that night, and in consequence he was very late the next morning.

Chapter Forty
The Doctor Plays Magistrate

Do I mean Nic did not get down till breakfast was ready, about eight o'clock?

No, I do not. This was Australia in its earlier days of the colony, and people's habits were different from ours.

Nic Braydon's lateness consisted in his being fast asleep when the piping crow began to run up and down its scales to announce that the stars were paling faster, when the laughing jackasses chuckled at the loud crowing of the cocks; and he was dreaming about Mayne being brought up to the station by mounted police when the sun had been visible an hour.

Nic started up in a profuse perspiration, jumped out of bed and dressed rapidly, eager to get out in the paddocks to see that the bullocks and horses that brought the party on the previous day were properly attended to.

He now met the three men who had come with the waggon busy enough unpacking, and he found that Brookes, old Sam, and the three blacks were all hard at work. The fresh milk was being brought into the dairy, the horses were being fed and rubbed down, and all was going on in the satisfactory way which the boy felt would please his father.

Directly after he ran against old Sam.

"Does one's eyes good to see the master back again, sir. How well he looks!"

"Yes, Sam. By the way, I didn't see the horse. How does it look?"

"Splendid, sir; but a good run in our enclosure won't do it no harm."

"Let's go and look at it."

"Look at it?" said the old man, grinning. "Well, you'll have to wait till the master comes back."

"Comes back! What, is he up?"

"Up, my lad? Hours ago, and his nag saddled and gone."

"And I asleep!" cried Nic, in a tone full of vexation. "Which way did he go? I'll saddle up and ride to meet him."

"He's gone over to the Wattles."

"To Mr Dillon's?"

"Yes, sir. He had a few words with Brooky, and went off directly. Here, let me clap the saddle on for you, sir."

"No, thank you, Sam," said the boy, with the tone of his voice changing. "I don't think I wish to go now."

The old man looked at him compassionately. "Don't you be downhearted, my lad," he said. "You've done right enough. You out with the plain truth, and you call me for a witness 'bout Leather. My word's as good with your father as Brooky's. Don't you be afraid. You and me's going to win."

"Yes, Sam, I hope so," said Nic; and he walked away, to busy himself about the farm stock till breakfast time.

Just before it was ready the doctor rode back, threw the rein to old Sam, nodded to Nic, and, looking unusually stern, he entered the house with his son.

Breakfast was ready, the governor and his wife up, and the latter kept the conversation going merrily enough, for she could read the doctor's face, and felt from Nic's looks that something was wrong—something for which he was about to be blamed.

Every one was glad when the meal was at an end, and the doctor rose, when Mrs Braydon darted an imploring look at her husband, the two girls one of commiseration at their brother, whose forehead did not wrinkle, but became crumpled and pitted, just as it used to at the Friary when he had to deal with a knotty sum or equation.

"Oh dear!" said Lady O'Hara. "I thought we had left all the business at home. Are you coming with me, John?"

"No; my dear; I think Braydon wants me."

"If you please," said the doctor. "Nic, my boy, fetch the two men round to my room. This way, O'Hara."

Nic went out to obey his father's order and the governor followed the doctor into the room which stood at the end of the house, and was used by the doctor for his own study, library, surgery, harness-room—storehouse for everything, in fact, in connection with the station.

"It's not very serious, I hope," said the governor, as soon as they were alone.

"Serious enough," replied the doctor. "Dillon has told me all about it, and I am half pleased, half angry with the boy."

"Then he can't have done much amiss, doctor," said the governor. "Plus kills minus. If Nic is half and half, he ought to be a very decent sort of boy."

"You'll help me if I want help?"

"Of course," said the governor. "There, I dare say there's not much amiss. Boys of seventeen, or so, are not at their worst age. It is over that trouble about your assigned servant?"

"Yes; the boy likes him, and I am not sure about him."

"He may be honest enough now; but he was always a strangely soured fellow, and I don't think I liked him much."

"Prejudice, perhaps."

"I'm afraid so; but here comes the boy."

In effect Nic came now to the door, followed by the two men, both of whom looked uneasy, while Nic's countenance was disfigured by rather a sullen, ill-used look.

"Come in," said the doctor sharply. "You too, my men. Nic, stand there."

Nic took the appointed place, and the men were nearly opposite, both stroking their heads carefully, Brookes his hair, old Sam his skin, for there was no hair on the top to stroke. The governor, who looked pale and weak, sat back in a rough chair.

"Now, Brookes," said the doctor sternly; "I have been over to Mr Dillon and heard about this trouble, one which ought not to have happened in my absence. I should now like to hear your statement."

Brookes gave it, and old Sam kept on uttering grunts till the man had done, when he gave his version.

"Now, Dominic," said the doctor sternly, and the governor sat watching the boy keenly. "You have heard what Brookes says. Speak out, sir, like an English gentleman and my son. Let me tell you, first of all, that I do not believe you would be guilty of such an offence against the law as Brookes suggests; but—"

"Oh, it's true enough," grumbled the man.

"Silence, sir!" cried the doctor angrily. "You have spoken; don't interrupt again." Then turning to Nic: "I was going to say, my boy, as this charge has been brought against you in the presence of our governor, that you have aided and abetted a violent convict, I call upon you to clear yourself at once. Now, boy, speak."

"Yes, father, I'll speak," said Nic firmly; "but I can't clear myself."

"What!" cried the doctor angrily. "Do you own that this accusation is true?"

"Yes, it's true enough," cried Brookes. "He helped him to get away from the Wattles."

"Silence, sir!" cried Sir John sternly.

"Speak, Nic. Did you help this man to escape?"

"No, father."

"There!" cried the doctor in triumph; but his countenance fell directly.

"I went to help him if I could, but he got away without."

Brookes chuckled.

"Then he is somewhere about here in the bush, as Brookes says?"

"Yes, father."

"And you know where?"

"Yes, father."

"And you have been in the habit of visiting this desperate man?"

"Yes, father, all that is quite true."

Brookes chuckled again with satisfaction, and rubbed his tawny brown hands as if he were washing them.

"Nic, you astound me!" cried the doctor. "You have, then, encouraged this man about the place during my absence, when I had placed confidence in you and left you in charge. Had you no respect for your mother and sisters?"

"Why, of course, father," cried the boy indignantly. "You don't suppose I should have done what I have, if I hadn't felt sure Leather was innocent?"

"Hear! hear!" said a voice, and Nic looked up to see that Lady O'Hara was at the door, and now came and stood behind Sir John.

"Innocent," cried the doctor, "and hides in the bush, and kills one of my sheep whenever he is hungry!"

"He doesn't, father. I'm sure he wouldn't," cried Nic indignantly.

"And pray, why not?"

"Because he likes me too well."

"Indeed," said the doctor. "Nic, how can you let yourself be imposed upon so easily by a scoundrel?"

"He is not a scoundrel, father," cried Nic, flushing up. "He was condemned for what he never did, and sent out here as a convict."

"I'm afraid they are all innocent, eh, Sir John?" said the doctor.

"A very large percentage, by their own account," replied the governor.

"But this man really is, father," cried Nic.

"How do you know?"

"He told me all his history, father, and I am sure he is honest."

"And takes advantage of my absence to break out and nearly kill one of my men. Then he escapes to the bush, and now steals my sheep."

"It was Brookes who took advantage of your absence, father."

"Oh, Master Nic!"

"You did, sir. You always behaved like a brute and a bully to poor Leather, and you struck him, and of course he struck you again; and then;" cried the boy rapidly, in his excitement, "you told lies to Mr Dillon, and had him fetched over there to be flogged; and do you think," he continued, turning his flushed face to Sir John, "if I knew I was innocent, and I was dragged away to be flogged with the cat, I wouldn't run for the bush? Why, I would to-morrow."

Sir John frowned, and the doctor looked pained and angry, but he did not speak.

"Well, all I know is, I've got the mark o' the chopper on the back o' my head still," said Brookes, rubbing the place softly.

"Mark of the chopper!" cried Nic contemptuously. "You ought to have the mark of the cat."

"Silence, Dominic!" cried the doctor. "It is very clear to me that you have let this man impose upon you by his insidious ways, and I am bitterly hurt by your folly. You ought to know better. However, the past is past. Now make amends by helping to have this man taken. Where is he?"

"Out in the bush, father."

"I know that, sir," said the doctor sternly. "No evasions, if you please. Where is his hiding-place?"

"Don't be angry with me, father," said Nic, in a pleading tone. "I can't tell you."

"You know?"

"Yes, father."

"Then where is he, sir?"

Nic was silent.

"I desire that you tell me at once."

Nic's brow grew more puckered, but his lips tightened. "Look here, boy. Are you going to disgrace me here before Sir John O'Hara by your disobedience, and by refusing to give up this criminal to the law?"

"Father, he is quite innocent, and he has trusted me. I can't be such a coward—such a wretch—as to give him up."

The doctor took a step forward as if to seize his son's arm.

"One moment, Braydon," said Sir John. "Let me speak to him."

The doctor drew back, and stood frowning.

"It is an error of judgment on the boy's part. When we were his age we thought we knew better than our elders; but we know better now. Look here, Dominic, my boy. You are in the wrong. This man, your father's assigned servant, was tried by a jury of his fellow-countrymen, found guilty, and sentenced to transportation. Well, my boy, we are all under the law, which protects us, and we require its protection very much in a new colony of such an exceptional kind as this."

"But the law was unjust to him, Sir John, and cruel."

"I think not, my boy. Certainly mistakes have been made. But here, you see, the law was not so cruel, but said to this man, 'You have served a certain amount of time; now go and prove your sorrow for your crime by making yourself a faithful servant, and in good time you shall go free, with an opportunity for commencing a new career.'"

"Yes, Sir John; and Leather—his name's Frank Mayne—has been a good servant. Hasn't he, father?"

"Yes, he has worked very well."

"And so he did, father, while you were away, till that man drove him to desperation."

"I cannot argue about all this, Dominic," said Sir John. "I have to judge this matter, and I am afraid, my boy, that you have been imposed upon, for matters look very black against this man."

Nic shook his head.

"Well, my boy, they do to me. But look here, Dominic. Now, more than ever, do we all need to join hand in hand—boys as well as men—for our mutual protection. Even during the past few weeks has a desperate gang of scoundrels broken away and taken to the bush, where our warder-guard and the soldiery have been unable to hunt them down. These men must be taken, and your friend too. Now, listen to me, boy. For your sake, as the son of my best friend, I promise you this: if you will enable us to capture this man, he shall have a fair examination before me, and I will carefully balance all evidence, and the good in him against the evil. You will trust me, Dominic?"

"Yes, Sir John; but I can't betray the man who has made me believe in him, and whom I look upon as a friend."

"Then—" cried the doctor.

"Stop!" said Sir John firmly. "This case is adjourned for a week, Dominic. Take time to think, my boy. This man must be taken—he shall be taken. It will be better if you show us where he is, than for him to be seized and driven to desperation. Blood may be shed."

"Here, I can show you where he is, sir!" cried Brookes.

"You know?" cried the doctor.

"Ay, sir. I ain't been keeping an eye on young master here for nothing ever since you've been away. I'll show you where he's to be found, and where he takes the sheep he steals."

"Stop," said Sir John. "We will wait a week to give Dominic time to think. And now, doctor, I think I'll take my airing out on your breezy hills. I'm much stronger to-day."

Sir John rose, and the doctor made an imperative gesture to the men to leave the room before offering Sir John his arm and leading him out; while directly after Mrs Braydon and her daughters entered, Janet going at once to her brother and whispering:

"Thank you, Nic: it was very good and brave."

"Ah," cried Lady O'Hara, "what's that ye're saying, gyurl, to this young criminal?"

"I was only speaking to my brother, Lady O'Hara," said Janet indignantly.

"Only shpaking to your brother. I heard you. Only, eh? I only guess what you said. Ye're encouraging him in his wickedness and his rising against the law. Nic, my boy, you've behaved very badly; you're a disobedient son, and a bad citizen, and I ought to be very angry; but somehow I can't, for I like the spirit in you."

"But you wouldn't have had me betray that poor fellow, whom I believe to be innocent, Lady O'Hara," cried Nic, in choking voice, "and give him up to be flogged, and sent back to the chain gang?"

"Bedad, I wouldn't," cried the lady, turning very Irish, and dragging him to her, she gave him a sounding kiss. "I'd have called ye no boy of mine if ye had, and your mother wid the gyurls say the same, don't ye, my dears?"

"Oh yes," came in chorus.

"But it's all very wrong, Nic; I say so who am the governor's wife; and this black sheep-thayving convict of yours'll be coming and killing us all in our beds."

Chapter Forty One
Right Wins

One idea uppermost in Nic's mind was that he must go and warn Frank Mayne that his father was back, that the governor was at the station with two men, that—as he had since heard—a party of mounted police were coming up to scour the country for escaped convicts, and of course they would search for him as well.

But how to warn him and tell him that he was sure Brookes must have been always watching, and knew pretty nearly if not surely of his hiding-place?

Nic felt that he could not go to the cavern tunnel, nor even approach it. Brookes would for certain be on the look-out, and the trouble would be made worse.

The governor had said that Nic should have a week for consideration, and three days glided by rapidly without an allusion being made by the doctor, who took Sir John about with him for long rides, and in every way expressed his satisfaction at the state of affairs about the station.

"You've done wonders, Nic," he said; but the boy felt no better. There was that sensation of being half guilty always to the front, and there were times when he felt as if he would rather the seven days had come to an end, the subject been broached again, and the horrible suspense over.

"I can't do anything," he said to himself. "It is like going more and more against father's orders to warn poor Frank; but what can I do?"

It was the evening of the fourth day, and as Nic was hanging about the garden outside the fence, listening to Lady O'Hara's cheery voice and his sister's answers, while the governor and Doctor and Mrs Braydon were seated in the sunlit verandah, Janet suddenly stood before him.

"Nic," she said in a low voice, and her face was very pale, "you and I are both sorry for that poor fellow Leather?"

"Yes."

"Lady O'Hara has been telling me that there will be a party of mounted police here to-morrow on purpose to hunt down escaped convicts."

"So soon?" said Nic excitedly.

"Yes; perhaps sooner. You know where this man is hiding?"

Nic was silent.

"You need not tell me—I feel sure you do. Ought he not to be told, so that he may escape?"

"Yes," said Nic; "but if I try to warn him I shall be followed, and the way into his hiding-place found out."

"Janet!"

"Yes."

"Here: Lady O'Hara wants you."

"I must go," whispered Janet hastily. "Pray do something, Nic. It would be too horrible for that poor fellow to be hunted down."

Janet hurried away.

"Do something, when I cannot stir without feeling that Brookes and these two men of Sir John's are watching me!"

Then a thought occurred, and the boy lounged leisurely about to where the dogs were playing, with the blacks looking on; and watching his opportunity he crept up close to Bungarolo.

"Look here, Bung," he said in a low voice.

The black turned round and stared.

"No, no: look at the dogs," said Nic.

"What for mine look at dogs? White Nic going hit mine in back."

"I'm not going to hit you," said Nic hurriedly.

"Kick mine. This fellow pidney."

"Nonsense! Look here. You know where Leather is."

"No pidney—no pidney."

"I say you do," said Nic sternly. "Now look here. You go to him to-night and tell him that the white police fellows are coming to hunt him out. You pidney?"

"Yes, Bungarolo pidney."

"Tell him he is to go right away and hide till the police fellows are gone."

"Bungarolo pidney. Mine tell Leather fellow jump right away, and police fellow baal find."

"That's right. Go as soon as it's dark."

"You come along see?"

"No, I won't watch you."

The black nodded, and then laughed at some antics performed by the dogs, while Nic walked away feeling more comfortable in his own mind than he had since his father had returned—though that did not mean much.

He was fully on the *qui vive*, and several times went out into the dark, still night to listen for the tramp of horses, but the police did not come, and he went to bed to dream of Leather being shot down in the bush because he would not surrender.

The next morning, as soon as he was up, Nic went to look for his black messenger, but he was missing, and the other two blacks professed ignorance of his whereabouts.

"He has gone and not come back," thought Nic; and he felt hopeful that, knowing his danger, the convict would escape right away along the gorge, and hide in some far-away fastness where he would be safe. But about the middle of the morning, to the boy's horror, he saw Bungarolo come crawling up to the station driving a flock of sheep.

Nic hurried up to him.

"Did you go and tell Leather?" he whispered.

"No go tell Leather fellow. Leather say mine come nigh get mumkull."

"But I told you to go!"

"Leather mumkull Bungarolo. Mine not want mumkull."

Nic uttered a low groan.

"Brooky look at mine. Come along, see where mine go. Doctor tell mine fetch sheep fellow. Mine go fetch sheep fellow."

"It's of no use—I must go," said Nic to himself; and then, casting aside all hesitation, he started off at once straight for the fern gully, crossed the bridge, and then made a sharp turn off to the right along another path and down by the little river, where, upon reaching the clump of rough growth which bordered the pool where he had fished that day, he suddenly crouched down in among the tree ferns and listened.

There was cause for his suspicion.

He had not been hiding five minutes before he heard a rustling sound, and directly after he caught sight of the barrel of a gun, which was followed by the man who bore it.

There was no mistake. It was Brookes following him, to see which way he went.

Nic's countenance grew dark as he waited, meaning to slip back; when, to his surprise, Bungarolo suddenly crept into sight, following Brookes's trail, and he too disappeared.

The boy did not understand this, but he knew enough. Brookes had gone off on a wrong trail, and now was the time.

Running back, whenever he could do so unseen, Nic passed round the far side of the house, and started right straight away across country, so as to strike the side of the great gorge not far from the well-like tunnel entrance.

It was a long, hot walk, for Nic felt it would be wise to take advantage of every bit of cover whence he could look back to see if he were watched. Then, satisfied that the coast was clear, he went on and reached the dense belt which ran all along by the edge of the precipice, feeling that a couple of hours' more walking would bring him to the mouth of the cavern.

He would not be back before dark, he knew, even if he found the convict directly; but he felt that perhaps he would not be questioned, and he would have placed the fugitive upon his guard.

Nic went pretty boldly onward, till he came within a mile of the opening, and then he sat down to rest and think.

He dared not now go straight to the place, as it was still possible that he might be watched. For Brookes had been so long amongst the blacks that he had picked up a great many of their habits, and for aught he knew, the man might be tracking him still—in all probability was.

To meet this difficulty, then, Nic started again; but went away at a right-angle, struck off again, and zigzagging here and there, he slowly drew nearer and nearer to the opening.

The sun beat down heavily in the treeless parts, but Nic heeded it not. He was anxious to reach the convict, give him a word of warning, and get back as rapidly as possible, unseen; and how to do this exercised all his thoughts.

Every now and then, as he crept along, stooping amidst the bushes, he startled some wild creature—bird, reptile, or one of the numerous kangaroo family—and, the animal darting away, Nic's heart throbbed with satisfaction.

For it was a good sign: nobody had been there lately.

At last he was within a few hundred yards of the opening, and he took a fresh curve so as to approach from the farther side, meaning to creep among the rocks and drop down into the hole almost at a bound.

And now his excitement culminated, for in a few more minutes he would be in the tunnel, and if fortune favoured him, would soon reach his friend, warn him, and return in comparative peace.

He was congratulating himself upon having succeeded so well, when he suddenly stopped short, half stunned by the thought which struck him. There was that long tunnel with its many forkings to descend, and he had no light, neither the means of getting one, nor candle, nor wood.

He went on again with his teeth set fast. He would do it, he thought, even in the dark, for it only meant keeping in the water and wading. He must go right.

A hundred yards onward through the wilderness of rocks, trees, and scrub; and he stopped short again, grasping his gun nervously, for he fancied he had heard the crack as of a trampled-on piece of dead wood.

But there was no sound now save the hum of insects. The birds were silent in that torrid midday.

"Fancy!" thought Nic, as he crept on again, stooping low and keeping a watchful eye in every direction, till once more a chill of apprehension ran through him, for there was a crackling, rustling noise.

He knew what it was: a twig bent back had sprung to its natural position; but who had bent back that twig? was it he or some one following his trail?

He listened, with every nerve on the strain, but there was no sound; and after crouching low, perfectly still for some minutes, he felt convinced that it was his own act: the twig had caught a leaf, been held by for a minute or so, and then released.

"I wish I was not such a coward," thought Nic, as he once more started off, satisfied now that he was close at hand, for he could just see the piled-up rocks from beneath which the spring bubbled out.

And now, as more cautiously than ever he crept on, so as to get within springing distance of the hole, he began to think of the long, deep, cool drink in which he would indulge—for his throat felt dry, and he was suffering from a parching, burning thirst.

Closer and closer and closer he crawled, now on hands and knees, with his gun slung over his back—so near that he had but to spring up and take a few steps to be there, but holding back so as to preserve the greatest caution to the very last.

In this way he reached to within five yards of the hole,—stretched out a hand to press aside a frond of fern, and gave one good look round.

He did so, and held on as if paralysed, feeling as if he were dreaming of being back on board the *Northumbrian* on his voyage out, and watching the convicts having their daily airing.

For there, just in front of him, and one on either side of the hole, half hidden by clumps of fern, crouched, like a couple of terriers watching a rat-hole, two of the convicts whom he had forgotten, but whose features and peculiarities were once more filling his brain.

Yes, there they were; he did not remember their numbers, but their features were clear enough: those of the pitiful, hang-dog, pleading-looking convict, whom he had set down as a sneak; and the good-humoured, snub-nosed, common scoundrel who had amused himself by making grimaces whenever he encountered his eye.

But that which startled Nic the most was the fact that they were inimical to the tenant of the cavern, for, as they watched so intently that they had not heard the boy's approach, each man held a native war club or nulla-nulla—poised ready to strike the poor fellow who raised his head above the edge of the hole, and a blow from one of those clubs meant death.

For some moments Nic felt too much stunned to even think, while the silence and the rigid motionless position of the two men before him added to the idea that it might be after all imagination.

Then all at once one of the men showed him that it was no fancy, for he raised his eyes looked across at his companion, and made a mocking grimace, just as he had been wont to do on shipboard, getting as answer a deprecating shake of the head.

And what did it mean? Death to Frank Mayne as he came up. For it was easy to see these were two of the convicts who had escaped. They were to blame for the missing sheep, and they must have seen and tracked Mayne to his hiding-place and meant his death.

This last was hard to comprehend, for why should one escaped convict wish to injure another? But Nic had no time for arguing out problems. The men intended harm to his friend, and it was his duty to try and save him. He had his gun, and if he could only hear Frank Mayne coming, a shout of warning would send him back.

But that gun: he wanted it for his own protection as well; and a shudder of horror ran through him as at that moment he again recalled the deck of the ship, with the convicts marching round and round, the soldiers resting upon their muskets, the stern-looking warders with their cutlasses, and that other man with the lowered, restless eyes and savage, wild-beast aspect, who passed him by from time to time looking ready for any evil deed.

How well Nic remembered now, and the old warder's words! and the cold shiver ran through him once again.

For suppose that wretch had escaped as well, and was lurking about free so near the Bluff? The idea was horrible, and but for Frank Mayne's sake Nic would have gloried in seeing the mounted police at hand.

But that gun! How could he have been so idiotic as to sling it across his shoulder just where he could not get at it without making some rustling sound!

Still it must be done, and he very softly drew his fingers toward the buckle at his breast, meaning to undo the strap instead of drawing it over his head. He kept his eyes fixed upon the men as they still watched that hole waiting for their prey. The nulla-nullas were balanced in their hands, and moment by moment, as his fingers busied themselves over the tongue of that buckle, which would not yield, Nic expected to see Frank Mayne's head rise above the surface by the moist mossy sides. The water bubbled and gurgled, the insects hummed overhead, and that tongue would not yield till he put more pressure on, and then, with a sudden rush, it was loose.

The two men sprang up quickly, and Nic was in the act of rising too, presenting the gun, when there was a quick rustle, and a tremendous load fell across his back, driving him forward; the gun went off, and the boy was wrenched round and over upon his back, with a man's hands at his throat, heavy knees upon his chest, and the horribly savage eyes of the ruffian of whom he had been thinking a minute before glaring into his.

"Hooroar!" cried the droll-looking convict, pouncing upon the gun and dragging it from Nic's hand; "just the little tool I wanted! Where's its bread and cheese, mate? Why, deary me, if it ain't the little chap as used to look at us aboard the ship! How do 'ee do, mate?"

He made a droll grimace, with his tongue in his cheek; but he turned serious directly, as the savage convict roared at him:

"Look round, you fool! See if any one's coming."

The other two were startled for a moment, and looked round wildly. Then there was another grimace.

"There ain't no one to be coming. Our bunny won't show out of his hole after hearing that row; so you won't have no chance of knocking him on the head to-day, mate. Here, I say, don't choke all the life out of the boy."

"What!" growled the ruffian. "Why, I'll cut his very heart out if he don't speak. Here, how many's along with you?"

Nic made no answer, and the ruffian drew out a knife.

"Did you hear what I said?" he croaked, in a low, guttural tone. "Who's along with you?"

"Don't kill him," said the other fellow, with his smooth aspect gone. "It's murder. Take him to the edge yonder, and let him fall over by accident."

"Yah!" cried the other man, making a grimace: "let him be. Here, young un, they won't hurt yer. You and me's old friends. But you must oblige me with them shoes, and that there nice warm jacket and clean shirt. Tain't had one for weeks. And I'll just trouble you for the powder and shot. Let him get up, mate. He won't try to run, because he knows I should have to wipe his head with this little nutcracker. Why don't you let him get up?—Yah! Quick! Look out!"

As the man spoke he swung round the gun and took aim at a figure which came rushing up. He drew trigger, but the hammer struck out a few sparks—that was all, for he had forgotten that it was not loaded.

What followed was very quickly done. Frank Mayne—for it was he—sprang at the savage ruffian who was holding Nic, and struck at him sidewise with the stout stick he held in his right hand. It did not seem much of a blow, but he delivered it in leaping through the air, just as a mounted soldier would direct a cut from his left.

The effect was wonderful: the man rolled over and over, and Nic sprang up, free to gaze after Mayne as he sprang at the other man.

The scoundrel struck at him savagely, and Nic heard the blow take effect. Then he had to fend for himself; for the man with the gun came on.

"Here," he cried: "out with that powder and shot, or—"

He raised the piece with both hands by the barrel, and swung it back as if to get force for a blow. But, boy as he was, Nic sprang at him.

"Give me my gun!" he cried, and he was too close in for the blow to have any effect, as he seized the fellow by the throat and clung to him with all his might.

But Nic's muscles were not yet hardened, and the man swung him round and round just as he liked, the boy gradually growing weaker; while, as he struggled, he saw with despair that Mayne was evidently getting the worse of it, for the man he had attacked partially disabled him at the first blow, and had now got his hand free and was striking brutally with the club.

Mayne evidently felt that he was beaten, but he clung to his adversary tenaciously, bore him backward with his hands fast at his throat, and, bending down his head to avoid the savage blows, he leaped forward so that he and the convict fell, the latter undermost.

"Joe, mate—quick!" roared the latter; and the big ruffian, who had now risen to his feet, stooped and picked up a piece of stone, raising it with both hands to bring it down on Mayne's head.

"Leather!" yelled Nic; "look out—look out!"

"Surrender!" roared a stern voice which sounded familiar, and the man with the stone paused for a moment to glance about like a wild beast. Then, seeing that he was surrounded by mounted police, who covered those present with their carbines, he hurled the stone with all force at the nearest man and made a rush to escape, when there were three puffs of smoke, three reports, and the convict tripped and fell.

Taking advantage of the smoke and excitement, Frank Mayne's adversary struck at him once more, and made a leap to escape, dragging the half-insensible assigned servant with him; but the grasp was too tenacious, and though he tried hard, Mayne held on to the end; only sinking back when a pair of handcuffs had secured the prisoner's hands behind his back.

"Now then, you with the gun there, surrender!" shouted the man who led the mounted police.

This to the convict who had confined his fighting to his struggle with Nic.

"'Course I do," said the man, making a grimace. "That young shaver's got all the powder and shot: where's the good of an empty gun? Here, ketch 'old. No, I forgot; it's yourn, young un. Well, how are you all?"

The police laughed as the man held out his hands for the irons.

"We've had a nice little 'scursion out here, only the nights was rather cold. Well, Mr Government clerk, you won't have a chance to pull your friend a topper now. How's old Joe? What, more company?"

This was accompanied by another distortion of the face, as two blacks came running up, followed by the doctor, the governor, Brookes, and Sir John's two men.

"Got them?" cried the governor.

"Yes, Sir John," said the leader of the police, whom Nic recognised now as the chief warder whom he had talked with during the voyage out; "but we had to shoot one of 'em down."

"Here, quick, 'fore he goes!" said Brookes to the warder, huskily. "Handcuffs," and he pointed to Mayne.

"Eh? What? Him?" said the warder. "Why, he helped to take one of 'em."

"Yes," cried Nic; "he was fighting to save me."

"I surrender," said Mayne faintly; "I'm satisfied now. Dr Braydon, I never told you I was an ill-used man, but did my work. Still, I told your son. Dominic, lad, Heaven is just. That handcuffed hound is my old fellow-clerk, for whose sins I have suffered all these years. There are miracles in life, for it fell to me to take him when he was escaping."

"After he had watched to take your life!" cried Nic. "He was waiting, you know where? There, Sir John—father, will you believe it now?"

The doctor had been kneeling by the fallen convict, roughly bandaging a bullet wound when, as he turned to rise, Frank Mayne struck him aside, and flung himself upon the wounded man.

The doctor turned fiercely upon Mayne, but the next moment he grasped the truth, just as a blow from the butt end of a musket struck the ruffian back; for as soon as the wound had been bandaged, the man had waited an opportunity to draw a knife and strike at him who had tried to assuage his pain.

In a short time the party was on its way back, the wounded convict borne upon a roughly made stretcher, and Frank Mayne walking with the warder, to Brookes's great disgust, for the doctor had said that he would answer for his not attempting to escape.

The next day the police rode off with their prisoners, taking with them a light waggon, in which the wounded convict was laid, Dr Braydon having said that he was in no danger. But Frank Mayne was not of the party, for Sir John had heard the simple tale.

"And that man was your fellow-clerk in the government office? Yes, I remember something about his coming out in the same ship as my wife. I remember the case, because he was the second man charged with embezzlement at this government office; and I remember, too, saying that matters must be badly managed there."

"Yes, he was my fellow-clerk, Sir John," said Mayne. "He was found out at last, but the time has seemed very long."

"And you say you were unjustly sentenced?"

"In Heaven's name, Sir John, I do. I was faithful to my trust."

"I believe you, Mayne," said the governor, looking at him keenly; "and there shall be a thorough investigation of your case. In the meantime, what I can do I will. You hear, Nic, for your sake as well as his, Mayne is free to go anywhere in the colony, and I will see that justice is done him in every way."

"Thank you, Sir John," said Mayne hoarsely; "it is more than I could expect on my bare assertion."

"Some bare assertions are better than oaths, eh, Braydon?" said Sir John. "What do you say?"

"I say that I have much forgiveness to ask of Mr Mayne: I ask it now of the man who saved my life."

There was silence for a few moments; for the doctor had held out his hand to Mayne, who stood looking at it with his lips quivering.

"I am only your assigned servant, sir," he said at last.

"Not now," said the doctor. "I was offering my hand to a brave man who has been misunderstood. I offer it, too, to my son's friend."

Nic looked dull the next day, but he brightened up when his father proposed that they should ride a part of the way with Mayne, who was going to take some despatches to Government House, where for the present he was to stay.

"You see, Nic, it will be better," the governor said. "The poor fellow would be miserable here with his old fellow-servants. So I have arranged for him to go and wait till I come. His story's true enough, and I shall see that everything is done for him before he goes back to England—to take his old position, I hope."

But Frank Mayne had no such ideas. England was dead to him, and he was content to stay. And to Nic's delight, his friend received a grant of land some ten miles away, close to the great gorge, where the boy spent all the time he could, watching the erection of the house by convict labour; for in this Mayne was helped largely by Sir john, while the doctor had become one of his firmest supporters.

Of course Frank Mayne had formed a very warm attachment to the lad, who had believed in him from the first; but Lady O'Hara used to laugh and joke, and say *she knew*, though she never said what it was she knew. Time, however, gave the explanation, about two years later Mayne had received a free pardon from his Majesty the King, "for suffering a great deal and nearly being driven mad," as Nic said.

But Frank Mayne said he was very happy and quite content, and we need not go into the causes of his content, especially since every one, from Lady O'Hara and Mrs Braydon downwards, was in the same way of thinking.

"Besides, Mr Mayne, it was worth it all, sure," said Lady O'Hara banteringly at the wedding. "Now don't you think so, Nic?"

"Of course I do?"

"Then that's right," cried the lady. "But tell me, Nic, how long is it since I brought you out?"

"I don't know," said Nic.

"Too busy; but about three years. Look at that now, and him grown quite a man."

"Yes," said the doctor, "farmer, cattle raiser, squatter."

"Yes," said Mayne, laying his hand on his brother-in-law's shoulder. "One of the first in the field, and my true friend."